Jacques Derrida: A Biography

Also available from Continuum:

Dissemination (Impact edition), Derrida

Positions (Impact edition), Derrida

Understanding Derrida, Jack Reynolds and Jon Roffe

Jacques Derrida: Live Theory, James K. A. Smith

Jacques Derrida: A Biography

Jason Powell

continuum

Continuum International Publishing Group
The Tower Building
11 York Road
London
SE1 7NX

80 Maiden Lane
Suite 704
New York
NY 10038

First published in 2006
This edition 2006

British Library Cataloguing-in-Publication Data
A catalogue record for this book is available from the British Library.

0-8264-9449-8 (paperback)

Library of Congress Cataloging-in-Publication Data
A catalog record for this book is available from the Library of Congress.

Typeset by Servis Filmsetting Ltd, Longsight, Manchester
Printed and bound in Great Britain by MPG Books Ltd, Bodmin,
Cornwall

Contents

Preface   ix
Introduction   1

1 **Algeria**   9
  1.1   The Tradition   9
  1.2   Family   10
  1.3   Culture   13
  1.4   During the War   16
  1.5   The *Lycée*   18
  1.6   André Gide   20
2 **Paris and ENS**   22
  2.1   Boarding School   22
  2.2   Husserl   25
  2.3   Husserl's Development   27
  2.4   'Violence and Metaphysics' [1964]   28
  2.5   Levinas   29
  2.6   Althusser and Marxism   30
  2.7   The Student Generation of the   32
        1950s and 1960s
  2.8   Psychoanalysis   34
  2.9   Michel Foucault   36
3 **After ENS**   39
  3.1   Harvard   39
  3.2   The War of Algeria   41
  3.3   Cerisy-la-Salle, 1959   42

3.4 Derrida's Early Critique of the Science of Science 46
3.5 The *Prix Cavailles* 47
4 The First Book 49
4.1 Husserl's 'Origin of Geometry' 49
4.2 *Husserl's 'Origin of Geometry': An Introduction* [1962] 50
4.3 Freedom 51
4.4 Writing: The Linguistic Turn 52
5 Against Structuralism 55
5.1 Thoughts on Althusser 55
5.2 'Force and Signification' 56
5.3 1963–65 58
5.4 'Structure, Sign and Play' 60
5.5 'Freud and the Scene of Writing' 63
6 Structures in French Thought 65
6.1 Structuralism 65
6.2 Post-Structuralism 68
6.3 Psychoanalysis and Jacques Lacan 69
7 1967 74
7.1 *Speech and Phenomena* [1967] 74
7.2 *Of Grammatology* [1967] 77
8 Avant-garde Philosophy 80
8.1 May '68 80
8.2 *Margins of Philosophy* 83
8.3 *Dissemination* 87
9 America: Derrida as Literary Theory 92
9.1 The 1970s 92
9.2 Travel 92
9.3 Life Death and the Other 94
9.4 America 98
9.5 De Man's Response to Derrida's *Of Grammatology* 102
9.6 Derrida and the Literary 103
9.7 *Tel Quel* 105
9.8 1972 106
9.9 *Spurs*, Nietzsche at Cerisy [1972] 106
10 *Glas* 110
10.1 *Glas* [1974] 110
10.2 Psychoanalysis in *Glas* 113
11 GREPH 116
11.1 GREPH 116

11.2 The Estates General for Philosophy   118

12 Yale   121

12.1 After *Glas*   121

12.2 Yale   122

12.3 Paul de Man, *Memoires*   124

12.4 *Limited Inc.* [1977]   125

13 *The Post Card*   128

13.1 Derrida and the Post/*Geschick*   128

13.2 The Postal System   130

14 Nietzsche and Heidegger   133

14.1 A Late Start   133

14.2 *Given Time*   135

14.3 *Living On: Borderlines*   137

14.4 *The Truth in Painting*   139

14.5 *Otobiographies*   140

15 The 1980s   144

15.1 Influence and Opposition   144

15.2 Levinas   145

15.3 'Of an Apocalyptic Tone' [1980]   147

15.4 'Psyche: Inventions of the Other'   149

15.5 The Early 1980s   150

15.6 Literature, Aesthetics and Politics   152

15.7 The International College of Philosophy   156

15.8 The Mid-1980s   157

15.9 'Khora'   158

16 1987–90, Deconstruction and National Socialism   160

16.1 Crisis in the Politics of Deconstruction   160

16.2 *Of Spirit* [1987]   163

16.3 The Assault on de Man and Heidegger   167

16.4 'Force of Law' [1989]   169

16.5 The Gulf War   171

17 Autobiographical Years, 1990–91   174

17.1 *Memoires of the Blind*   174

17.2 *Jacques Derrida* [1991]   177

18 The Future of Democracy and the Very Worst Moment of Capitalism   182

18.1 'The Right to Philosophy from the Cosmopolitan Point of View'   182

18.2 *The Other Heading*: Europe   183

	18.3	*Resistances of Psychoanalysis* [1993]	187
19	**Derrida's World: Confronting Marx**		189
	19.1	Final Major Works	189
	19.2	*Spectres of Marx* [1993]	190
20	***The Politics of Friendship***		196
	20.1	*The Politics of Friendship* [1994]	196
	20.2	'Nietzsche and the Machine'	201
21	**Derrida's Religion**		204
	21.1	Messianism	204
	21.2	'Faith and Knowledge'	205
	21.3	Late Publications	207
22	**Thoughtful Welcoming of the Other, Death**		211
	22.1	'On Cosmopolitanism'	211
	22.2	'Derelictions of the Right to Justice (But what are the *sans-papiers* lacking?)'	212
	22.3	'On Forgiveness'	214
	22.4	'As if it were Possible'	215
23	**2000 Onwards**		218
	23.1	A Contemporary Philosopher	218
	23.2	*Philosophy in a Time of Terror*: 9/11	218
	23.3	Life Death	223
Conclusion			226
Notes			231
Works Cited			246
Index			256

Preface

I began this book in 2003, less than a year before Jacques Derrida's death, as a 'critical biography'. I intended a sketch of a biography which would be complete, given the work on and knowledge of Derrida's life then in print. I present a comprehensive continuous narrative of Derrida's life, an appraisal of his works and a summary of his philosophy.

One or two books were of great value to me as I set out on the writing of this biography. In particular I would like to acknowledge Geoffrey Bennington's *Jacques Derrida* (Bennington 1999), of which the section entitled 'Curriculum vitae' formed the early backbone of my research. Particularly useful biographical details were also found in Catherine Malabou's *Counterpath: Travelling with Jacques Derrida* (Derrida 2004a).

I would like to thank Dr Karl Simms of the University of Liverpool, who supervised the research for this biography. I would also like to thank my wife, Melisa.

Introduction

Jacques Derrida was the most famous philosopher of his day, and also a great and original thinker. But his work was born into controversy, and the mixed interpretations of his work and his basically Heideggerian 'deconstruction' have not yet settled into a more balanced picture. The familiar image of Jacques Derrida is the image of a destructive critic of historical philosophy and culture, who undertook to upset established facts and practices, in the name either of good or of wicked causes, depending on the point of view. One view saw him as anti-Western, and maybe there are Arab, Algerian elements of his thought on the law as a non-territorial based, international set of commands. On the other hand, his cosmopolitanism is the epitome of North American national identity, and his view of the law is both secular and also based on faith. He has a reputation amongst some philosophers for aggression towards philosophy, which he attacks by using literary reading styles. He has stepped out of literary studies, bringing with him emotions and rhetoric. Others see Derrida as the most complex and effective of academic philosophers, a fighter against orthodoxy and idleness, an unworldly cynic, involved in changing the way students are taught. Roger Scruton (2005), and many other Anglo-Saxon philosophers and commentators on culture, see Derrida as one who worked on behalf of the new, low, pop, culture – a 'culture of denial', even though few genuine, transcendental philosophers have ever dwelt at such length on the importance of memory, ancestors and our duty to the as yet unborn. Some see Derrida as an ultra-elitist reader of texts associated with Nazism, as well as with Soviet communism in a parochial way, recognizing in his work the symptoms of a thought based on nationalist feelings, and idolization of Dead White Male Europeans.

Throughout his career in France he was suspected of being 'the French Heidegger'. Others, more sympathetic, picture deconstruction as a progressive type of critique of the history of philosophy, producing works which could conveniently replace the old tradition, and make it superfluous. Derrida is a contradictory philosopher if we go by academic hearsay. His works are those of a mischievous outsider; a strong leader and excellent teacher, in the lineage of a Nietzschean 'aristocratic radicalism'; he was professorial and conservative; but above all, his life and work was definitely not something which one could ignore, whether he was understood or not (and maybe the controversy itself shows a lack of attention and caution in those who were supposed to have read his works).

Derrida rose to fame in the mid-1960s in Paris, while his fame had to wait until the mid-70s in America and Great Britain, if we except Paul de Man's admiration for him, which originated at a 1966 Johns Hopkins conference.[1] Papers on him abounded from the start, in a quantity which was unusual for a writer who had not a great deal of substance at the time, no positive doctrines, beyond, perhaps, his 'grammatology'. The increasing attention given to what was perceived as 'deconstruction' gave either an image of someone who was overrated,[2] or else of someone who had more than met the eye. Something seemed to be right about a school of thought which was 'deconstructing' during those years; there was something fashionable and worthy about deconstruction. Derrida had come from a complex background, a culture mixing French and German living 'theorists', and a tradition of grand Europeans with whom he was in close communion in his reading. Never at home, not in structuralism, or in Paris, and not in America, or even at any university, there was a secret desire in his work which made him the centre of a new attention, and a new industry. He summed up the thinking in philosophical studies, and high culture, for a large part of the university. He was never, from the first, a mere scholar, but seemed to have a method, which people wanted to put in the perspective of the age, to question, to learn, to summarize. It was a new 'ism'. His evasive and super-cautious doctrine frustrated many, but even in his 'doctrine' he was seemingly at odds with himself: there was no doctrine or method. Derrida read texts with a single intention, no doubt, but not with a method, or a concrete, realizable objective.

Attempts were made to summarize deconstruction and the new way of thinking during the 1980s, by English-speaking writers predominantly. These attempts focused on the aspect of Derrida that seemed to be common to philosophers of all ages. Richard Rorty (1982) saw him as a pragmatist;

Rodolph Gasché (1986) as a post-Kantian transcendentalist; and in Great Britain Christopher Norris (1987) and Geoffrey Bennington (1992/1999)[3] presented him as a linguistic philosopher. Each of them could see that Derrida enjoyed reading the history of philosophy, and that a special teaching, a deconstructive 'philosophy' was involved, but they could not, in retrospect, quite locate it. They did not dwell on Derrida's ethics at that time, the desire for purity, for the very best, or Derrida's vision of the future, his vision of the nature of beings, his interest in nationalism and his relationship to the past. Positive critics of the 1980s assumed a political bias to his work, but could not, at least not on the strength of his own avowals, express it, nor could they see the ethical basis for his works. Finally, there was no discussion of the type of person Derrida was, what he was really trying to achieve. Negative critics, not so sympathetic to the presumed politics, were more straightforward. They assumed that Derrida was an anarchist without social responsibility, and that he merely enjoyed attacking the West's culture, and, disliking this, they too attacked his works, which they little understood. A common complaint was that Derrida did not subscribe to rational argument; although, even if his critics were well intentioned, their criticism of Derrida was never very reasoned, or accurate as to the facts. A famous example of the great quantity of these critics and their lack of attention was given in the 'Cambridge Affair' of 1992, in which twenty academics from several countries unilaterally ridiculed Derrida and also attempted to impede his professional career (Points 1995b, 419–21).

By the 1990s the debates over Derrida and modern studies at university level had reached a crisis, since the culture wars were at their height, and the level and kind of teaching at universities was seen to be in decline: Derrida was assumed to be one of the key reasons for the decline. Self-appointed defenders of morality, and of educational standards, were picking at Derrida's name with greater frequency and with a concerted will. The attacks revolved around a Derrida who was perceived to make a joke of philosophy by academics who wished to expel 'deconstruction' from the university body and its curriculum. Controversy in the USA and the UK centred gloomily on what deconstructive thinkers and their models had done during the war. Derrida for his part seemed to respond when in the early 1990s he issued several lengthy and high-quality works which were explicitly concerned with the political and ethical problems of the twentieth century and with the future of democracy and morality. Steadily Derrida was telling his audience who he was, who the man was and what the secrets were, behind the names of 'Derrida' and 'deconstruction'. By the end of his life, in October

2004, there was enough information to compile a biography of Derrida from his statements alone,[4] and provide a complete account of the aims of deconstruction, though in Anglo-Saxon circles of philosophy the same stories were doing the rounds, of a Derrida who had no positive doctrine, a nihilistic politics and ethics and an inimical stance towards higher educational standards. John D. Caputo (1997a and 1997b) was working on Derrida's religion, and debates over his work were more concerned with the politics and ethics of deconstruction, but vocal supporters of Derrida, once many and strong, were fewer in number, although a general recognition was coming about in the popular media.

Admirers, critics and 'deconstructionists' alike would, perhaps, scoff at the very idea of a biography of the philosopher of deconstruction. It was always thought that deconstruction had no author, that it neglected genre distinctions and disposed of factual things. From a glance at the early combative deconstruction of work prior to *Glas* (Derrida 1986a) one could be justified in thinking this, if one were not interested in Derrida's 'targets': Hegel, Nietzsche, Rousseau, Freud, Heidegger or Kant. Not enjoying reading these in a new way, critics may have seen no point in 'deconstructing' them either, and would see no guiding intention or personality beyond the deconstructive critique. In Derrida's early work, authorial intention, politics, ethics and the sense of responsibility are not overtly presented. But Derrida was writing with the intention of letting these things fall silent so that they could appear more 'primordially'. Derrida's intention was lost on some 'anti-Western' admirers too, who did not foresee the intense self-centredness of his late work, his subtle patriotism and his faith in both France and America; they did not get to grips with the person and history of this important thinker. Everyone knew who Bertrand Russell was and what he stood for while he lived, but few knew anything, or wanted to know anything, about Derrida the author and the man. Deconstruction was something which seemed to belong to all.

In retrospect one can see that Derrida did have a philosophy which went well with his evasions and his secretiveness. It is an ontology of ghosts, a ghostly writing which follows the insubstantiality of all things, anything, including and especially of the self, the writer, the state or nation, philosophy itself. It was a philosophy which attempted not to change things, but only to describe them as a post-Heideggerian ontology must see them. Every 'thing' which exists does so only in a distant manner, as if it were a ghost of itself. When the philosopher sets out to find a true and real thing, he inevitably ends up with only a shadow. The truth of this claim, the core of deconstruction, cannot very well be doubted; on the other hand, it could also be refuted by commonsense philosophy, which would rightly point out that if all things are ghostly, then nothing is so. Derrida's reason for pointing out that all writing is trace [*trait*], each public person a ghost, and each tradition a history of spectres, is that for each ghost there is a promise of something truly real. The truly real is not in a distinct realm, however, but is a promise which the ghostly existent thing holds out, the promise of a purer version, a non-existent, better version of itself, which is hoped for, but not to be realized.[5] Derrida proves or gives reasons for this theory in terms also of the obvious machine-like process of life and death, the way in which so much can be predicted, the way in which so much is known, that there is no mystery, and everything which is possible is almost already actual. This means that it is very rare that a real 'event' ever takes place. In such a technological world (and deconstruction is *also* an attempt to reform technology), most existent things are therefore just spectres of what they could be, and we must await the truer coming of things.

With this theory of the messianic structure of events and things, elaborated in as many ways as there are texts by Derrida, and deeply congruous with each other, how could such a storm of controversy or such a sea of critiques have come forth? One reason for his remarkable fame and for the body of scholarship on his work is that his thought was genuinely representative of the deep questionings of his era. Beyond the proofs and discussions of spectrality, which are manifold, and beyond Derrida's other theories, which please because of their numerosity, what counts most is Derrida's overall vision of our culture which this basically Platonistic theory holds on to. Derrida belongs, perhaps, to a tradition of philosopher-kings, who wish to have a say in the future of politics, ethics and culture, and it was his vision of a promise concealed in time which seemed so appropriate to his age, and especially to the forward-looking USA, more than to Europe. It is a philosophy in which the author, for example Derrida, does not matter as he might be expected to matter because he is a ghostly writer, of traces, but he still matters. In the case of the biography of the thinker of deconstruction, a biography is the more urgently needed since the theory of spectrality and traces always involved itself in the person of any writer, and the psychoanalysis of the subject in its individuality, rather than in its universality. It is notable that the anger aroused by this deconstructive ontology is due to the frustration which conservative, authoritarian minds feel when they find that their ideals are truly real only because they insist that they are real, and that in fact they are spectral ideals for a half-present world.

By and large Derrida devoted himself to a campaign for a better version of justice, and a better version of the truth as known by philosophy. In his critiques of Heidegger he devoted his attention to Heidegger's nationalism, and the way in which 'Being' is almost synonymous with 'Germany'. He did this on the basis that texts, laws, commandments, works and systems are, and can only be, traces of a better, hoped for version; or, in other words, while Heidegger may be right about the home-coming being equivalent to reaching the origin of philosophy, it may be as well to unsettle the certainty which Heidegger felt that Germany, even Nazi Germany, was the source of the most true philosophy. There is nothing in this which writers such as Scruton, or the many enemies of deconstruction, or even the enemies of university philosophy and teaching, should have taken umbrage over. Derrida was a genuine philosopher, and his politics, as well as his cultural commitments, providing for the furtherance of the Western tradition in a progressive form, rather than a dead one, infused with faith, have nothing of blame attaching to them. His lifelong meditation on Heidegger's 'originary' thinking yielded a thought of equal depth, but more cautious results. He was a man of extraordinary single-mindedness and energy, very self-defensive no doubt, but a power in cultural matters to the advantage and furtherance of education as it has stood hitherto. A whole and coherent study on this basis is as yet lacking.

While this book was being written, Derrida's natural life ended unexpectedly. There were instant announcements of the fact around the world, often as front-page news. But the man beneath the name remained a mystery, as he always will, and as deconstruction insisted that each individual always will do. However, his teachings, and there are teachings, remain, like works before their time, to be lived up to, by modern culture. No doubt their effects will be minimal, but against the aggressive critics at least, and against the forgetfulness of the grandeur and the purity of the ambition of the West's philosophical ambition, this ideal of the philosophy should have a fair reckoning. There now exists a complete body of publications at least, since Derrida has ceased to write, even if we do not yet possess a collection of letters, which is usually necessary for a biography.

Derrida was a great traveller of the world, supremely learned, and yet with all of these signs of greatness and extravagance, he was also, above all, very cautious, and his style, the rhythm of his ideas, and of his prose, were all very slow. It often feels as if Wolin, Scruton, the signatories to the letter to *The Times* in 1992, and the rest, including his admirers, were far too hasty in their judgement on him, not because they should simply take more time to read and think about his work, but because they should change their own pace, and adjust to this calm, very wide-ranging gaze, which always took in the distant past and future, and was always painfully aware of the injustice of hard-and-fast distinctions, over-simple judgements and the disregard for genuine predicaments. A biography is an essential aid to revealing the value and respect due to Derrida in just this way. In an inversion of time and influence, familiar to those who have read *The Post Card* (Derrida 1987a), one could say that Heidegger was too hasty in his rejection of Derrida's messianism, too bold in his pushing aside of a theory of events which will never occur, a theory of Being in which Being will never reign.

There is an enormous amount of work in print under Derrida's signature, and a critical commentary out of all proportion to what is usual for a thinker who has only recently died. Derrida published several works per year during his adult life, from the age of thirty-two to the age at which he died, when he was seventy-four. At no point in his life did Derrida slow down or cease activity; his momentum and his course, sheltered and guided somewhat by his position at the *École Normale Supérieure*, were more or less unchanging throughout his life, following a path from obscurity to world fame. The list of destinations, and what was taught at each one, plus the regular teaching responsibilities, not to mention his private life, could well demand an enquiry into whether, with all of the information available potentially, a biography could ever be completed which took account of it all, as well, finally, as the content and intention of each of his works. A truly complete biography of Derrida would be a very big task indeed, requiring several volumes, especially if it were to accept Derrida's own demanding standards of reading and commentary.

The age in which Derrida lived saw the decline, and virtual neutralization, of the political entities in Western Europe, and with that the neutralization of its culture; other nations tended to become as good as or better than Europe at its own game. For whatever reason, Derrida more than almost any other writer and thinker took in and understood this culture while it was in decline, and unlike many another, particularly in English-speaking countries and universities, he found a way of keeping it relevant without any nostalgia or conservatism. If the West and its culture has run out of steam, then so too Derrida will have become irrelevant, but if it has a future, and is now merely in a sort of limbo, then Derrida's sketches of a 'heading' will always be of value. As he said and assumed in his works, for many reasons, not least of which are the catastrophes which it has brought about, the culture of the West cannot turn back and become what it was, even if this unnatural process were possible. It now faces the challenge of Westernizing, and incorporating into itself, the rest of the world, and deconstruction is essential to this, since what looks like an act of undermining, of 'destruction', is actually the process of realizing the future.

If other biographies existed of Derrida I should have to apologize for my own contribution. Doing so, I would insist that this short account of his life emphasizes the continuity between himself and Nietzsche and, to a lesser extent, Heidegger. Just as Nietzsche came to German thinking, to Hegel, Kant, Fichte and Schopenhauer, as well as to the positivism of his day, and pronounced judgement on them, bringing a future time of a vastly different sort than the present time with which they were obsessed, so Derrida brought a future to the structuralists, existentialists, the neo-religious, the nationalists and the analytic philosophers. Like Nietzsche, he brought only a few solid doctrines, but many new ways of thinking, and he said things which common philosophy was too afraid to say. It is in this way that Derrida is the continuation of a long tradition, as well as a cultural event of some magnitude, whose effects may well last for some time, before they become a memory, or are fully incorporated into the way people see existence.

1
Algeria

1.1 The Tradition

Derrida was to become one of the many thinkers who were schooled in the thinking and Enlightenment world-view of Kant, only to have to adapt that thinking to something more appropriate to a world which, after the twentieth century's excess, has to rethink itself. These thinkers found a culture in crisis about its past, one trying to forget, not able to remember, overburdened by guilt, and suffocated by machinal capitalism and philosophical subjectivism. Derrida's life is thus an involvement in Kant and his descendants, as one amongst them, most specifically Hegel, Nietzsche and Heidegger, nationalistic thinkers whose destiny as nationalists was to them a precondition of thinking at all, since they were also self-consciously descendants of the Greeks, descendants of the egoists and nationalists *par excellence*. The thinking and the dreams of these places and times constitute the biography of a thinker today, almost predetermining it. If, that is, it were not for the coming of the unexpected, which, being impossible to prefigure and foresee, literally is impossible, as Derrida was to say in his late metaphysics.

But while he made of his life a place in which justice and better things could be discerned to express themselves in old European works of thinking, Derrida himself was no less unjust, of course, in his own readings and the violence of his alliances. Kant, Husserl, Heidegger, Nietzsche, Freud, Marx and the Greek thinkers more or less saturate the content of Derrida's work from early in his career to the end. Derrida championed these, and has been received best by other critics of them. But Derrida, facing the event of life itself, thought of it as different from things in life; 'life' was hidden within them, and always or almost always he found it to be hidden because he was the first to make the point that 'existence' is a problem, and that it is a problem because it does not take place in normal time. His reading of the great tradition, and his unrelenting flow of work on the great tradition, shows a desire for purity in the appreciation of life and existence which is the hallmark of high culture. But his purity went beyond the given greatness of high culture, in order to find a purer purity, as he himself says (Derrida 1998e, 46). He posited a deeper, purer, more just, promised culture beyond the given one based on the mundane grasp of what genuinely is the case, and the ordinary acceptance of what is just and true.

1.2 Family

Derrida's family were Sephardic Jews resident in Algeria during its history as a French province, and messianism, the sense that this world has not been fully revealed, was, to an extent, native to him. Derrida's type of Jewishness, his family's kind of religious observance, was marked maybe by many years of having to dissimulate belief and to perform its rites in secrecy. The name 'marrano' was given by the Spanish Catholics to the Jews who converted to Catholicism in public but remained faithful to Judaism in private. Derrida's family did not need to dissimulate quite so much in Algeria, and were happy to become North African in their way of life, he says (Derrida 2004b; 2004a, 85), until they were naturalized, when they rushed into becoming French and bourgeois at an unnatural rate.

In 1830 when the Safar, maternal side of the family were already installed in Algeria, the French government launched its massive assault on North Africa with the ostensible project of ridding the Mediterranean of piracy. In 1848 Algeria became officially part of France. In 1870 when Algerian Jews were granted European rights by the decree Cremieux, of the Algerian population, one in ten were French descended, of whom one quarter were Jewish. From 1870 onwards the Algerian Jews became French in the genuine sense that they became bourgeois, and their existence, their relationship to the land they lived on, changed into a rather spectral, doubling, French one.

The maternal great-grandfather, Moses Safar, came to Algeria from Portugal in the first half of the nineteenth century. Moses' wife, Derrida's great-grandmother, was, Derrida later recalled, attentive to her appearance, her clothing, her makeup and her manners, as was her daughter, Georgette,

who was born on 23 July 1901 (Bennington 1999, 125). Both were attentive to their status as bourgeois colonists of French Algeria. Derrida's mother
was God-fearing in a sentimental way. She was never to read any of her
son's books, but cared that he may or may not believe in God. Judging by
the annual holiday to El-Biar, which took place during Derrida's childhood,
she enjoyed a simple, uncomplicated routine of work and relaxation. She
was to have several sons, two of whom died in infancy, and one daughter.

Abraham Derrida, whose brother Elie Derrida abandoned his wife and
children to make a life for himself on mainland France (Bennington 1999,
186–7) was Derrida's grandfather on the paternal side. He had two sons,
Aimé and Eugène Eliahou Derrida. Aimé Derrida, Jacques' father, was to
become a sales representative for a French, Catholic family. He travelled four
days a week throughout his life, and although he never spent a night away
from home, he would call himself a travelling salesman, or a 'traveller'. The
Catholic family for whom he worked, the Tachets, were dealers in wines and
spirits. They had their own brand of anisette (Derrida 2004a, 31). Derrida's
father worked for three generations of the Tachet family as a docile
employee and spent his whole life 'on the job'. Each morning he had to be
up early to do the accounts on the dining-room table, and the job as a whole
was exhausting, humiliating, and made of this man one whom Derrida later
refers to as 'my poor father'. He felt himself, in later life, often, when doing
his own work of lecturing, writing and travelling, just like his poor father,
with that feeling of humiliation which was part of his origins (2004a, 32–3).

His father began work at the age of twelve for the Tachets as an appren-
tice, then as a commercial traveller. He was 'always behind the wheel of his
car' (Derrida 2004c, 107), stopping at every café, every grocery store, taking
orders, and 'I always saw him in the persona of the petitioner or the appli-
cant' (2004c, 107). 'The word "sacrifice" came up constantly: "He is sacrific-
ing himself for us."' Derrida suffered with him through adolescence, telling
his family they did not appreciate their father (2004c, 108), who worked all
of the time and never took any vacation. Derrida felt that his mother did not
recognize his father's suffering, and his father began to confide in him during
adolescence in default of any other ear (2004c, 109). 'My father lacked
authority, while also being prone to anger and I regretted the fact that he
always came to me to complain' (2004c, 109).

Aimé Derrida married Georgette Sultana Esther Safar in 1923 and they
moved together to rue Saint-Augustin in Algiers in 1925 (Bennington 1999,
325). The same year René Derrida, the first child, was born. And four years
later, Paul Derrida was born to them at a holiday home in the summer.

He died less than three months later. Then in 1930 came the birth of Jackie Derrida, at El-Biar, in the same holiday home, to parents who were still mourning the deceased son Paul. Jackie, or 'Jacques' as he later called himself, was to suspect throughout his life that he was merely a replacement or 'supplement' for the dead brother. He was born towards dawn during a game of poker, which his mother was reluctant to interrupt, as it was the passion of her life. Two months after Jackie was born the family went back to the house in Algiers, located on the rue Saint-Augustin (Caputo 1997a, 19). There was a dark hallway, a grocer's down from the house. Holidays were spent in the same villa, in the hot summers, with games of poker at night (Bennington 1999, 130).

Derrida was circumcised in the usual circumstances some days later. The rite, performed on the seventh day, is attended by the father, the *mohel*, or priest, an uncle, and, at least in spirit, by the prophet Elijah who is given a chair at the ceremony. It involves the removal of the foreskin with a knife, and afterwards the application of a tight bandage on the penis, with orange water to attenuate the pain, and some wine for the child to taste. By the same ritual the child is named. Derrida speculates and dreams in *Circumfession*[1] of the tradition of the mother eating the foreskin, and of sucking it, mixing blood and wine. As an indication of how indelicate they found it to be too Jewish, the family called the rite, which allies the child to the Jewish God, 'baptism' rather than circumcision (Bennington 1999, 72).

The name 'Jackie' was what his parents considered to be an American name. They were inclined to that sort of thing, although it was not peculiar to them since, as Derrida was to recall in numerous interviews, his native culture was hardly a real culture at all, being a mixture of French, and Arab cultures, the Judaic religion, and the general Western/American media culture which was then being propagated around the globe randomly. Later he changed his name to 'Jacques', feeling that its tone was more French and more intellectual, more stylish. However he considered his surname 'Derrida' to be beautiful and rare. His parents also gave him, as is traditional, a secret name, which he learnt only much later: 'Elie'.

The family lived on rue Saint-Augustin in Algiers until Derrida was four years old, when they moved to El-Biar, 13 rue d'Aurelle-de-Paladines. Once installed there in 1935, Derrida was hardly to leave El-Biar before his nineteenth birthday, when he moved to France to pursue his higher education. The family bought this villa with a loan which they would only finally pay off when they left in 1962 for France, nearly thirty years later, remaining there until the eve of the independence of Algeria when they forfeited the property. Janine Derrida was born when Derrida was four years old, his only sister.

In his early years, and well into his teens, Derrida suffered from ill health – from otitis, and from various other infirmities which were hard to understand but easy to placate. He often seemed on the verge of death, so that his mother used to pray for him, and he seemed to cry for nothing, always weeping over himself and finding it hard to sleep. He says of himself that he was more gracious than pretty, which is to say delicate, and pitiful, needing attention and appreciating it (Bennington 1999, 173), crying every night until his mother let him sleep near the paternal bed on a divan.

1.3 Culture

Thinking of his homeland with Heidegger in mind, no doubt, and the equivalence with Being which Heidegger assigned to Germany, Derrida said of France, which was the putative capital of Algeria, that it was always for him, and perhaps the first example of, the Ghost (2004a, 83). The origin and core of Algeria, and the Derrida family's culture, was a spectre, not a deep 'well', a source of life, security and definite borders. The essence of France was spectral and its outlines and borders were traces. The Derrida family lacked any genuine culture, being properly Jewish in descent, and yet *pieds-noires* French – 'pieds noires' being a familiar term used for the Algerian French, referring to the dirty condition of the workers who manned the coal bunkers on the Mediterranean ferries to and from mainland France. They had three countries: France, the USA and Algeria; Derrida also had several cultures or homes, Arab, French and Jewish cultures, with a curious intermingling of each with the other, undermining each other, and binding together: the Algerian enamoured of France, the Frenchman's love for Algeria, the romance of America with France. Meanwhile as a youth he rebelled against Judaism because it was practised as an outward ritual but had been disavowed inwardly (Derrida 2004a, 82). Thus he had a Christian critical viewpoint, even though it was the Christian French culture which had ruined his Algerian Judaism to begin with. His language was not properly his own either, nor was it properly the native language of any of the French in Algeria. He grew up with an Algerian French idiom and intonation, but was to change his accent to the purest correct French. Occasionally his old *pieds-noires* Maghreb accent surfaced when in states of emotion, but even then only in private, with family. On behalf of France and Paris he contested his own voice throughout his life, held it back, his accent, his native language and idiom (Derrida 2004a, 89). His desire to contest everything, even himself, in the name of a higher standard of purity, is very characteristic.

The linguistic turmoil was universal to all inhabitants of Algeria in one way or another. One was allowed to study Arabic, but it had no use for students in Algeria, except for masters of Arab farms, and so on (Derrida 2004a, 81). He was to take great pleasure in extending, destroying and enlivening the French language throughout his life.

Of course, Derrida's future destiny cannot be explained even in part by his cultural origins. He was never raised to be a successful man, nor was his success anticipated by his family. René Derrida, his brother, says that their mother read a lot, but had not read any of Derrida's works. Following him in later life, the family were astonished by what Jackie became, by each new idea, and by his ambition. They were not intelligent, and the way in which Derrida excelled at thinking was unaccountable to them. It would not have been such a surprise if the family had had the resources to give him an expensive education, but they were not wealthy, and his talent was simply unforeseen, like genius (Kofman and Dick 2003).

11 January 1938 saw the birth of Norbert Derrida, who died of tuberculosis barely two years later, the second death for Aimé and Georgette. At the same time Derrida was attending junior school at El-Biar. One can conjecture that he would not have done extremely well at school, since at times in his late adolescence he failed various exams, and felt ill at ease in schools or colleges. Photographs of him (Bennington, 1999; Derrida 2004a) show him to have dark, thick hair, and a complexion slightly darker than those of his classmates, 'a little black, and very Arab Jew' (Bennington 1999, 58).[2] He later said of himself that of his generation (in philosophy) he was the most melancholic, the least joyful (Derrida 2001b, 215). He did however have many friends later in life, or working associates, and if one can project the later life on to the earlier, in the belief that one's character does not change in any great degree, then we can speculate that Derrida probably had in his early youth a predilection for belonging to groups. Early memories consist of scenes of semi-rural, colonial life amongst farmers, some form of elevated status and ease, mixed with touches of civilization and barbarism, such as the motor car which killed one of his cousins a few years later, the doctor's surgery and the nurse who took blood from his arm with a syringe (Bennington 1999, 7); and then again the vastness of the Algerian desert which surrounded the urban areas, and into which he drove the family car once he had learned to drive (Derrida 2004a, 32). The Derrida family lived

at El-Biar on the edge of the crushingly poor Arab district. They lived on the outskirts of civilization, playing outdoors on dusty streets, surrounded a few miles away by murderous deserts, and feeling the vague thunder of coming civil war. He and his cousins stole grapes from a rare Algerian-Arab bourgeois vineyard.

He was an active child, one whose parents gave the casual and untraditional name of a film star, and whose father was often too busy properly to look after him. He felt that coming civil war in animal fashion, feeling the end of the world. His imagination was formed in these circumstances too. In dreamy moments the adult Derrida dreamed of making love or else of being a resistance fighter in the war, blowing up trains and bridges (Bennington 1999, 209). As well as wanting to be a writer, he also enjoyed life on the sports field, and wanted to be a professional footballer. Later he was part of a gang. His friendship and understanding of Jean Genet was more than an affected sympathy for a lifestyle and a style of writing and thinking vastly different from his own. There may not have been that much difference at all, given the amount of travelling he did, and the troubles which he caused, the way in which he throve off being misunderstood, blamed for various ills, and generally set aside as a mischievous villain.

During his childhood he had a collection of silkworms, a diversion which only a sensitive and inquisitive, secretive child could follow. He would have had to search for maple leaves during the summer so that he could observe the cycle of these maggot-like worms, which spin a cocoon of floss-like silk for themselves, and eventually become dark moths, an event which always surprised the young Derrida. The moth's change brings a burst of red, almost black colour, giving a sense of reality bursting forth, which Derrida likened to an image of a world without evil coming like a revelation from behind a veil. This event, he explained, and his collection, was a singularity which signed, as a memory, him alone (Derrida 2001a, 355).

Derrida's schooling was disrupted by the war in Europe when, at the age of ten, it came to North Africa. Immediately there was the Pétainization of the school in an Algeria which was never occupied, and never saw a German soldier. Derrida considered that his French citizenship was taken from him by the French themselves, because of an innate intolerance. The subsequent exclusion from school affected his identity, when all of the Jews became hostages of the French (Derrida 2004a, 86). Derrida remained in school two years more, though his older brother was subject to the quota for Jewish students and expelled at the beginning of the Pétainization. Jackie began the first year of secondary education at Lycée de Ben Aknoun in 1941, near to El-Biar.

1.4 During the War

The former Israeli President Ariel Sharon once said of the French that they are the most anti-Semitic people on earth. At the time this statement went uncontradicted (Barlow and Nadeau 2004, 93). The French have a famous self-regard and pride in both their land and its culture, which goes along well, perhaps, with a certain exclusivity, although one cannot align French culture with anti-Semitism. The Vichy laws in 1940 barred Jews from public offices, and from all state jobs, even teaching. The government went on to produce 168 anti-Jewish laws and regulations. The Law of Exclusion ordered officials to confiscate Jewish business. There were quotas for Jewish students, doctors, lawyers and other professionals. They were made defenceless, and people took all the Jewish goods they could get their hands on. Jews were rounded up in France and Algeria for the first time in 1942 by 6,000 French police. The persecutions in Algeria were unlike those of France. Jewish children were expelled from school, and Jewish teachers were laid off. In Algeria and El-Biar there was physical and verbal violence, including against children. Derrida suffered it at firsthand and for the duration of the war until liberation. Derrida confesses that he suffered a great deal of the basic elements of anti-Semitism. It went on around him, and he did not learn of it by hearsay. He suffered insults in the streets, from his classmates, and being beaten up as a 'dirty Jew' (Kofman and Dick 2003).

On the first day of the school year in 1942 at Ben-Aknoun, he was sent to the Principal's office and then home, not really knowing why. A Jewish high school had to be formed from the expelled pupils and the unemployed teachers, on rue Emile-Maupas. But Derrida, in his torment and fear, and probably suffering some sort of nervous debility, was absent from any sort of schooling for the following twelve months, playing truant, usually hanging around the brothels after the liberation, watching the Allied soldiers. During this year of exclusion he was also expected to attend 'the Alliance'. The Alliance was on the rue Bab Azoun, in a Jewish building where at thirteen he had to sit exams for his 'first communion' or *bar mitzvah*. There he pretended to learn Hebrew.

The Allies landed in 1942 on 8 November, but the return to normality had to wait eleven months, until October 1943, when the authorities realized that anti-Semitism was no longer justifiable. During adolescence anti-Semitism was *the* tragedy for Derrida. It was present in everything else. A desire to enter non-Jewish society was the result, and an over-sensitivity to little signs of racism. In his late essays and speeches on the immigration/race crisis in France in 1996, as well as in his statements on Bill Clinton's policy on the death penalty in the USA, which by and large targets African-Americans, there is a genuine and intense expression of hatred, with a rare bitterness and irony. He was victimized in his homeland, and also knew the pettiness, the emptiness of the reason for this victimization. He despised, for a time at least, the Jews themselves too, who seemed to welcome their segregation, their victimization, and the new feeling of community which their suffering brought them.

From 1943 to 1947 he was back at the Ben-Aknoun school, although in 1944–45 the school was transformed by the English into a military hospital and a prisoner of war camp for Italians, so that the students had to study in huts (Bennington 1999, 327). In years nine and ten, by 1944, when Algiers had become something of a cultural capital, Derrida was dreaming of writing books, and was reading Nietzsche, Valéry and Gide. He especially admired Gide, who visited and spent some time in Algiers like other French intellectuals who made it the literary capital while Paris was still occupied. Derrida said that for Gide he had a fetish, and that he knew several of his books by heart (Derrida 1995b, 341). The effects of Rousseau and Nietzsche in forming a mentality composed of key religious and atheistic concepts such as Nature, God, and Writing, are incalculable. These writers, these texts, like that of St Augustine, the north African Christian bishop, are confessional, they are soaked through with the life of their authors, with, as Derrida pointed out, their tears. They were all quick to tears, these writers whom he admired, and they all mixed their personal questioning of what man is, who they themselves are, with the infinity of time and of Nature, or that way of interpreting the meaning of things. Rousseau and Nietzsche were his two positive heroes, he said some forty years later (Bennington 1999, 33).

The way in which Bennington (1999, 327) describes Derrida's schooling after the war brings out that, being taught in huts, and in the general impoverishment of the post-war world, intellectual matters took second place to more basic activities of educational life such as football, track and field, and competitions, which diverted the scholars rather than raised them. The post-war years were austere and brutal, as they were in Britain at the time, with demobilized soldiers bringing home notions of discipline, aggression and the manners of the barrack room. The disorganized schooling itself, and his reaction to it, probably contributed to his later fascination with education, and especially to his campaign for philosophy teaching in schools. He only did well at philosophy, but had little formal recognition for it, and he probably suffered because, though he could read philosophy, he could not, during his teens, express his ideas in terms of how they were relevant to him. One must conjecture on the point of his recurrent and very painful failures, which were repeated, that they were caused to some extent by the fact that Derrida's reading was very wide, and was also undertaken largely in private. He developed a thoroughgoing love for French literature. Schoolmasters of whatever calibre and of whatever status never really are in a position to appreciate private study, and paradoxically, indulgence in study which is extracurricular is almost always punished by teachers.

1.5 The *Lycée*

Derrida began his adult thinking and research with the urgent question, on which he was to attempt to base a *Thèse d'Etat* when he had completed study at ENS, 'What is Literature?' (Norris 1987, 13). In Algeria he had ploughed through lessons on French geography, and French history, with none of it making any impression. But classes in French literature were different (Derrida 1998e, 45). French literature brought out in Derrida an indomitable desire to find and retain purity, the very heart of deconstruction (1998e, 46). The austerity and elite status, the pretensions of the literary canon, worked on him such that he could never stand, afterwards, any lack of purity in thought and language. He expressed this in *Monolingualism* (1998e) as both a desire for the purest French accent, style and text and, accompanying this, the demand on himself to go beyond even this mundane purity, and to deconstruct what did not seem pure enough in the tradition of literature and thought. This demand is not ethical, political or social, it is deconstruction itself, born straight from a desire to gain the heights of Western or European culture, and to carry it forward from this age in which a tawdry pop culture reigns. It was at its origin a desire to revive and match up to the great, and dying, European high culture, born in provincial Algeria, in an already mixed-up and rootless society, over which a distant and phantomatic homeland held sway. Well before he travelled to America, America had already become his 'homeland' (Derrida 2004a, 27).

Though Derrida's interest in culture for itself grew, his failures in formal examinations began to cause him embarrassment and suffering. His first major academic failure occurred where most people had already ceased formal study. He failed the *baccalauréat* at the Lycée Gauthier on the first attempt. The experience of sitting the *bac* can be traumatic, as it was for Derrida. At the same time he suffered physical illness, but he kept a private journal imitating Rousseau, Gide, Nietzsche, Valéry and Camus. He was doggedly following his own path at writing, since he also achieved publication for some poems which, he said, were terrible, in little North African reviews. Despite his mental suffering, which must have been cruelly poignant given his ambitions and his talent for reading and thinking, and his physical pains, which were probably psychosomatic, he was always to retry his formal examinations, and never to have time off from studies.

Back at the Lycée Gauthier in Algiers he pursued his baccalaureate as well as deep readings of Bergson and Sartre. He began to believe he could be a writer, and recognized, in a pragmatic manner, that since he had to earn a living, teaching could be his only option, even if he did not look forward to it. Derrida returned to the *lycée* in order to retake the baccalaureate examinations in 1948 at the time of his eighteenth birthday. This time he passed.

At eighteen he learned to drive and loved using the car to travel south into Algeria. His Algeria seemed to have death in its soul; it was wounded and murderous. This aspect of Derrida, the African side, is perhaps fully developed in his work in the fascination with death, the mixing of life and death, and his rejection of the here and now. He was always to incorporate a fascination with the infinite and the endless, the perspective of one who sees beyond conflict and opposition, the appearance of things, to the totality, which he saw as infinite, in which life, which always changes, and passes with time, is already, because it must change and die, infused with emptiness and inhuman deathly qualities, like the desert itself. But apart from the odd excursion with his father, he was never to go far from El-Biar as a youth, never at least more than seventy kilometres away, 'as far as the beaches of Bab-el-Oued, Saint-Eugène, Deux-Moulins, Madrague, or to Guyotville, Sidi-Ferruch, Zeralda, Cherchell, or Tipsa' (Derrida 2004a, 290).

He considered himself to have been a rebellious adolescent, and in his way despised the French sophistication which he found in literature and in those from the *Metropole*, as France was known. Throughout his life, like Paul de Man, he always preferred and returned to the great originality and passionate, nationalistic, troubling, questions of the Germans. In continental philosophy after Hegel there is an essential, creative, literary fictionality and daring in the quest for what matters in the here and now, at home. He dreamt of a great explosive Book and whiled away time by belonging to a gang. It is not impossible to reconcile the little philosopher with the 'hooligan' who despised restrictions.

Jean-Paul Sartre opened up the philosophical and literary world for him, but he had some damning things to say in later years about Sartre. Namely

that Sartre, in spite of his appalling lack of understanding of all of his contemporaries, was still accepted as the intellectual giant and the speaker on
behalf of them all. Sartre dominated the scene while misreading everyone.
Derrida wants to know what is it, or who is it, that grants authority to him,
or those like him (Derrida 1995b, 123)? Sartre played a major role then, and
was always loved, as a model, though nefarious and catastrophic. That first
question, 'What is literature?', was also Sartre's.[3] 'I learned a lot from
Sartre's "What is Literature?"' (Derrida 1995b, 345). But he only really got
to grips with existentialism and Sartre when he arrived in Paris as a boarder,
when he also began reading books of Simone Weil, and a brand of Catholic
mysticism. While still in Algeria he discovered Kierkegaard and Heidegger
and was 'awed', overcome, by the mental and spiritual 'leap' which they
demand by various rhetorical strategies (Bennington 1999, 328), into a discovery of what is most real, and what is most near at hand.

1.6 André Gide

Derrida's early 'Bible' was André Gide's *Fruits of the Earth* (2002), a book
which itself was written by a young man. Gide was twenty-eight when he
wrote it, and, suffering from tuberculosis, thought he was going to die. That
it was Derrida's most important book as a youth is not in itself important
since it is aimed at youth, and lends itself to appropriation by any semi-
religious but rebellious sort of mentality. Derrida only developed as a writer
much later in life, by which time many of the early influences were forgotten. But this text, semi-religious and anti-Christian, in love with the present,
pantheistic, and also anxious about losing what remains of experience, gives
a taste of how Derrida felt and saw his life at the turning of his youth into
early manhood.

Fruits of the Earth has the same quality of swerved Nietzscheanism and
superhuman closeness to nature which many early interpreters of Nietzsche
found and espoused. The narrator of this highly artificial and mock-naïve
text tells his understudy, Nathaniel, to give up reading, to give up following,
and to live. The book accounts for travels in Italy and North Africa, forcing
itself to name foreign fruits and places, describing empty landscapes, without
mention of the sophistication amidst which Gide had grown up. It requires
a great deal of energy and resources to live in the superhuman self-exposure
to dehumanized culture and the nudity of soul which Gide prescribes almost
desperately. Above all, like Nietzsche apparently, it prescribes the use of the

will, of willpower in order to desire more, to experience more, and to love everything. It is a book or a reading for those perhaps who are afraid of the banality of experience, the banality of orthodox religious answers, and of growing pains, something Nietzsche would probably have called, in its artificiality and nervous distraction, *'décadent'*. In its refusal of all tradition, and desperate desire to be at one with life or nature, *Fruits of the Earth* is the book for those afraid of the death and non-self-presence which the later Derrida was to accept as wholeheartedly as Gide fears it. In it, Gide is very metaphysical and unreflective, following the old metaphysical concepts of presence, God, experience, the soul and natural process, as if they had only just been blended in this way. Is not all of this what present-day post-metaphysical philosophy is in mourning for? Here one can see how Derrida was once anti-Judaic and anti-Christian in sentiment, maybe with passion, and how he continued in reading Kant, Heidegger and Levinas, to seek this same ultra-ontological site where a pantheistic God could be located. This dream of full-presence was to be that which Derrida would soon commemorate and mourn, calling it just that, a dream, although his love of 'life' was to emerge in his last years as a theme, and his desire for a purer life, a purer world, was never to cease to be followed.

2
Paris and ENS

2.1 Boarding School

After the baccalaureate Derrida spent a year at the Lycée Bugéaud in Algiers doing the *khâgne*, with a view to entering the *École Normale Supérieure*, in Paris. He would move to Paris and develop as a thinker and writer in an academic community, and undertake a personal study of Husserl. He would develop the kind of writing he dreamt of, following Rousseau and Nietzsche, transfiguring his identity, and his religious intuitions, which had been refined against the disappointment of his familial Judaism.

During the summer of 1948, having passed the *bac*, he enrolled for the ENS, never having heard of this famous institution before. By his own account this momentous change of the direction of his career, which set him on to a path which ultimately led him to becoming the friend and colleague of the most distinguished philosophers of Europe, and becoming the leading French thinker, occurred after hearing a radio programme in which a French professor of *hypokhâgne* talked of literary studies as being of benefit, and also of a writer from Algeria, named Camus, who had become internationally respected after attending that Parisian *école*. Derrida went to see this teacher the very next day, enrolling for the *khâgne* at the Lycée Bugéaud, preparatory to entrance to the ENS, still not knowing properly what the ENS was. Four years had to pass before he was accepted to study at ENS, having passed the entrance examinations. The *École Normale Supérieure* is the leading French college specializing in educating the teachers and professors of the French education system, and it only accepts the very best pupils. It was still, at that time, the *éccole* which supplied France with its leading political figures too, although since the war this role had gradually been taken on by the ENA, the School of Administration. Entrance is dependent on a competition held open to all French students, known as the *concours*. Post-baccalaureate education in France involves a year of study called the *khâgne*, followed by a course called the *hypokhâgne*, which Derrida began, at the age of nineteen, in Paris, at Louis-le-Grand. Instead of it taking him one year, though, it took Derrida three. These were years of suffering and torture for him. In October 1949 he first travelled to the *Metropole* on the *Ville d'Alger*, landing at Marseilles, a twenty-hour voyage, which he spent with a memorable sea-sickness, then took the train to Paris.

When Derrida spoke of his lack of authentic culture whilst growing up (1998e, *passim*), doing so in a depressed mood, he also meant that he did not have any knowledge of French and European culture until a late stage in his development, for the only culture he was ever really to have was the one he learnt at the ENS. This meant, to judge by how much of it he later learnt, that he had to do a great deal of cramming. This crammed reading of philosophy, history and literature began at around his time of leaving secondary education and the beginning of the baccalaureate studies, a study which with his great talent for reading he ought to have had little trouble with, but which, because he had been schooled and raised in such a haphazard and confused way, had to be paid for with repeated failures and physical ailments.

Arriving in Paris, his first lodging was at the 'sinister' boarding house of Louis-le-Grand, or 'Baz' Grand' (Derrida 2004a, 76; 1998e, 44). His first years were a bad experience. He had difficulty maintaining his health and getting used to his new solitude, and little luck with his studies, save in philosophy, which he enjoyed. Except in this discipline, nothing seemed to harmonize in his mind. He turned to intense readings of Simone Weil, of Christian mysticism, and of modern existentialists (Bennington 1999, 325–36). In 1950 he had to return to El-Biar for three months due to ill health. There was nervous collapse, lack of sleep, nightmares, and prescription of amphetamines. In his third, and what turned out to be his final year at Louis-le-Grand, he met many who would remain his friends, whether they went to the ENS with him or not, including Michel Serres and Pierre Bourdieu (Bennington 1999, 329), who were, along with him, to survive structuralism, and rise to prominence in its wake.

Louis-le-Grand was a prestigious boarding-school, but Derrida suffered from the pressure, was sick all of the time, and frail, on the edge of nervous breakdown. This was not solely due to the difficulty of the tuition there, which was preparatory for entrance to the elite *écoles*. Derrida had always been sickly and 'quick to tears'. He was now an exile, and without family. He had never been far outside of El-Biar before, and failure meant ignominious return to that provincial and communal life which he despised. It is quite marvellous that he had the determination to continue what he had by chance begun, but then self-sacrifice and doing without vacation were the traits which he had inherited from his father. Derrida's problems will also have sprung from a feeling that all that he knew, all that he was confident about and strong in, his family, friends, his status as Jackie Derrida, were no longer of any use to him, and that he was having to stake himself on his philosophical interest, an interest which itself was not certain, since he had been largely self-taught, and it is very likely that he was barely recognized as a talent for years after his move. (He later insisted on teaching philosophy properly, and from early on.) From the early 1950s colonial Algerian politics and society were unbearable to him, and yet his situation in Paris at Louis-le-Grand would have been no comfort. It was at this stage of his life that Derrida entered into the life of self-determination, and he seems to have found it very difficult to come to terms with. After these experiences, schools and colleges always gave him physical symptoms and anxiety (as, it might be pointed out, they did Nietzsche). But having made himself here, in these schools, he always feared and hated the thought of leaving, like his fellow-Algerian, Louis Althusser. Despite having been in despair at the ENS, he took up the post of lecturer in philosophy there in 1964, and always preferred *écoles* to universities. It was in these dark and isolated years that Derrida began his struggle with what he saw as the pinnacle of modern philosophy, its most up-to-date and most genuine exemplar, Edmund Husserl's phenomenology, which he would have had to toil with, gratified, if at all, by the vision of ultimate truth, the most sure description of science and scientific objects which philosophy could yield.

In his final year at the *lycée* (1951–52) he spent a year in a 'minuscule maid's room without running water at 17 rue Lagrange, near the Place Maubert' (2004a, 291). Derrida failed the *concours* twice before finally entering the ENS on his third attempt. He did so in 1952, aged twenty-two. He was to make a few journeys home to Algeria in the coming years while at ENS but not according to the strict regulations. He would travel home 'on board cargo planes that didn't look very reassuring (a less expensive way to travel, but which could be rather frightening when they hit air pockets with altogether more vertiginous results given that one was seated on a bench in the middle of cases full of vegetables)' (Derrida 2004a, 290). Derrida's time at ENS would also include annual holidays, with a visit to a ski resort in the Alps in 1953, the Loire Valley châteaux in 1955, and Normandy in 1956 (Derrida 2004a, 291). His final year at Baz' Grand was brighter, and he met many of his lifelong friends there, including his future brother-in-law (Bennington 1999, 329).

2.2 Husserl

With entrance into the ENS Derrida settled down into a confirmed study of Husserl, and a normal student life. He settled into the district in Paris in which he was to live for the rest of his life. The course of Derrida's study went from 1952 to 1956,[1] during which time he was studying Husserl, and wrote *The Problem of Genesis in the Philosophy of Husserl* (only published in 1990). He was not taken by the more engaging Husserl of life-world phenomenology which Merleau-Ponty made famous in the days of French phenomenology, but rather by the most rigorous and abstract, the most scrupulous, even tedious analyses of signs, meaning and ideality to be found in Husserl's *Logical Investigations* ([1901], 1970).[2] Derrida began studying Husserl in 1949, and his commitment to him increased as his formal education continued, until, at the time when he was teaching, ten years after his return from his compulsory military service in Algeria, he was giving papers, and publishing texts on him; the better part of the publications up to and including 1967 are on Husserl. But just so intense as this involvement with the one particular author was, so the end came with an avoidance of further involvement after *Speech and Phenomena* in 1967 (Derrida 1973), and in the arch non-Husserl, non-logocentric text *Of Grammatology* [1967] (Derrida 1997b), which asserts the revolution against Western idealism as exemplified by him. It was a technical training (Caputo 1997a, 56). What is remarkable, therefore, is that this intense and long study gave Derrida his own style of thought.

Husserl was the 'test case' wherein the grammatological opening was first seen (Derrida 2003, xiii). Derrida developed deconstruction by attending to Husserl's difficulties in explaining what properly 'exists' and, at another level, to his conception of the nature of language, the sign, speech and writing. The study of Husserl was not that of a follower, or one who considered this 'science of science' to be the source of knowledge; it is not the study undertaken by one who is convinced. He read internally, which means he read like a true follower. Maybe he read Husserl so as not to get involved in the prevailing orthodoxy of 'life-world' existentialism and phenomenology at that time while still doing philosophy, for he always preferred to avoid any 'community' or any sort of hegemony. Derrida was close to the existentialists, but he was not sympathetic, and he went his own way.

Husserl as a test case raises a problem. Husserlian transcendental subjective phenomenology was the predominant French philosophy of the time, and, following Sartre, more or less every French philosopher was trying to do what Husserl and Heidegger (then still flourishing) had done. This means that Derrida was studying the fashionable philosophy, and 'philosophy' *stricto sensu*, as opposed to 'thought' in general, humanities in general. The problem would then be, how did Derrida's become an original thinking by following a backward and already over-subscribed school? The answer is that as a 'test case', phenomenology was only a means to critique philosophy so as to bring grammatology and deconstruction's post-metaphysical, post-nationalist philosophy to light. It also means that Derrida maintained a distance from Husserl throughout, which explains why, when once he had expressed his 'grammatology', he never returned to Husserl again.

The study resulted in his first thorough essay, 'The Problem of Genesis in Edmund Husserl'; his first research work proper, at Harvard; his being awarded a prize for research (with Husserl's 'Origin of Geometry'; *An Introduction* (Derrida 1978)); his first book-length publication, the *Origin* again; and his first conference – at Cerisy, delivering 'Genesis and Structure' (Derrida 2003, 193–211). One must see Derrida as a Husserl specialist, or one of those involved in promoting knowledge of Husserl, and if not a specialist, then a Husserl scholar. For although his knowledge of the history of philosophy, ancient and modern, was great, including knowledge of Kant, Hegel, Heidegger, Plato and so on, as well as of modern existentialism and phenomenology, structuralist linguistics, ethnology, and up-to-date literature and theory, he concentrated on Husserl when producing finished work. Because of what we know about Derrida's random course through education, blessed by excellent good fortune as it was, and of the very practical nature of 'deconstruction', as opposed to the abstractions of phenomenology, we are able now to see that Derrida was not quite as interested in Husserl's project for itself as he may have seemed. It is true that Derrida was always to be interested in the history of concepts, and the use of concepts in the various sciences, but to master Husserl (who is a very difficult thinker), and to overcome and then discard it, having won a victory over it, was perhaps a greater motivation for the young Derrida. Derrida's scholarship, as he himself began to see, when he put it beside his literary interests in 1957, was never completely sincere with respect to Husserl.

Husserl's philosophy was very widely studied amongst French academics in the mid-twentieth century. The propagation of the teaching, which Derrida joined as he did not join the communist revival, involved Levinas, someone with whom, in general, he had sympathies. Levinas had translated Husserl into French, along with another acquaintance and teacher of Derrida's, Paul Ricoeur. Derrida took part in this work himself with his own translation of the 'Origin of Geometry'. We must also consider Derrida's remarks on Husserl and Heidegger in light of the necessity of the questioning philosophy, or the demand to question.

Husserl was a neo-Kantian, who produced some powerful new ideas which have been very useful to the Continental tradition in the last century, such as the transcendental reduction of phenomena to ideas inside the openness of intentionality. Heidegger meanwhile developed his new 'fundamental analysis' of Being by adapting intentionality. In general Husserl's was a thinking through of the way in which things are experienced, like a psychology, or, more basically, like a scientific understanding of science. It has retained its interest in the modern era since it lends to knowledge the human aspect of being 'intended', and of being the product of a living consciousness, an interesting distinction in the age of machines and computers.

2.3 Husserl's Development

For Husserl, the first glimpse of this new concept of a scientific study of science was seen from a study of mathematical objects in *The Philosophy of Arithmetic* which he published towards the end of the nineteenth century. Husserl refused to accept that maths and its structure, its numbers and laws of mathematical series, had fallen from some heavenly place (Derrida 2003, 197), and so he had set out in the *The Philosophy of Arithmetic* to give them a history from the perspective of both the psychological and the objective.

Thus he had to navigate between the Scylla and Charybdis of logicizing structuralism and psychologistic genetism (very much in the subtle form of the 'transcendental psychologism' of Kant). He had to open up a new direction of philosophical attention and permit the discovery of a concrete, but non-empirical, intentionality, a 'transcendental experience' which would be simultaneously productive and revelatory, active and passive (Derrida 2003, 198–9). The transcendental intentionality solved a puzzle both psychological-projective and empirical-receptive. His problem was the problem of the foundation of objectivity (Derrida 2003, 199), although as it turned out it was the one place which escaped description. His theory, in a nutshell, was to posit an 'open space', a transcendental space, which joined, like a line, the human consciousness and the phenomenal world, while also dividing them. The open space is the location into which the consciousness first emerges, and in which the world as objective thing first appears phenomenally. It was always how this open space or 'transcendental' opening was generated in the first place which was a problem for Derrida. This opening was perhaps Husserl's main discovery, and as such was exploited by Heidegger, his student. The transcendental opening became, in his hands, 'Dasein', or 'Being-here'.

Of course, Derrida's study of Husserl was always also a study of Heidegger, following Heidegger's exact pathway away from Husserl. (While Derrida was studying, Heidegger himself was still writing what Derrida was to learn so much from: his *Elucidations of Hölderlin's Poetry*, *The Question of Being*, and so on. Heidegger, in fact, only died in 1976, after Derrida's *Glas*, and Derrida was, perhaps, shy of being too involved while this was the case.) Husserl's value was that he was a serious and original thinker, building on the past, and demanding answers which could work and convince today. But he was very similar to Kant, largely by accident in fact, because he was uneducated in the history of philosophy, and yet orientated towards science and mathematics. He was early on crassly empiricist, only turning to a more Kantian, transcendental idealism after a severe criticism from Frege on the publication of his *Philosophy of Arithmetic*.

2.4 'Violence and Metaphysics' [1964]

In following Derrida into his early studies it will be borne in mind both that Husserl was a respected master for his early training in thinking, and that Husserl was a 'test case'. The study of Husserl, which began in earnest in 1952, was to be to the detriment of the study of Heidegger therefore, and of other sympathies. We will now try to make good this lapse by reading ahead to 1964, when Derrida began to write on Heidegger and Husserl together.

The essay 'Violence and Metaphysics' (2003, 97–192), shows to us a defence of Husserl, and of Heidegger, against criticism of them in *Totality and Infinity* (Levinas 1969). Heidegger is accused by Levinas of being unethical, because of his supposed disregard of the Other. There is a proper explanation for this complaint, in that the consistent relationship which, Heidegger maintained, was most basic to thinking of the highest and most enduring sort, was to Being or the reign of truth which metaphysics reveals, particularly in one's own origin, which, as more important than, and prior to *other people*, was also an excuse for never considering them. But Derrida surprises us by pointing out what is obvious. Heidegger's 'Being' [*Sein/Seyn*] was always conceived by him as prior to the Other, or the pure singularity of the Other as a person, and, thus, letting Being be also lets the Other be.

Levinas in any case made gross, very hasty readings of Heidegger. His writing has a simple style, of reducing complex texts to simple statements. Heidegger's work is called 'ontology' even though this is something which Heidegger had revolutionized, and after *Being and Time* he had denied the fundamental value of ontology in his theory and practice. His work is also concerned with *power*, says Levinas, but at what point did Heidegger cease to campaign against power interpretations, Derrida asks?

Later on, Derrida would admit that Levinas was a thinker with whom he never disagreed over fundamentals. Levinas represents the religious interest for Derrida, and as an antagonist of the two German thinkers he is also an external perspective. Not that Levinas was an equal to these two in terms of how well and deeply he thought. He made gross errors and simplifications. But his religious sense was good and his ethics were serious, even if his thought is, in essence, aimed at an impossible and pure empiricism, capturing the individuality of each individual. In despair of achieving this, it outlines a thought in terms borrowed from the most gratuitous of Grecian metaphysics.[3]

2.5 Levinas

In general Levinas only began to seem sympathetic when the structuralist movement had ended, but if a non-structuralist element was part of Derrida's thinking from the first, then Levinas represents it, as Bernasconi noticed (Wood and Bernasconi 1985; Bernasconi 1992, 136), because Derrida did not ever wish to deconstruct Levinas, only to deconstruct his empiricism. John D. Caputo was later to show himself to be a very committed follower of Derrida and his 'religion'. He says of Levinas that while in Jewish theology the characterization of sanctity is reserved for God, Levinas extends it to the Other, or other person, with a gesture which neglects to explain how this is possible (Caputo, 1997a, 136).

The essay on Levinas, as almost a third of *Writing and Difference*, has all the appearance of being the crucial part of the collection. In this essay, originally published in the *Revue de métaphysique et de morale* [1964], Derrida goes over the most important influences on his philosophy. Husserl, Heidegger and Levinas are all treated, and are made to interact with one another. It returns Derrida to a more homely place, the religion of his ancestors, and a patient, meditative, non-Marxist, non-Freudian place, which was also the place of a brand of purest philosophy.

Husserl had taught Levinas that the absolute need to keep up the questioning which philosophy undertakes is the most essential thing, it is the essence of freedom and responsibility. He and Heidegger, in Hegel's shadow, were involved in keeping questioning alive as a necessity (Derrida 2003, 99–100).

2.6 Althusser and Marxism

French 1950s philosophy, in its academic heartland, the ENS, was dominated by phenomenological concerns (Dosse 1998a, 37), and it was, above all, Sartrean, emphasizing a consciousness able to know itself. This meant that Heidegger and Husserl were the *koine* of philosophical students and teachers. As we saw, Derrida was not keen to join in, however, since Merleau-Ponty, who taught at ENS, was changing philosophy into something akin to a social science, and was transforming *Being and Time*, which was intended as an explanation of how Spirit develops from commonplace origins and our actual birth and life in time, into a mere anthropology. There was also a good deal of Husserlian scholarship which treated Husserl as a psychologist. Heidegger and Nietzsche therefore had to be rediscovered somewhat. It is in this way that, moving away from the 'anthropological' Heidegger of *Being and Time* [1927] which Sartre had popularized, he was to dwell on the late Heidegger of 'What Are Poets For?' (in *Holzweg*, Heidegger 1950, and Heidegger 1975) and *The Question of Being* (Heidegger [1955], 1959). He also particularly admired Heidegger's *Elucidations of Hölderlin's Poetry* (2000b), which harbours all of Heidegger's later period attitudes to philosophy and literature and, not coincidentally, resembles, in its outline of the scheme of Being as 'destining', Derrida's grammatology.[4] On the whole the next decade was to see philosophy decline further, however, with Foucault's *Madness and Civilization* dealing something of a deathblow to pure French philosophy (Dosse 1998a, 41).

ENS in the 1950s, while Derrida was there, was also dominated by the 'go-tos' who attended communion, and the communists, who were mostly Left-wing Christians (Dosse 1998a, 148). Only in 1960 did Althusser introduce 'scientific' Marxism into the ENS, and in 1961 began giving his 'young Marx' seminars in which he considered this early Marx as more radical and more scientific than the Marx of *Capital*. Lacan began lecturing there also in 1963, invited by Althusser, with seminars on Freud against humanism and psychologism. But ENS in the 1950s was still a place where philosophy, as opposed to structuralism, even if it was existentialist, was taught.

Entrance saw the start for Derrida of a normal sort of training, and new failures, in ethnology and psychology. He met Marguerite Aucouturier, his future wife, a Czechoslovak. The two met when Derrida was on a skiing holiday with a friend of his from ENS in winter 1953. She was the sister of the friend who had invited him; Marguerite described her first seeing him from afar in the snow. Some time later she invited him to dinner at the family home (Kofman and Dick 2003). Derrida belonged to militant extreme-Left-wing groups intermittently, but not communist ones. Communism along Stalinist lines was dominant in the rue d'Ulm, but Derrida consistently refused to become involved.[5] On his first day he met Louis Althusser (Bennington 1999, 329).

Derrida and Althusser, who was his director of studies, and like himself from Algeria, rarely discussed philosophy together and thus remained friends, Derrida later recalled (Derrida 2002a, 149). Teachers at ENS never did talk openly about their personal studies and research with each other in conversation. Everything was assumed and never said. When assumptions did become vocal there could be trouble and chaos. So when Althusser and Derrida met, they talked of Algeria rather than philosophy, setting up a secret accord due to their shared background. But Derrida was reticent with him on the subject of Marxism, because it seemed to lack an understanding of the historicity of ideas. In later years Althusser's success caused Derrida some embarrassment since, in the last instance, Marxism, and Althusser's version of it, had an anchor in the economics of production, which Derrida rejects (Derrida, 2002a, 172), because he has a concept of a general economy, rather than one restricted to exchange values and products.

Born in 1919, only eleven years before Derrida, Althusser says in his autobiography that he misled his contemporaries, since although he was continually associated with Lacan and Freud at the ENS, where a Lacano-Althusserian orthodoxy took hold in the early 1960s, and where his type of Marxism used a Freudian approach (Dosse 1998a, 300), he had not really

31

read much Freud, and, indeed, he often asked Derrida for help on this matter (Derrida 2004c, 104). He became a student at the ENS at the age of twenty-seven after the Second World War and never had to leave, becoming a *caïman* – or a tutor, in philosophy. He taught in the rue d'Ulm and also lived there. His ironic and confused reasons for being a communist are characteristic of Left-wing behaviour in France at the time it seems, for they witness a confused grasping at justice and equality in the state, atheistic materialism, and self-centredness, even a kind of lunacy in self-promotion and safety, and above all, the ambition to be in charge.

After studying at ENS Althusser became *caïman* for Foucault as well as for Derrida. In fact, in this 'womb' he had a profound and well-known effect on the whole generation of French professors and teachers, with his 'scientific', structuralist-linguistic version of Marx's work. His teaching was Marxist, but also anti-PCF (Parti communiste français) from within the PCF. Although he objected to family and state, hating his parents and ultimately strangling his wife, he idolized his country grandparents for their physical lifestyle (Sturrock, 1998, 45). This plain, country life was his redemptive future for France and the West. He suffered from psychiatric problems, and it is estimated that he was admitted into hospital every three years of his life. After the murder, in 1980, he was put into care and not into prison.

2.7 The Student Generation of the 1950s and 1960s

France was in these years very conservative and inward centred, as indeed were its thinkers, who took little notice of specifically British or American culture.[6] It had not yet suffered its humiliation in Algeria, and had not been turned towards Europe by Charles de Gaulle. In intellectual things, the era was dominated by a sense of crushing conformity, almost intellectual policing in conformity with structuralism, Marxism and a basically Freudian psychoanalysis. All of these influences were internalized in the members of the community, not imposed from without, and were thus more difficult to overcome. Marxism and Freudianism differed in their types of imposition of authority: Freudianism was just a culturally formative power, while Marxism governed ideas and politics.

These were years of intense ideological debate at the ENS, with Marx as constant reference, but with no sure 'scientific' grounding; years of debate because the conventional bases of the Left were in trouble. Krushchev's anti-Stalinism mattered in France, and called for a reappraisal of Stalinism. Italian

Marxists were vocal, and published in *Les Temps Modernes*. New Marx manuscripts were being published, and Rosa Luxembourg, the German communist, was back in fashion. Above all, everyone questioned the PCF. The PCF represented order and stability, while the student unions wanted change and were against stability, wanting to take the place of the French Communist Party.

The Algerian War, which began in 1954, opened the eyes of this genera-tion and moulded its attitude to politics and to France as it had been. With the atrocities committed there, authorized by the French government, these students did not have any faith in democracy. They also admired the revo-lution in Cuba, and supported the Vietnamese in the war from which the French military had just withdrawn; the Third World became important, a situation in which Lévi-Strauss' anti-Westernism was popular. It was a polit-ical culture which believed in changing society by means of politics. The primacy of the political domain was, throughout the 1950s, unquestioned, and since the PCF was contested, separate Marxisms developed critiques, rereadings, debates, new ideas. With all of this, however, Derrida was to have little to do, and belonged to the various small groups on rue d'Ulm only 'intermittently' and half-heartedly (Bennington 1999, 329). A far-Left Stalinism was dominant there.

When Derrida arrived at the ENS and Paris this is the environment which he found, post-war and austere, inward-looking and conservative, with a hard disillusionment with democracy amongst the students and some of the staff: ENS was not a university, but was rather avant-garde and abreast with radical thinking. The new revolutionary temper was to climax with the intellectual shambles of 1968. While sharing most of its main ideals, Derrida was suspicious and shy of involvement and cultivated a genuine intellectual detachment. He found it most offensive that he had to join or not join the various communities. And although he shared the main objectives, and throughout his life adhered to socialism, as if it dominated his frame of mind and his conceptual framework, he still found fault with the way that the various individuals dominating the scene viewed essential matters, particu-larly the status of the concepts they were using.[7] What they lacked was a knowledge and application of the dominant motifs of Husserl and Heidegger, especially of the latter, in regard to history and the questioning of the subject, and finally in regard to the status and use of questioning-thinking itself. Heidegger's technique is often to reveal the real nature of words, their real meanings. By the time Derrida was twenty-two and entering ENS he already had a largely self-taught grounding in these matters which conflicted with the assumptions of Althusser and Foucault, his teachers. Caputo (1997a, 178) says that Derrida's late democratic messianism is attuned to the excesses of both the Left and Right of the twentieth century, which is the historical matrix from which deconstruction was born in the 1960s, drawing on both, but avoiding their desire for realizing, concretely, the impossible. Derrida's fixation with Heidegger and Nietzsche would have been seen as rather Right-wing in those times. As he later recalled, a critic of his work in the early 1970s attacked *Tel Quel* for publishing thinkers who were associated with the German Right. It was with the more pride in his secrecy and non-commitment, and the more determination not to be side-tracked, that he continued with these personal studies, precisely because the study of them had ruined his chances at each formal examination hitherto. He considered that this determination would one day pay off, if he only per-severed. All the same, he failed examinations in psychology and ethnology, perhaps, this time, because he was simply not interested in these anti-philosophical sciences.

Another of Derrida's teachers in philosophy was the Hegel scholar Jean Hyppolite, who guided a generation of students at ENS towards Marx and Hegel. Hyppolite, following Kojève, stressed that the essential attribute of Hegel's thought was the master-slave moment of the dialectic. Lacan was to call it the 'iron law of our era' (Lacan 2001, 29), an era in which the 'Other' was having to be recognized by the subject. It was Hyppolite, along with Althusser, who was to find Derrida his job at ENS in 1964 when he himself departed, and to invite Derrida to stay on as a substitute teacher when his formal studies were concluded.

2.8 Psychoanalysis

The psychoanalytic science and way of thinking was, with Marxism, an orthodoxy in the 1950s. It formed a sort of conscience in ENS, and in Paris at large. In effect, the general tendency was to cure the mind, and to direct those thus cured towards a socialist politics.[8] If it was not a pure Freudianism, it threw people on to themselves, isolating them and aggriev-ing them, though the Unconscious took away personal responsibility. The resulting mixture, incorporating the already metaphorical and intangible element of the self-as-psychoanalysis, with an ideal image of how things ought to be, made of the thinking of Derrida's contemporaries something which Derrida's work does not so much deconstruct as epitomize.

Deconstruction itself is a sort of cure of philosophy's historical illness, and most of Derrida's narrative, invention and reading styles have psychoanalytic tendencies. While at ENS Derrida read Freud in a 'fragmentary, insufficient, conventional way' (Derrida 2004c, 169), which probably means he read the *The Interpretation of Dreams*, *The Psychopathology of Everyday Life*, *Civilisation and Its Discontents*, and so on. Even up to the time of *Of Grammatology* [1967], he did not know much of Lacan, and had only looked over a couple of his shorter papers superficially. He was failing his examinations in psychology at the ENS while there, but as he said to Elizabeth Roudinesco many years later (2004c, 179), psychoanalysis itself, as opposed to psychology, is never really permitted in state institutions, and Freud was probably not on the course of studies there.

One cannot really understand, perhaps, Marxism and socialism, the sense of liberty and of the destruction of classical reality, without also understanding psychoanalysis. Foucault, Althusser, Lyotard and Lacan are each, along with countless others, so similar to one another, both as critics of bourgeois cultural and political reality, and as theorists of the subjectivity of the self along Freudian lines. Derrida entered into this culture and did things with it from the start, self-consciously no doubt, but without attempting to exit from it. He disagreed not with its arguments, but with the whole basis of these sciences of the subject, of logocentrism, so that a mere exit was not of any use. Changes had to come from within.

What made Derrida stand out in this culture is mostly the serious value which he accorded to the origin of any science, an origin implicating any science in religion and poetic founding: he remained a philosopher. His vision of the true Unconscious as a really pure 'unknown' was stronger than Freud's, but his vision of what constitutes a self, or the psyche, was to become, especially in *Of Grammatology*, quite Freudian, picturing it as a set of forces and traces, but written, archived ones, rather machine-like, a process in which the self, the whole psyche, is seen to be spectralized, shot through with traces, rather than substantial and whole. The problem of distinguishing psychoanalysis from within his work is the more difficult in that the terms and notions which Freud had developed, chiefly the Unconscious in *The Interpretation of Dreams* (1991 [1899]), had become so much a part of the culture of Europe that practically every discourse owed something to Freud. Freud's later theories, of the superego, the ego, and the like, which took on a life of their own, were aspects of Freudianism which, of course, Derrida did not believe in, but for all that, the idea of curing the mind, of utilizing fictional descriptions and methods, of making progress by means of invoking

35

unconscious motives, by way of a communicative therapy in which facts are mental and in which myths mean something, reverberates in Derrida's style.

The ENS culture mixed literature, philosophy and psychoanalysis as it seemed appropriate, in an effort to produce well-educated teachers, and as Derrida was to do later himself, in *The Post Card* for example. It was not a university, but the breeding ground of an elite corps of teachers, and, strictly, there was no orthodoxy or tradition of classicism there. ENS was avant-garde. In *The Post Card* and *Glas*, which draw on Lacan and Freud in an almost doctrinal way, Derrida shows that in the main he conceives of the living mind broadly in Freudian/Lacanian terms, that is, linguistic ones, although he disputes the vitalist version of things in the one, and the structural quality of the other's thought on language as 'sign', and as capable of speaking the truth. In *Glas*, *The Post Card* and *Circumfession*, Derrida takes the science of psychoanalysis at its own estimate, and speaks its own language, but changes 'full speech' into traces, and living mind into machine. Above all Derrida was trying to make use of the neglected thinking of Nietzsche in this field. He also probed the drastic and simple Freudian way of positing an Unconscious in which practically anything could occur, and he wished to map it out and to free it up in *The Post Card*, while he subjected it to Hegel's Absolute Knowledge in *Glas*. In fine one must say that it took until the mid-1970s for Derrida to comment fully on psychoanalysis, and when he did so it was with reference to the Lacanian side of it, considering the applied aspects to be none of his business, and limiting himself to Freud and Lacan as writers and authors, rather than as doctors.

But in the last analysis, Derrida kept his distance from psychology. If anything, a prevailing sexualization of the mind, a commonplace orthodoxy on the mind's form, which gave very little and took away a great deal, would have been embarrassing for Derrida, in that it produced almost no genuine enquiry or thought on the mind, for which Husserl would have been a welcome remove. The quite banal notion of curing a mind, treating it as a simple object, which permitted simplistic sociological and anthropological descriptions of man and society, was drastically reversed by all of Derrida's texts with their heightened sensitivity, intelligence and lack of dogma.

2.9 Michel Foucault

Derrida heard Michel Foucault, with whom naturally he has many affinities, lecture in 1951 when he arrived in Paris as a student of the *khâgne*.

He became a friend of Foucault's in 1954, at the time when he made a journey to Leuven (or Louvain) to inspect the Husserl Archives for his dissertation. Despite their proximity, he and Foucault were always wary of each other and their work is, in its style, very different, though both had high standards of scholarship. In the main their search for social and political justice was the same, but as well as their style, their ontology was at variance.

Foucault is rightly seen to be an enemy of pure philosophy, which he was not shy of describing as a hindrance to liberation, and part of the ancient, Western logocentrism. Foucault published *Madness and Civilization*, a critique of logocentric reason, in 1961 (Foucault 1989), and Derrida wrote on the text in 1963 in 'Cogito and the History of Madness' (2003, 36–76), a lecture delivered to the Collège Philosophique, and published in the *Revue de métaphysique et de morale*, expressing himself with a self-confidence that shows a long familiarity with Foucault and with certain ideas of what he thought psychoanalysis and philosophy should be. Despite Foucault's dealing with fairly socialist and revolutionary themes in his work – the prison's history, rather than the government's, for example – Foucault deals with his subject in a straightforwardly academic way, a way, in fact, which the government of any era would find sympathetic. Like Levinas, he uses logocentric metaphysics to undermine logocentric metaphysics, which, despite its deconstructive appearance, does not effect a change. In his accommodation of the Other, but within reason, and in the name of justice rather than prejudice, Derrida's approach to problems will have more of a future, as territorial law is superseded by international law in the future of the West. Perhaps deconstruction is a genuine accommodation and resolution of otherwise insoluble problems between the 'West' and the 'rest'. Derrida thought so.[9] In his conference paper which was written and delivered well after he had left the ENS as a student, he points out that such a manner of dealing with troubling themes will change nothing about them, and that one must write from the perspective of the imprisoned if their history is to be written, and if such a thing is possible. Foucault responded aggressively when he reissued the work, with an appendix on Derrida's essay, and the two fell out. Derrida was not unaware of the offence he could cause Foucault with his paper, delivered in the latter's presence, but he seemed to have felt that saying what he thought was more important than their acquaintance. Derrida was never restrained in print about what he saw as the shortcomings of his contemporaries in the efforts they made to embody their ideals. But Derrida admits that Foucault had taught him something in that massive and revolutionary book (which was Foucault's *Thèse d'État*): 'What Michel Foucault teaches us to think is that there are crises of reason in strange complicity with what the world calls crises of madness' (Derrida, 2003, 76). That is to say, Foucault taught these things by showing the crisis, and by trying to unravel and separate the poles of madness and reason, though he failed. Derrida took the view that they were not so separable. Derrida was to see Foucault as a father of his own thought, and to revolt against this father, as indeed he was to revolt against the other structuralist 'fathers'.

3

After ENS

3.1 Harvard

Derrida in the later part of the ENS course had opted to become a teacher of philosophy, but failed the oral portion of the *agrégation*, and abandoned the third, written, test under the same conditions as he had failed the *khâgne* in 1951. The *agrégation* is the third-year exam, usually terminating the course of three years, which thus took Derrida four years. He eventually passed in 1956.

The award of a grant as a special auditor, after passing the *agrégation*, allowed Derrida to go to Harvard to study the microfilm collection of unpublished and unedited Husserl texts. It was a pretext for visiting the USA, and seeing Harvard Square. He also began his work on Husserl's late essay, the 'Origin of Geometry', beginning the translation of the edition by Fink there. He spent a lot of time reading James Joyce in the Widener Library, which offers, Caputo says, a revealing portrait of him, as both the serious Husserl scholar and, at the same time, the devotee of the experimental novelist (Caputo 1997a, 182). He saw some work of his in print at this time, in a journal, an article which, ironically, was a translation into French of an essay by Willard van Orman Quine, the renowned analytic philosopher who was then relatively unknown himself.

While at Boston, in June 1957, Derrida married Marguerite Aucouturier with the confidence that, having graduated from the ENS, he could support a family. They were to have two children, Pierre, born 1963, and Jean, born 1967. His wife was not Jewish, and his sons were to remain uncircumcised. Derrida's choice of wife is indicative of his character; he married outside of his religion, it seems, because he desired from his heart the internationalism which jettisons any particular religion or place. He also married a woman who was in origin Eastern European, and from a recently Stalinized country, almost as if embracing with feelings of unity and daring the people of that dispossessed and endangered state. The couple left for France in the same month on *La Liberté*, after having journeyed by car to Cape Hatteras, South Carolina (Derrida 2004a, 291).

Derrida planned a doctoral thesis on Husserl's phenomenology once back in France, but abandoned it, embarking instead on a more random study of Husserl, German idealism and phenomenology, thus exiting formal study for good at the age of twenty-seven. It seems that, after ENS, and the year spent studying Husserl at Harvard, he did not wish to slow down in his trajectory of writing and sitting exams, and wished fully to complete his education and achieve professorial status. The proposed title for the award of the *doctorat d'État* was to have been 'The Ideality of the Literary Object' (Norris 1987, 12), the wording of which later confused Derrida himself, since although the thesis was to deal with how the effects of the literary seem to confound Husserl's type of ideal objects *qua* concepts, it seems that Derrida had not fully emancipated himself from Husserl even while planning to criticize him. This external critique would take many more years to achieve and would require a new vocabulary. It was also, as a doctorate *in philosophy*, unsuitable. It was ultimately this unsuitableness, and the lack of hope that the thesis could be defended adequately, which decided the matter for Derrida. He did not complete it, he said (Norris 1987, 13) in his 1980 doctoral defence (based on *Speech and Phenomena*, *Writing and Difference*, *Of Grammatology* and other works), because Husserl had led him to problems of writing, inscription and certain 'literary' aspects of philosophy. These matters were to be contributory to his *Introduction to Husserl's 'Origin of Geometry'*. 'My most constant interest, coming before even my philosophical interest I should say, if this is possible, has been directed towards literature, towards that writing which is called literary' (Norris 1987, 13).

So in 1957, fresh from his schooling and newly married, he instead began his compulsory military service as a French citizen in the war in Algeria. He asked to be given a post as a teacher during his mobilization, and was sent to Koléa, near Algiers. 'At my request I did not wear uniform and was assigned to teach in a school for the children of servicemen at Koléa, thirty kilometres from Algiers' (Derrida 2004a, 291). During more than two years he was a soldier of second class in civilian clothing, teaching English and French to young French Algerians, while living with Marguerite and her friend Bianco in a villa near the deprived school. He also translated news-paper articles during this time.

3.2 The War of Algeria

Derrida always condemned the colonial politics of France in Algeria, but had hoped, until the last moment in 1962, that a form of independence could be possible which would render cohabitation with the French possible. He had also tried to persuade his parents not to leave in 1962, but returned to Algeria to help with their 'exodus' from the country when they did leave that year (Derrida 2004a, 291). He often talked of his nostalgia for his home-land (1998e, *passim*).

The crisis which brought about civil war was the result of the whole history of mistreatment of the Arabs by the French since the invasion in 1830. On VE day in May 1945, the Setif region of Algeria suffered national-ist riots which were put down brutally, signalling that France intended to keep its colonies. There followed nine years of peace. The French had already had to fight for eight years in Vietnam since 1946, withdrawing in 1954, only to be drawn into Algeria a few months after final defeat there. This Algerian War was arguably the most dramatic event in European decol-onization, although it is confined largely to the French recollection of history, and not often recalled as the disaster which it was for colonial France. After this, France turned towards a European identity. De Gaulle came to power after the Fourth Republic voted itself out of existence due to the war, and he was expected to end the troubles by bringing a strong hand on behalf of the military. Although France won Algeria back in the end, the colony was given up due to adverse reaction inside France to the ethical dimension of colonialism.

Derrida wanted the French to stay, as he attempted to persuade his parents to stay, until final conclusion of French efforts in 1962. He wanted Algeria to have self-rule but to tolerate differences between Arabs, French and others. However the expulsion and voluntary removal of all the French was unavoidable, so there were population movements as one million French Algerians left for France. Derrida's family resettled in Nice.

De Gaulle's Fifth Republic lasted ten years from 1959 to 1969. He demanded extra powers so as to re-establish order, and drafted a new con-stitution in which the president became the effective head of state with special powers over the Parliament.

3.3 Cerisy-La-Salle, 1959

On his return to France, Derrida took up his first teaching job, at the Lycée du Mans in *hypokhâgne,* with his friend Genette whom he had known at rue d'Ulm. He had an episode of depression at the end of this school year. The school system and education in general had always affected him negatively, and would continue to do so. He made his first journey to Prague with the family of Marguerite. It was in this year, not having attained a place at a university or *école,* and still working as a teacher, that he attended a conference where he delivered his first paper, the ' "Genesis and Structure" and Phenomenology' lecture at Cerisy-la-Salle (Derrida 2003, 193–211). The conference at Cerisy on this occasion was in fact devoted to 'genesis and structure', a structuralist problem, and Derrida's paper was to involve Husserl in this structuralist conference. Husserl could not reconcile structure with genesis and, as Derrida says at the start of the lecture, he would not have used these terms. The problem, which was recognized early on to be inherent in structuralism, was that it could never account for the becoming of history, because it relied on the synchronic, pure structure of time and history. Derrida's inclusion of Husserl at this structuralist conference is unusual, and out of place, striking perhaps the wrong note, but Derrida had become an expert on this philosopher, even if he had to speak about him at a conference arranged around a movement which was in essence anti-philosophical. Derrida must have been hoping for eventual inclusion in the staff at the ENS, and was in fact substituting there already for Hyppolite and Althusser (2002a, 150). His attendance at Cerisy was of a piece with his determination to remain in the circle.

The annual ten-day conference at Cerisy is held in a château in Normandy, and is devoted, from year to year, to a given subject or thinker, with discussions after each paper, usually by a distinguished specialist. Derrida was to attend many others, and some of them, four to date, were upon himself. The titles included 'Nietzsche' (1972), which he was fond of remembering since it gathered so many of his generation who had come to prominence, 'Ponge' (1974), Derrida himself ('Les fins de l'homme') (1980), and 'Lyotard' (1982). A conference was again held on Derrida as recently as 2002 on 'The Democracy to Come'.

'Genesis and Structure', written when Derrida was twenty-eight, sees the first manifestation of clear deconstructive practice, with the features of deep and highly informed reading, multiple references to the cultural inheritance, a thorough, even poetic recreation of the given system in the space of a single textual presentation, a generous internal reading, which by and large raises no petty objections of bad reasoning, or of inapplicability of a system to empirical fact, and a guiding questioning which results in the location of an irremediable paradox or crisis in the system itself, but only the one problem, as a result of internal difficulties rather than external, partial frames of reference. Derrida has told the story of a piece of Husserl's history, but located a great rift within the fabric of that history. Bernasconi (1992, 137–66) has pointed out in his reading of the criticisms of de Man by Derrida, and of Derrida by de Man, that the part which storytelling plays in Derrida's work is the chief literary quality of his work, and the point at which Derrida becomes blind to the rhetorical quality of his philosophical thinking: it is his blind spot. This criticism was levelled at Derrida by de Man himself and can be made more use of, as Bernasconi does. Derrida himself is blind to this power of his because he refuses to acknowledge that he is able to tell a story. For, by Derrida's own admission, he only feels forced to recognize his own storytelling power, and his need to submit to it, when an ethical demand imposes itself, that is, when not to narrate a story would be unethical. All the same, Derrida's power to create a history or a story is evident even in this earliest piece. There is, for example, a greater coherence and narrative structure to Derrida's own reading of Husserl's history of the transcendental subjectivity and its ideas than there is in Husserl himself. In fact, by outlining his precise reading of Husserl's work he lends to it a completely new form, even if he does not deviate.[1]

In 'Genesis and Structure' the problem which deconstruction sets out to redress is the subject-centredness of Husserl, his voluntarism, the origin of mastery and control over the world by a subjectivity. This is achieved by reading the outline of the transcendental subjectivity as a structure with a history. But a structure cannot have an explicable history unless it changes beyond recognition at each stage of its history, that is, its change cannot be explained.[2] This means that the structure must not be as structured as Husserl thinks, but more fluid, more open, less exclusive, and less unjust than it attempts to be. It is Derrida's task always to paint the totality and the imposing mastery of a system first, so that he can then undo it. For better or worse this talent is supremely his.

The gist of this early piece is the Kantian nature of Husserl's thought when it reaches its extremes. To be more precise, Derrida showed that when Husserl attempted to prove that eternal concepts in the sciences developed over time, Husserl resorted to the gesture of saying 'there must be regulative laws or Ideas governing the development, otherwise my system, or the very actuality of experience and knowledge explained by it, would not be possible'.

The work of Husserl's with which he is concerned is the later stage of his investigations, particularly *Ideas I* [1915], and its popularization in *Cartesian Meditations* [1926].[3] Again, Derrida is attempting, by lending more coherence to Husserl than he really possessed, to complete the theory to its limits and then show the tension at those limits. By the way, before considering this simple but expert paper, we could point to a residual trait which is in fact definitive of Derrida's type of reading/criticism, namely that he does not find fault by arguing against or along with the text he reads, but goes for the whole 'world-disclosive' picture set forth in the text, enjoying its poetic power as it were, and taking for granted that it is neither right nor wrong, only then to show that by its *own* standards and its *own* argumentation it cannot work and become a coherent textual artefact. That is, his method is contrary to Anglo-Saxon types of reading, and is contrary to the way in which philosophy is generally taught in universities. His reading is not objective or part of a greater analytic enterprise; it is always internal, taking it for granted maybe that, for example, 'Husserl' is a given and effectual part of history and the present, and that to that extent, right or wrong, Husserl's thinking is, because people read it and put it to work, already proven to be classifiable as true. One may even say that in his readings Derrida has already assumed what truth is, or has assumed that there shall be no absolute truth; but if people, especially Husserl himself, believe that Husserl's theories and thought are workable, then this will be granted, and this generosity is extended to them because they are encyclopaedic and genuinely involved in the extremes of reason and of factual reality. In the end, Husserl manifested a dream which was constructed in his works; Derrida appreciates the ideal and the dream, yet directs us to a purer version of it.

The essay finds fault in the incompatibility of the origin and history of intentionality and the structure of it, where the description of genesis, or history and change, ought to cohere with the description of the structure as it stands at any point of that changeable developing history. But the nature of this structure contradicts the description of its genesis: how can a structure be examined concretely when it is always on the move? Husserl set up his speculative intentionality in the Kantian way, one which precludes genetic description, because the Kantian Idea was, for him, the overwhelming self-evident result of his scheme of knowledge and its conditions (Derrida 2003, 209–10). Derrida also calls attention to the ultimate telos of Husserl's system, namely God.

As was seen, Derrida had an early and maybe dominating interest in the question of concepts and structures which continued throughout his career to shape his studies. The historical genesis of concepts used for example by the Marxist critics, who used them as if they had always been available, and did not need to be analysed *qua* concepts, had posed a problem for him while at ENS as a student. It was seen by him to be a question of the history of science, and the status of scientific answers, their value as truth or the like. In this paper it is Husserl's naïve application of structure and genesis, his 'historico-semantic' naïvety about what these concepts mean, and how they arise from an initial unity, which is his fault or weakness, and this arising from unity to conceptual difference is also the origin of transcendence itself (Derrida 2003, 210). Derrida says in the Cerisy paper that the reason that Husserl falls back into Kantian metaphysics, in which Being is thought, and the mind (intentionality) is transcendental, is that he cannot allow himself to give a precise description of the origin of intentionality itself, since intentionality precedes descriptions, it precedes accounts of historical genesis and actual structure. Intentionality has no genesis or structure, if both are to be described together, *unless as heading towards a telos which will unite them*. The Kantian idea was regulative, acting as a telos, rather indescribable until the telos had become attained and static, something which would never occur for an infinite project. This telos was God.

The core of consciousness, intentionality, as described in *Ideas I*, is an opening which receives impressions and is an appropriately volitional-based entity, located firmly in the present moment, receptive and creative. It has features of the volitional aspect of the mind, but is also a place of openness in which things just happen, whether because of the will, or because of what goes on in the world. This basis of all phenomenal experience, which turns them into transcendental objects so that the mind may meet them, and vice versa, is, however, necessarily, a construction placed on our limitless experience, limiting it for the purposes of science and metaphysics, to an absolute moment, a finite moment in the infinite. Derrida often described it as a Kantian idea, this basis of phenomenology, similar to the Kantian idea of the soul, as described in the *Critique of Practical Reason* (Kant 1883). It is unproven, but necessary. To it, objects are given, neither in themselves, nor subjectively organized. This Kantian idea is explained in the *Introduction to Husserl's 'Origin of Geometry'* as the Kantian idea of unified experience, a pre-supposition of the unity of experience for the intentional opening.

In Derrida's easy familiarity and mastery of Husserl one can see that he had been studying these same themes for many years. One can imagine him mulling over the opening history, the genesis of ideas over time, and time itself, while facing the rather obtuse dogmatism of Althusser, Hyppolite, Foucault and maybe Lacan, as well as Merleau-Ponty, who were merely unreflectively using such given ideas and historical configurations in the present, without reflecting on the giveness of the present, or the nature of language and of the self. One immediately notices on reading this paper, Derrida's first, an extraordinary faculty with abstraction, lexicon and general intellectual prose styling. At no point does Derrida's style flag from a very rarefied flight amidst the technicalities of this scientific examination of science.

3.4 Derrida's Early Critique of the Science of Science

In his neo-Kantianism, Husserl was similar to some other Jewish intellectuals of his time in Germany (Derrida 2001a, 135–88). Hermann Cohen, who preceded Heidegger at Marburg (just as Husserl preceded Heidegger at Freiburg), for instance, was a pre-eminent neo-Kantian, who was confident that Germany was well adapted, in its Enlightenment, Prussian history, to being the leader and home of culture and progress in Europe.[4] Husserl was a Protestant German of Jewish origin in the same way. He was a German nationalist whose sons died in the Great War, on the German side. The idea of Germany was associated intimately, at least for Cohen, with the idea of a certain Kant, and a Kantian *Aufklärung*, a philosophy of scientific and rational progress, and a politics of citizenship and ethics on the grounds of reason alone. Kant's is not a rationalist description of existence and knowledge of it, but one which calls on the imagination, the understanding, and certain semi-mystical but decidedly human, subjective faculties of a living being. Husserl belonged to this type: neo-Kantian, Protestant, idealist, and transcendental in thinking, that is to say, like Kant, instituting a new ground for religion, and the Protestant observance of religion, when such grounds would otherwise be intellectually lacking, or unsatisfying, alongside a faith in reason and scientific practice. Prerequisite for any adequate description of the facts of experience presented to the religious and scientific consciousness is a description of the conscious receptivity to scientific and mathematical objects, or an epistemology. It seems, from the 1959 lecture, that Derrida began his original research in *epistemology*, then, as he has himself said (Derrida 1995b, 345), and there is no reason to doubt that his first concern was with the truth conditions of science. In Husserl's transcendental account of the conditions for the existence of anything as occurring within a clearing of intention and phenomena, Derrida masterminded his own sort of thinking by finding problems with Husserl's epistemology. It was around this time too, while preparing this paper, and translating and introducing the 'Origin of Geometry', that he first asserted the importance of writing in the intentional structure, and thus found access to a universal problem of traditional metaphysics in the thematic of writing, although, as a theme, 'writing' did not become explicit for Derrida until the 1962 publication.

3.5 The *Prix Cavailles*

In 1960, the year following his address at Cerisy, and his first job as a state-school teacher in Le Mans, Derrida began teaching at the Sorbonne, and was still helping at the ENS, where he had an office, helping the *agrégatifs*, mostly in Althusser's absences. On his return to Paris from Le Mans he was offered an assistantship at the Sorbonne, where he remained for four years. He and Marguerite travelled to Prague for the first time 'in a tiny Citroën *deux chevaux*' (Derrida 2004a, 291). In 1961 Derrida won the *Prix Cavailles* for his translation of, and introduction to, the 'Origin of Geometry' which had appeared in journal form in this year, and he was warmly congratulated by his friend Althusser.[5] The *Prix Cavailles* is awarded for works on epistemology, related to progress in the philosophy of science. Derrida had made his translation from the German text, edited by Eugen Fink, and introduced it with an essay almost three times its length which is faithful in its reading, and concluded that the science of phenomenology fails because it requires a philosophical ontology if it is to be comprehensive. This bow to Heidegger was probably not lost on his fellow-Husserl scholars. The translation and introduction was published the following year in 1962, his first book publication, the work of about five years, since the translation was begun in 1956, and the introduction was signed in 1961.

Derrida and his wife travelled to Prague again in 1962 in the same Citroën, and had a vacation in France. Derrida's later holidays would always be in France; his travelling would, on the other hand, be for the sake of lectures and teaching. The preferred holiday destinations were 'Charente (a village near Angoulême) or Nice' (Derrida 2004a, 291).

Work continued on Husserl while at the Sorbonne when Derrida was already in his thirties, with 'On the Phenomenological Psychology of E. Husserl', published in *Les études philosophiques* in 1963. 'Force and

Signification' (2003, 1–35), an essay on the literary criticism of the structuralist critics, was also published in 1963, in *Critique* (June–July), indicating that, after the structuralist conference of 1959, Derrida had become
aware of this movement and had been studying it. During this year Pierre
Derrida was born to Jacques and Marguerite, a birth coinciding with
Derrida's first book release, as he said in *Circumfession*, noting the symbolic
coincidence of double good fortune, relating his son's birth to the birth of his
other 'children'.

4
The First Book

4.1 Husserl's 'Origin of Geometry'

Derrida's first published book-length study was a translation of Husserl's 'Origin of Geometry', released in 1962. Derrida's introduction had a scope vastly greater than its object since it followed Husserl's last period as a whole. It was, above all, a success, and marked Derrida's release from the failures of his past, and gave solid proof of his ability as a scholar and as an original mind.

Husserl's 'Origin of Geometry' was published after his death by his friend Fink. Both because it was posthumously published, and because he had translated it, Derrida felt that the short text needed an introduction to situate it in the 1960s. He also saw it, no doubt, as the opportunity to write on Husserl's later work. The 'Origin of Geometry' is a fragment, part of a broader context of late works by Husserl. Bernet (1989, 139–53) says that Derrida defends Husserl, and repeatedly frees him, to confront the scholarship of the 1940s and 50s, and that this is one of Derrida's reasons for his introduction. In line with his belief that mathematics was not a gift from heaven, Husserl, in 'The Origin of Geometry', discovered that the fact of tradition, and the development of ideas by successive generations, and by individuals in a community, had to be decisive factors in the development of the ideal sciences. Husserl's problem was to explain how an actual person had to have started geometry off, because it was never a personal project as such, but a reaction of a single mind to what was always from the first universally acceptable. Ideal objects, which is what geometry deals with, are acceptable to any mind, and in any language. So how is the ideal discovered in one time rather than another, if they are already potentially and always universal? These, the ideal and the historical, are reconciled in the fact that pre-geometrical minds would have had intuitive knowledge of the science over periods of history, but would not have objectified the knowledge into a science until they had begun to speak of it. The first point at which such speaking of it occurs is, vaguely, at the time of, and in the person of, Plato. Speech is therefore central to the history of science. The thematic of the ideal object seemed immediately self-evident to those who had communicated it amongst themselves and deposited it in the memory, and due to its being true to the ideal nature of things for intentionality, and to the intentional opening of the mind, it would have been evident to all, and ceaselessly amenable to being reactivated as scientific and exact knowledge, by means of repetition.

4.2 *Husserl's 'Origin of Geometry': An Introduction* [1962]

The *Introduction*, in which Derrida situates the text of the 'Origin' amidst the work from which it had been removed, roughly around *The Crisis in European Sciences*, sees a renewed effort at describing the intentional opening, but now under the name of the Living Present, the Absolute, revealing a greater awareness in Derrida of time's importance to this structure.

To begin with, Derrida states his purpose. The intention is to recognize and situate one stage of Husserl's thought, with its specific presuppositions and its particular unfinished state (Derrida 1978, 27). This is in fact what occurs, although with a thinker of Husserl's kind, one involved with a guiding thought throughout a lifetime, and with 'unfinished state' being a central theme, this situating of one moment in the thought of the thinker draws on the entire *oeuvre*. For as he points out (Derrida 1978, 28), Husserl's first important work could have been called 'The Origin of Arithmetic,' and interest in that origin is not very different from the work of fifty years subsequent to it. While the early work had described the origin in terms of psychological genesis, the later describes it as phenomenological history, where both approaches avoid treating the origin as a cultural and factual history. He then proceeds to an exposition of the text lasting until Section VIII, when he moves on to more general considerations which derive from Husserl's general project, and thus address that project in its presuppositions. These presuppositions will be found to treat of experience, not existence, and present times, not time itself.

Phenomenology itself then, by the time of the 'Origin', had become a description of the process of history which is also the recognition of Ideas, or the intervention of the ahistoric into history, the eternal Idea within history (Derrida 1978, 141). In Section XI Derrida describes this late version of phenomenology before placing it within the question which Heidegger asked of it, the question of why there are things at all rather than nothing, which phenomenology cannot ask, but which, Husserl says, phenomenology equips philosophy with the means to ask, causing a delay in asking the question, since first the Living-Present is explicated before the question of Being can be answered.

4.3 Freedom

Phenomenology is characterized by its being the interaction of freedom with ideas, or responsibility. Here Derrida has lighted upon responsibility and freedom as lessons from Husserl. The other lesson which Derrida seems to have learnt is the power of thought as questioning. The most crucial thing in deconstructive thinking, and in what Derrida learnt from Husserl, and which Levinas noticed in Husserl, was the questioning power of thought, the challenging aspect of it. The institution of philosophy is an institution based on questioning. This is so because the infinite task of science is one for which one must be responsible, and for which the mind must play a role as the investigative consciousness. The decision to reduce things to ideas, is its first moment. The first moment is subjective and classically volition based. Derrida asks and answers some doubts about this scheme in which search for the ideal, and interpretations of it in language, may seem to lack freedom because the Idea is self-evident. Derrida explains that the Idea, being outside of history, has to be interpreted, made sense of, and hence does not govern history, or deprive Reason of responsibility and freedom. And Reason too is not eternity working inside history, realizing itself in a Hegelian manner, and outside of human volition, since it is not external or apart from history, but Reason is the mind itself, and is also essentially responsibility, and the freedom to be responsible. Reason is subjectivity itself, and is only beyond us because it is a telos, the telos of self-explication. Derrida is not afraid to point to the late appearance of God in all of this, though he makes no comment (Derrida 1978, 147), in that Husserl's God is the end to which this moves, the Entelechy of history, by which the history can be fully described. When God and Logos are seen to cooperate, then history becomes the ultimate reality, and nothing is outside of history.

> God speaks and passes through constituted history, he is beyond in rela-
> tion to constituted history and all the constituted moments of transcen-
> dental life. But he is only the Pole for itself of constituting historicity and
> constituting historical transcendental subjectivity. The dia-historicity or
> the meta-historicity of the divine Logos only traverses and goes beyond
> 'Fact' as the 'ready-made' of history, yet the Logos is but the pure move-
> ment of its own historicity. (Derrida 1978, 148)

Within this self-enclosure there is just isolated self-responsibility (Derrida 1978, 149), from the Ideal Living Present, to the ideal godly Entelechy. By making a summary and passing silent judgement on this Husserlian-Kantian Enlightenment scheme of freedom and objectivity, Derrida makes prepara-tion for his own notion of the new Enlightenment, only explicitly announced much later and based on responsibility to the Other, not on freedom.[1]

4.4 Writing: The Linguistic Turn[2]

At the time of publishing his introduction to the 'Origin of Geometry' Derrida insisted on the status of the written thing in the history of science (Derrida 1995b, 345). His initial idea conflicted with the original assump-tions of Greek and Western mathematics. Finally it conflicted with Hegel and Husserl. His idea was somewhat obvious, but also neglected, and despised by the Western tradition, so that, looking back at its obviousness now, one can only suspect that the judgement of the merely supplementary character of writing must have been owing to a tacit prejudice, or even to an arbitrary and universally accepted judgement without grounds.[3] The history of the resulting science seems to have found the prejudice essential to its existence.

Derrida's emphasis on writing has a complex relationship to deconstruc-tion. Christopher Norris in his *Derrida* (1987) assumed that Derrida's philos-ophy was primarily about writing. Indeed, Derrida returned to writing in *Of Grammatology*, and devoted this systematic work to archi-writing. But to begin with, Derrida does not mean 'ordinary' writing, such as one carries out every day, but archi-writing, which uses 'writing' only as a quasi-metaphor. Moreover, in the larger perspective, Derrida concentrated on writing in these years because it was the most direct way of broaching the issue of the spectrality of the body, of ideas, of authors, and of readers. General grammatology is part of a larger vision of an ontological deconstruction of normally accepted philosophical reality. Derrida's theory of what words are – that is, that they are 'traces' – has, as is well known, an uncanny resemblance to Heidegger's formulation of words and poetry in the essays such as 'Hölderlin's Heaven and Earth' (delivered in 1959) (Heidegger 2000b) in which the word is 'sent', 'posted', destined, and in which the word is the means by which the world is created and ruled by its Origin [Anfang];[4] the purpose of the word is to divide the world into its fourfold unity, with a word which divides and binds. It is clear that this is not a 'philosophy of language', but a philosophy of the divisive unity of the world, which is affected by time, and the historical pathway of man, and in which language is constitutive of how Being is broken up. Words are essential to it because poetry and philosophy have to use words.

In *Of Grammatology* Derrida argues with Saussure's version of what language is, and says that Saussure's proofs about writing's technical side are oneiric, Freudian dream-proofs (Derrida 1997b, 45), because Saussure is determined to give a vocalic, human essence to language, rather than a destinal, metaphysical, 'sent' essence. Derrida's version of language is impersonal, and hence not decisively grounded on the human choice of whether to speak or be silent. 'Writing' speaks, regardless of its author: speech on the other hand, as logocentrism sees it, can only communicate when it chooses to do so. But even if the history of philosophy is right to assume that writing is supplementary to the human voice, Derrida in any case replied that the 'supplement', or prosthesis, is itself originary, and equiprimordial with the 'genuine', so that, again, his point is to undermine a cocksure ownership or appropriation of 'genuine things', and a philosophy which believes it has a thorough grasp of what it is dealing with. Derrida's clarity about writing, which is not a mere reversal of the two opposing poles speech/writing, with an argument which is convincing, and therefore respectable, and Western, is nevertheless, in the overturning of a prejudice which blocked the deeper reality of how writing 'owns' [ereignet] and rules over man, rather rebellious, even, it may appear, rebellious for the sake of rebellion against the mainstream of Western thought – if we do not take into account the Heideggerian provenance. It has a Foucauldian appearance. It has the same peculiar driven edge that Foucault's post-Marxist revolutionary thinking has; the idea of revaluating the dismissed and forbidden part of a binary set of concepts, in this case, speech and writing. It was still the era of socialism in France, of change, in memory in part of the French Revolution. It was not a valorization of the forbidden altogether, as Foucault's was, though, or a purposive erotic transgression in the way of Bataille; Derrida never sided with the opposite pole of a binary set, but always got to the place which superseded them – in this case the fact that they were different, and that the truest essence of language, *différance* (the absence within presentness) was hidden beneath the opposition.

With the discovery of the logocentric problem by the early 1960s, Husserl was primarily for Derrida the thinker of phenomena as present, ideal objectivities, so that the fact that they are shadowy and trace-like, spectral, is simply ignored by Husserl. Derrida's new notion was to find this imposed settlement on the play to be an imposition, underneath which was a reality which is never secure, but is ghostly. The ghost reality is constituted by traces, not words, difference, not meaning, and writing, not spontaneous spoken words. The play of différance between the written and spoken is loaded on the side of those things which produce immediate and present effects in Western philosophy: the voice of the living man, rather than his dead inscription; the full presence of his mind and ideas, rather than a book to be interpreted; firm, ideal meanings, rather than memory and the future. As Caputo writes: 'Deconstruction does not renounce the constitution of meaning and the transmission of scientific ideas. It is a certain Husserlianism, a theory of the constitution of meaning and ideality, but one that is already exposed to a certain Joyceanism' (1997a, 183).[5] The problematic of writing emerged and was bound to the irreducible structure of *deferrer* in its relationships to consciousness, science, history, history of science, the disappearance or deferral of the origin (Derrida 1981b, 13).

5

Against Structuralism

5.1 Thoughts on Althusser

In 1962 Derrida was still teaching at the Sorbonne, the University of Paris, in general philosophy and logic as assistant to Bachelard, Canguilhem, Ricoeur and Jean Wahl (Bennington 1999, 330). He gave courses on Husserl at ENS (Derrida 2002a, 150), and prepared students for the *agrégation*, but was embarrassed by the move to Marxism at ENS, following Althusser. He did not find Marxism pointed enough at the time, finding ontology more important, this being a feature of his later criticism of it in *Spectres* (1994); in fact the major theme of that book is that Marxism could not understand history. Derrida did not comment on communist arguments, both because he did not like to be thought a renegade, and because he did not like joining in for the sake of it, though he did not disagree fundamentally. Fundamentally he believed in Marx because of justice. He felt Althusser was doing something useful too (Derrida 2002a, 154). But the whole question became irrelevant when people began to hear what communism was doing in Eastern Europe (Derrida 2002a, 163). Althusser was in any case creating the end state of Marxism in France because, while the PCF was stagnant, it was nevertheless practical and envisaged revolution, but while Althusser may have renewed Marxism, and given it a new philosophical respectability, he deprived it of action.

Derrida tended to dismiss Althusser because, although Marxism was good on justice, and was a force of good in this way, both Althusser and his followers had not read enough Heidegger and were not sufficiently philosophical and cautious. Hyppolite spoke a lot about Heidegger at ENS, and most people had read the 'Letter on Humanism',[1] which was intended for the French (Derrida 2002a, 156); but more Heidegger would have been of great value to the Marxists (Derrida 2002a, 176). Such Marxism was not scientific enough because it did not understand what it was working with, namely concepts. How could it deploy a critique of events when it had not exhausted an examination of time, or of how things happen, or of what things are?

5.2 'Force and Signification'

In a bid to enter into dialogue and argument with the structuralist movement, Derrida started to think and write on structuralism. 'Force and Signification' (Derrida 2003, 1–35) was an article of 1963 on structuralist literary criticism. In that year Derrida already had in mind the end of structuralism, as an 'invasion' which by the same token could, or had to become, normalized or neutralized. In the essay, published in *Critique* in that year (June–July), he discussed some structuralist literary theorists, and while hinting that one day the event of structuralism would be only history, he said that it lived today as a questioned way of thinking which occluded the new thinking of Heidegger and of Nietzsche above all, and the notion of the Other. So although learning from structuralism (from Althusser, and the Cerisy conference of 1959), he, like Ricoeur and Levinas, was already keeping his distance. 'Force and Signification' calls on Heidegger and Nietzsche, with Derrida's own view of how writing constitutes meaning in the absence of its author. For him, a written text is one without author, while the world as a structure of interpretations is an interpretation without origin. Nietzsche wrote for others, and in others his meaning was realized, as his Zarathustra found in the down-going [*Untergang*]. Writing is the original Valley of the Other within Being, and it is from the Other that writing comes. This critique is applied to literary writing, for it, like *Zarathustra*, speaks to others, and makes a valley in the harsh inhuman landscape of Being, exiting from Being as Hölderlin's poet exits Being, to join the god.

Derrida found that the Other, or the Person, cannot be accommodated by a structuralist conception of culture or literature.[2]

It may be that there is a structure in, for example, *The Remembrance of Things Past* by Proust, but this was the intention of Proust, the author:

Proust's aesthetics and critical method are, ultimately, not outside his work but are the very heart of his creation, 'Proust will make his aesthetic into the real subject of his work' [Derrida is quoting Rousset]. As in Hegel, the philosophical, critical, reflective consciousness is not only contained in the scrutiny given to the operations and works of history. What is first in question is the operation of the consciousness itself. (Derrida 2003, 26)

If then the 'impersonal' structure faces this problem of having been forced by a 'personal' choice, how can the impersonal structure be genuinely impersonal? What way out is there, other than leaving this binary opposition behind altogether? How can a criticism relying on structure account for Marivaux's or Proust's intention as they wrote, for it is clear that there is a structure, a form, in *The Remembrance of Things Past*, and yet the structure was intended to be as it is by the author. Hence, force is indistinguishable from form. This means that a new conception of language itself is needed (Derrida 2003, 31). In the Barthesian era of the death of the author, and birth of the text, and the reader, Derrida spoke of the trace-language, the Other, repetition as constitutive of meaning, but no 'death of the author'. The end of the subject is only the reverse of the dominance of the subject and the mastery of meaning.

In the concluding paragraphs, Derrida begins to speak of Nietzsche, who had faced the same problem, but maybe not resolved it. His last printed words in *Ecce Homo* were 'Dionysus vs. the Crucified' (Nietzsche 1979), or at the beginning of his career, 'Apollo vs. Dionysus', form versus force (in *The Birth of Tragedy*). Force and structure together constituted the whole myth of being for Nietzsche, the eternal combat of becoming and eternity, which encompassed all things. The concepts were inclusive of all things, and so Nietzsche faced the same problem of not being able to reconcile them, as the structuralist critic cannot account for works adequately either. Rather in spite of himself (a tactic which Derrida will often use, turning a chance admission against the text he is reading so faithfully), Nietzsche had shown the way out, though he himself had failed to observe it. His Zarathustra actually begins to speak and write with meaning only for another person, during his *Untergang*. While Force and Form govern being, writing is an absence of being, and introduces the Other, so that the way out of Force/Form is the writing of/for the Other.

This notion of the Other as the opposite of Being is one of the premier ideas of Levinas, announced in his work as early as his 1951 'Is Ontology Fundamental?' (Levinas 1998, 1–11). There in the boldest and most simple terms, he opposes the Other to Being, and characterizes them as mutually exclusive, especially in the matter of ethics, in which the Other is the dominant idea, and in which Being cannot properly figure as ethical. Straying away from Husserl, Derrida has begun to use the terminology of Being and the Other, indicative of his growth out of his early studies of epistemology and the science of science.

This Derridean opposition of the Other to Being, or Levinas to Heidegger, is a dominant idea of the whole era in fact (Lyotard, 'Heidegger and "the jews": A Conference in Vienna and Freiburg' (1993, 135–47)). Jean-Luc Nancy and others, friends indeed of Derrida, while following Heidegger, and using his terms and ideas, still reject the primacy of Being, or *Dasein*, in favour of *Mitsein*, thus placing being-with other people, or the Other, in the most primordial place, the place from which to survey everything else. Of this, more when we speak of Derrida's later, more overt political and ethical, less scholarly, literary-philosophical work. The motive of Levinas' trying to escape or 'transcend' Being is that Being is, as Heidegger had it, an 'overwhelming sway', and controls human *Dasein* to its own purposes.

5.3 1963–65

1963–65 were years of some turmoil and progress for Derrida. They were the years when 'the trace' was worked out. The publications eventually contributing to *Writing and Difference* [1967] continue with work on Edmond Jabès and Levinas. Derrida describes a meeting with Jean Benoïste in this year also (Derrida 2001b, 107–10), a person 'complicit' with him at that time because of his distance from Marxism. But in their ideas they disagreed, Derrida believing that Marxism should not be opposed. Benoïste lived in London, and Derrida was to visit him there many times in the future. They took their politics too seriously, and disagreed in the end (Derrida 2001b, 110). Derrida began teaching at the *École Normale Supérieure* in 1964 too, as a *maître-assistant*, a junior, but permanent and responsible position. He had been working and teaching there for the past few years with Althusser and Hyppolite, and it was on their recommendation that he was taken on permanently. Hyppolite left for a post at a university, but recommended Derrida to be his successor (2002a, 150). Derrida seems to have jumped at the chance to work full time at ENS, since he was offered a position at the CNRS first, which he accepted, and then rejected when ENS made him an offer (Bennington 1999, 330).

In 1965 Derrida made contact with the *Tel Quel* group, an association which would last until 1972. He published 'La parole soufflée' in *Tel Quel* in the winter issue, 1965, although his major involvement was to come only in the late 1960s. He said in his funeral oration for Levinas at the time of the latter's death, collected in *The Work of Mourning* (Derrida 2001b, 197–210), that he met Emmanuel Levinas at around this time too. Levinas was a friend of Maurice Blanchot, and he was fortunate enough to see them together once. The friendship lasted until Levinas' death in 1995. Another sign of his becoming part of the general scene was a meeting which took place in 1966 with Roland Barthes, somewhat older than him, but on whom he had an influence by means of his greater concentration of vision and sense of purpose, for in 1966 he travelled with him from Paris to New York and then to Baltimore, to the Johns Hopkins conference, invited by René Girard, to deliver 'Structure, Sign and Play' at the 'International Colloquium on Critical Languages and the Sciences of Man'. It was a large colloquium, later celebrated, which marked the debut of a 'spectacular intensification' (Bennington 1999, 330–31) in the acclaim of certain French theoreticians and philosophers in the US; it was also Derrida's second visit to the US. There Derrida met Paul de Man, soon to be a close friend and colleague, and Jacques Lacan, who was also close in intellectual matters, but never to be on speaking terms. Others attending Johns Hopkins in 1966 as speakers were Vernant on Ancient Greece, Roland Barthes on literature, Georges Poulet on literary criticism, Tzvetan Todorov, and Lacan, who insisted on giving his contribution in his very bad English. Lacan was the leader of the delegation (Dosse 1998a, 328–9).

Derrida's fame – which announced that his thought was something which deserved more attention on its own terms – came when he arrived in America properly speaking, where his thought was received in the main as a theory of literature and reading called 'deconstruction' rather than what it in fact was, namely a 'pessimistic' ontology. But its force was due to its counter-movement status against a French cultural phenomenon, namely structuralism, which tended to dominate the humanities in education and the view of science. In America its counter-movement status was due to its opposition to New Criticism. Derrida had, along with the other attendants of the colloquium, gradually come to view himself as part of a general move-ment of the study of humanity, and humanities, rather than strict philoso-phy. Indeed Barthes and Lacan, and to an extent Derrida himself in his major work on Saussure in these years, were what was to become known as 'struc-turalists'. Paradoxically it was structuralism which Derrida was to attack in his paper delivered there, so that structuralism's arrival in the US was also, in Derrida's paper, the occasion of the announcement of its death.

Structuralism was a system of studying human activities on the basis of the structure which had been discovered first of all in language (more familiar to English-language speakers from the work of Noam Chomsky). Not only did this structure prove that human and cultural things could be studied with some accuracy and dogmatism, but it also gave the impetus to this study and this science in terms of human culture as an exchange of various signs. Lévi-Strauss discovered the structure of exchange and communication in primitive societies on this basis; Lacan described the mind on the same; Barthes did so in regard to the history of art and in general aesthetics; Althusser did so on the basis of the scientificity of idealism and the connection of ideas.

The essays on structuralism were those which made Derrida's name as the pioneer of deconstruction, as a post-structuralist *par excellence*. What else is 'deconstruction' but a counter-movement to construction, or structuralism, but from within?

5.4 'Structure, Sign and Play'

'Structure, Sign and Play' announces the death of structuralism and the birth of something else (something 'monstrous'). The paper is nothing more than an attack on structuralism, or maybe no attack since such an assault would be doing violence to what he announces is already dead and finished with. His talk is, then, the announcement that structuralism is no more, and at its conclusion the paper holds out a vision of a new practice of thinking. Insofar as Derrida came to some renown in the late 1960s, he did so at the expense of structuralism, both in terms of his writings on structure, and in terms of the various public events which he attended and where his aim was to undo structures.

The use of Heidegger, Nietzsche and Freud that Derrida made was maybe one of the events of this conference, at least in Derrida's own history. He had admitted his ancestors and told who he was. Although he had been studying and teaching Husserl for more than a decade, his real masters were only these three, a trio whose positive doctrine is largely negative and destructive.[3] From now on, he says, signs can only name a non-present centre or origin, like the missing God, or the absent Being (that is, absent 'homeland', or place of living), and if we align this with the conclusion of *Of Grammatology*, which he was then in the process of completing, the non-present origin dissolves structures, and makes the objects of histories and studies turn into differential, non-static structures. These new fluid structures form a game, or play, amongst their components, since there is no firm harmony or law for them beyond the rules of a game which leaves them fluid, whether the objects be words, signs or events. There is therefore no strict or hard-and-fast meaning in a deconstructed system, but, rather, meanings which can change depending on the condition of the system. This new situation for systems of thought and philosophy has already begun to work, he says, and is no doubt the way of this era. Freud, Nietzsche and Heidegger envisioned a world which had no centre, and they contributed to destroying such an original, central basis for the world; at the same time, they also destroyed the possibility of a transcendental signified, which had hitherto functioned as such a basis. With that, however, the signs, or the old products of the centre's rule, still remain.[4] Where once the orthodoxies of the West, and of culture, were founded on a belief in a certain metaphysical order of things, be it God, or full-existence, or the person and soul, now these orthodoxies are trace-laws, and embody a realm of half-entities and playful shadows.

The actual subject of the deconstruction in 'Structure, Sign and Play' is Lévi-Strauss, the ethnographer who described various cultural phenomena according to formal principles which applied universally, that is to say, he described the structure of cultures, as if they had a central point around which each one was organized (*The Elementary Structures of Kinship*). For Lévi-Strauss there were various types of cultural phenomena, but a signified language of signs which they used. Lévi-Strauss was the unlikely founding father of structuralism in France, unlikely because of how antithetical he was to the idol which he overthrew – Sartre. Derrida is looking at his first work, *The Elementary Structures of Kinship*, in which the universal feature of culture is symbolic exchange, specifically the exchange of females. In Derrida's response we see a problematizing of the origin, which is classically deconstructive, and also a way of showing that what is based on the origin of history, in this case philosophy, is made to tremble by finding the confusion of concepts therein, which reveals how a conflict points to *a unity*, a unity which is precisely absent. And since the origin is lacking, is not present, cannot be so any more, then the structure is an irreal, rather baroque, mathematical imposition on the variety of experience. For although we could have said that the incest taboo is inexplicably the origin of culture, it is better to say that there simply is no origin which could be thematized as being present, no origin capable of being described at all, and this incest origin contains contradictions. 'The overabundance of the signifier, the supplementary character, is thus the result of a finitude, that is to say, the result of a lack which must be supplemented' (Derrida 2003, 367). The absence is a lack of signification which our signs supplement. When there is no origin, the signs are set free, free of objects and of sense. What has been found is that, if there is an origin of culture, that origin which Lévi-Strauss suggests is just not pure enough.

The text is to be read not as a series of signs, but of traces, and likewise 'the female', as an exchange token or sign, is also a trace. That is how the deconstruction was carried out, in appropriately grand terms for the audience at the conference. Because of Nietzsche, Heidegger and Freud, works such as those of Lévi-Strauss, or of Foucault and Althusser, could no longer be considered good enough, for the age of taking structures seriously has passed. We are too sceptical of origins. Lévi-Strauss himself was aware of this and insisted that he was a *bricoleur*, and made his systems up from pieces he found here or there, so as to avoid philosophy, and to be trans-empirical, something which Derrida admired. He knew that philosophy could make his work seem incomplete, and he would have liked to avoid metaphysics. But still, he belongs to the age of structural metaphysics, Derrida says. Mirroring his work in *Of Grammatology* again, Derrida says that Lévi-Strauss is Rousseauistic, trying to find an absent origin on which to base his structure (Derrida 2003, 369), an origin of which Rousseau despaired.

The power of this lecture, which introduced Derrida to an American (that is to say, a more powerful and open-minded) audience, lies not only in its enjoyable destruction of an old sort of metaphysics, but also in its appreciation of the power of the three great German thinkers, and also, finally, in the figure of this thinker who becomes the spokesman for a new movement, heralding a birth which he welcomes for himself, only with reservation, as a monstrosity, and which all the same, he recognizes and characterizes in a firm and certain tone, as 'play'. Derrida seemed to have arrived with a whole outlook:

> I employ these words, I admit, with a glance toward the operation of child-bearing – but also, with a glance toward those who, in a society from which I do not exclude myself, turn their eyes away when faced by the as yet unnamable which is proclaiming itself and which can do so, as is necessary whenever a birth is in the offing, only under the species of the non-species, in the formless, mute, infant, and terrifying form of monstrosity. (Derrida 2003, 370)

He was no freak either, but an academic, and one who lectured and produced scholarly works. This was impressive; for Derrida was not a conven-

AGAINST STRUCTURALISM

tional academic in some quality of his work. He seemed to be another of
those Germans, a young Heidegger, or Freud, or Nietzsche, and he was an
excellent teacher. He had the confidence and skill to analyse the contemporary situation and yet not appear deranged or fanatical, with that lightness
of the Latin sensibility, the intellect and *ésprit* which the Germans lack. In
the year following the paper he further backed up what he had to say by
reaffirming it in three books, each different, and each one with the same
powerful message, or rather lack of message, with a programme of activity
without aim, the aim being the ceaseless enjoyment and study of the fluid-
ity of the mind, and the absence of origins, while we await the 'monstrosity', the coming from which we avert our eyes.

5.5 'Freud and the Scene of Writing'

'Freud and the Scene of Writing' (2003, 246–91) was also delivered in this
year at the *Institut de psychanalyse*, and was published in *Tel Quel*, summer
1966. If we seek an acknowledgement of what he owes to Freud in this
paper we will be disappointed. Rather we find what he has to bring to Freud.
In Derrida's 1960s work Sigmund Freud is as important and pervasive as
Nietzsche and Heidegger. With Freud he is so deeply involved that, as can be
seen in contradistinction to his borrowings from Levinas, he rarely mentions
this reliance. But then it is debatable, and Derrida does debate it, whether
the name and author 'Freud' fully saturates the science of 'psychoanalysis'
which he founded. Derrida never settled accounts with Freud as he did with
Marx. He never, that is, said in simple terms what was valuable about Freud,
what he believed was good, and what pernicious about the psychoanalytic,
mechanistic view of the soul and the mind of man. This may have been as
a result of the quite early revisions of Freud from within the psychoanalytic
community itself, so that widespread and unjust condemnations of Freud
have not taken place recently as they did of Marx.

The thematic of the trace is a direct borrowing from the image of the mind
or mental process as a pattern of shifting traces and effects, derived from
Freud directly as he himself says, as well as from Heidegger. Derrida's very
fictionalizing of history resembles closely the case-histories which Freud
constructed from his analysands. Throughout his career he held a distant
and savage debate with Lacan over what he saw as a well-timed revival of
Freudian psychoanalysis, aspects of which showed, however, the traditional
mastery of the sign/signified complex by a conscious subject.

The text on Freud is only a fragment of the lecture given at the *Institut*. At the time, he and his audience were interested in pursuing suggestions made in pre-published excerpts from *Of Grammatology*, which had appeared in *Critique* 223–4. Derrida's problem is then to establish the science of grammatology with the tools of psychoanalysis. Derrida answers with his most abiding way of reading and using/abusing Freud's text; he says it is a tale in which the human is made into a machine, and choices are pre-programmed by history, and destiny, or life-history. The Freudian texts approach the problem of memory, of how a virgin memory, always fresh to impressions, can also be inscribed, yet remain pure. Freud's answer, which Derrida's paper sets out to bring to light more clearly, is that a virgin space can be both inscribed and uninscribed, by a writing of traces. The meaning of the harmony and activity of the forces will never rely on presence, the plenitude of a given meaning to be read as final, in a present fulfilment:

> The metaphor of pathbreaking, so frequently used in Freud's description, is always in communication with the theme of supplementary delay and with the reconstitution of meaning through deferral, after a mole-like progression, after the subterranean toil of an impression. This impression has left behind a trace which has never been perceived, whose meaning has never been lived in the present, i.e., has never been lived consciously. (Derrida 2003, 269)

This is how Freud's version of memory functions; and it is also how Derrida perceived the trace-writing to function in the mind of the writer, reader, and finally, in any existent thing. The trace is constituted by its being erasable, and essentially absent at any given moment. Essentially absent rather than present, the trace exists not in the present, but in a time which keeps it repressed or lets it surface, in a space which is never here, but somewhere else, absent. But the correct term is not 'absent', the opposite of 'present', but, rather, it is the term 'different': the trace is deferred and self-deferring.

6
Structures in French Thought

6.1 Structuralism

Roudinesco (Derrida 2004c, 1) put it to Derrida that he was basically the heir of structuralist masters: Althusser, Lacan, Lévi-Strauss and Foucault. In the main, Derrida did not publish a great deal on any of these writers as compared to his work on Nietzsche, Hegel or Plato, for example. Nevertheless some discussion of structuralism is necessary because, if not a straightforward structuralist, he was one of the heirs of its work and, secondly, his work is structuralist. Primarily structuralism set the subject and the referent aside. It attempted to make the human, social, studies into sciences, and to do away with humanism in favour of making humanity less human, more machine-like, dominated by structures of signs. It was an avant-garde academic movement in its time, which competed with the Sorbonne classicism often, so that it was both a university movement in its practices, but outside of the mainstream of scholarship. The era of structuralism spans 1945 to 1980, the year in which (or around which) each of the main leaders in the movement died or disappeared spectacularly. As for its origins, it began by combating philosophy, and especially existentialism. Major philosophers in France at the time tended to be outside of the movement, so that Levinas and Ricoeur remained out of sight during the time. Lévi-Strauss dealt with Sartre in this sense, tending to replace him as the new father-figure, the new 'intellectual' of the age (Dosse 1998a, xxi). The other major figures tend to be leaders in distinct fields, so Lacan was the psychoanalytic structuralist, Althusser the political philosopher, Lévi-Strauss the ethnologist and cultural critic, Foucault the historian and philosopher, and Barthes the structuralist of literature. Derrida appears as the latecomer, even as the first post-structuralist, or 'hyper-structuralist'.[1] What disqualifies him as one of them is that he never really learnt much from Saussure's linguistics. In 1966, when Derrida 'arrived' and turned on structuralism, announcing its end, structuralism was in fact at its zenith and still had years of expansion and decline ahead of it. 1967 was the actual beginning of the end for structuralism, not insofar as it then seemed to all and sundry to be finished, but because the central core was exhausted. Although structuralism was to become more popular and was to gain followers, it itself lost vigour, and new structuralists, such as Derrida or Chomsky, began to round on its central basis, the basis in impersonality, in the scientificity of the linguistic sub-structure of events, and in its imperturbability in the face of history. It is therefore correct to say that even while it seemed to be most powerful, it was in fact facing a crisis from which it would not recover.

At structuralism's origin stood Lévi-Strauss, who initiated it after having read Saussure's *Course of General Linguistics* (Saussure 1960) and having met Roman Jakobson in New York in the 1940s. This extraordinarily long-lived thinker[2] had trained as an ethnologist and made the unusual step of actually travelling to a foreign land to study natives in their environment, rather than studying them in his library. His thesis for the *doctorat d'État* was submitted in 1948, recounting his travels in South America, entitled *The Elementary Structures of Kinship* (Dosse 1998a, 18), setting the standard and the method for all structuralist thinking thereafter. He had not studied the empirical behaviour of the tribes in their kinship alliances in order to draw out inductive inferences, but to discover the symbolic structures which governed this behaviour, the signs and tokens which they used, or which used them, irrespective of individual choices. For him, the structural network of symbols is autonomous and does not need a subjective mind or a context. The rules of the symbolic network are not confined to any circumstances, as he pointed out in his early *Introduction to the Work of Marcel Mauss*. Above all, the conscious intentional structure of the subjects of the tribes was not invoked to describe the behaviour, but the signs which they had to use, which, regardless of circumstances or individuals, are the same. The symbolic structure existed regardless of conditions and environment, as Saussure's signs and words do regardless of referents. Lévi-Strauss converted the study of language and grammar into a study of the grammar of cultural activity and laws, since these could be studied as objects of science.

The object was the symbol or sign. Crucially he centred on what he saw as the centre of kinship relations and marriage rules, namely the law against incest and its permutations from tribe to tribe (Dosse 1998a, 21). 'The kinship system is a language' (1998a, 23). So for Lévi-Strauss the most fundamental object for the science of man is the sign, and non-semantic objects act like signs. This position is clearly what impelled Derrida to see, in *Of Grammatology*, in which he studies Lévi-Strauss and Saussure, the object of the science of 'grammatology' as the reduced sign, or the 'trace'. Derrida of course only studied a small portion of Lévi-Strauss there, but this was always his method. His plan was to cover all of Lévi-Strauss' work by looking at a small section.

Lévi-Strauss had intended, like Marcel Mauss, to put signs in the place of things in order to account for the total social fact. So the structuralist 'scientific' revolution in social studies was to develop from Ferdinand de Saussure's linguistics of a sign arbitrarily related to its signified, through Lévi-Strauss' anthropology, to Jacques Lacan, who also recognized Saussure as the important additional factor in his basic material (Freud in his case), and finally to the other major structuralists. But in each of them, the system of signs was unable to change, and was incapable of accounting for time, something that was noticed by Derrida, who put this problem in terms of the literary theorists' inability to account for the author (in 'Force and Signification', 1963). However, he was not the first to say this, nor were such criticisms important to structuralist thinkers. The 1959 Cerisy conference which he attended was devoted to the problem of genesis in structuralist thinking. On the other hand, Lévi-Strauss and later Foucault, with his theory of discontinuous history, made a virtue of this lack of timeliness in their structures.

Ultimately, Derrida was to find problems with the notion of 'sign', not finding lack of reference radical enough. He dismissed even the possibility of reference; the trace is the sign stripped of any power of reference, and of any existence. While Saussure had stripped words of their naïve relationship to things, and given them the power to float on, alone, as phonemes and letters, like the words of schizophrenics, Derrida was to question even this free-floating status, and try to show that a sign is not a sign, but a mere trace, which can be made into a sign/meaning only after the fact, and by a certain choice made by the subject so to use the trace as a sign. His trace is not even a thing; it is a cut, a gap in a system consisting only of other gaps and cuts. It is the Heideggerian *Riss*.[3] (The gaps and cuts are incized, in the end, into the virgin world, the realm of pure Being.)

6.2 Post-Structuralism

In its rejection of diachrony, structuralism had made a problem of time, made it appear to thought in a non-natural way. This theoretical time, which gave way to space and structure, opened the way for a thinking in which the present does not figure, but in which past and future mingle together, at the point where the mind or memory are. The subject, who once was the point at which past and present meet, is now an absence where signs and time master themselves, rather than being mastered. In structuralism reason is no longer what governs structures, but is even despised, as Lévi-Strauss despised Western rationality relative to the multiplicity of other possibilities. The outcome of structuralism was always, naturally, the deconstruction of the canonical themes, objects, systems, beliefs and dreams of subjectivity, as well as of its world and metaphysics. Deconstruction, like structuralism, is the logic of signs which are their own masters, and of a time which cannot ever find a place in which to halt and be taken account of. But while structuralism is based on words and signs, the 'logos', it is logocentric: deconstruction would not be logocentric.

In Dosse's final chapter of the first volume of his *History of Structuralism* he describes the arrival of the 'post-modern hour', and most of what is said there of that hour applies to Jacques Derrida. After 1956, and the disowning of Stalin by Krushchev, he says, the intellectuals who took care to make announcements on what culture had as its objects in the West no longer had anything to hope for in the future. Post-modernism was against progress in principle and was disillusioned with evolution. The dominant class, the middle one, had reached the end of its history, so that in the thinkers who speak for it, perhaps, we see the same symptoms which the middle class embodies: senility (Dosse 1998a, 359), recycling of the past, commemoration, remembrance, mourning. In Derrida we find traces of 'the future', but a future which he has to plead for, one which he sees no hope in, nothing new, unless it is unforeseen, for in this thinker there seems to be the feeling that we have already seen the future, and that it is bleak, that the world is not capable of anything worth anticipating with happiness. Heidegger and Nietzsche indeed, the thinkers of a new future, are in fact preparatory for this hopeless era, since they above all took away all faith and usefulness from traditional things, such as progress, ideals, humanism. Nietzsche and Heidegger describe the decline of the West, even making us at home in it. They disliked the modern, destroyed it, in the name of a better future, but it was a future which has never arrived.

6.3 Psychoanalysis and Jacques Lacan

In 1968 Derrida discovered Lacan's *Écrits* and the notes from his seminars. He studied these texts for three years intensively, and with enthusiasm, until he responded in 1971 with a lecture on Lacan's 'Poe Seminar' (collected in the 1966 *Écrits*). His lecture disputes Lacan's thesis of a true place for any letter or sign and a correct truth of the Unconscious, as well as a meaning which a mind or patient must find, destined for them, which is what Lacan saw the purpose of psychoanalysis to be.

In a late interview twenty years after Lacan's death Derrida said that (Derrida 2004c, 8): 'In certain situations I am Lacan's ally against others; in other situations I object to Lacan.' He was, he said, closer to Lacan than to Foucault (2004c, 11), and more so than to any of the others of the structuralist era because he and Lacan shared an attention to the movement of language, not the signifier, but to the letter (2004c, 14). Lacan and he were both moved by Bataille's 'accursed share', and while Lacan made sense of it as the 'Real', Derrida said that it was governed by 'différance'. There are also more cosmetic similarities which conceal a true proximity such as the similarity of Derrida's différance to Lacan's *objet petit a*. This object being a sort of thing in itself, the other, with a small 'o' (or in French 'a'). It names the thing created which is unsignified when discourse and naming miss their object. Lacan wanted *objet petit a* to be an algebraic formula for this objective absence which is still something somehow.

Derrida and he met very rarely through their respective lives. They travelled to Johns Hopkins together in 1966 when Lacan was the leader of the delegation; they also worked at the ENS at the same time, but never spent time together. When Lacan was denied the use of a seminar hall at that *école* Lacan noticed that Derrida did not protest (although Derrida would presumably have denied this), and after a three-year period of reading him, Derrida in 1971 began to criticize him in public. Their characters were both dominated by the will to power, and they in general were antagonistic. Derrida couldn't stand Lacan's dominating and arrogant behaviour, and he contested the significatory value of signs in Lacan's brand of structuralism.

In the 1950s Marx and Freud's followers pretended to be an uncontested 'Enlightenment' to which Derrida tried to not give in (Derrida 1995b, 81). The problem of their being an orthodoxy made itself felt because not much change was taking place in the use of their thought, and concrete uses of their teaching were evident not so much in theoretical developments, as in the existence of Freudian institutions, developments in basically non-Freudian psychology (which had become biologistic (Derrida 2004c, 101)), and, in the case of Marxism, in the Soviet government and the French Communist Party. This was to change with Lacan and Althusser in the 1960s, at a time when Derrida had already himself begun to teach and write professionally. Lacan revitalized Freud in a number of ways, not least in setting up his own school of psychoanalysis after having been ejected from the International Psychoanalytic Association. Lacan then was the most dominant post-Freudian thinker of this era and made substantial contributions to its modernization in line with structuralism. Derrida points out that the foundations of his own transcendental system of traces and différance had already been worked out before he read Lacan and Freud in the new way, so that Lacanian psychoanalysis had no real effect on his *Of Grammatology* or the thinking of the trace (Derrida 2004c, 169).[4] Nevertheless Roudinesco put it to him that Derrida 'played an important role in teaching psychoanalysis' (Derrida 2004c, 166), especially after having made contact with René Major, an arch anti-Lacanian, in 1976. Major, who was prominent in the field after Lacan's death, owed a theoretical debt to Derrida.[5]

Derrida was never to write a 'Spectres of Freud' Roudinesco suggests, although he might well have done so, given how similar Freud's position as a theorist was for Derrida to that of Marx. Similar to Marx again, Freud's thought has something endangered about it, and like Marxism, today, its end is continually being announced (Derrida 2004c, 177) and in some states it is mocked, attacked, threatened. It is, in France, forbidden in the high spheres of republican teaching (at the EHESS for example) (Derrida 2004c, 178). 'It has at bottom very little influence in the university . . . it is rather smuggled in.' But if one took psychoanalysis seriously there could be terrible consequences, since institutions and laws are based on personal responsibility and the mastery of the individual as an agent, while psychoanalysis' main teaching has always been that the subjective agent is dominated by something unconscious or unknown. Nevertheless, though admiring it, Derrida considered psychoanalysis to be a type of fiction, a non-self-conscious literature. He never accepted the 'metapsychology' of the id, ego, superego, and so on, preferring instead partial, regional and minor analyses, the most 'venturesome soundings' (Derrida 2004c, 172). He admired Freud and Lacan for their theoretical daring. Since 1971, the time at which his naïve enthusiasm for Lacan had ended, he had criticized him for his belief in 'full speech', 'true speech', and the 'logic of the signifier' (Derrida 2004c, 171). 'The Purveyor of Truth', in *The Post Card* (Derrida 1987a) gave rise to disputes, collected in

The Purloined Poe (Harvey 1988), but Lacan never responded (Derrida 2004c, 171).

Lacan's work is indeed creative and daring. Its style, the flow of his pre-dominantly spoken prose (collected in volumes according to seminar series in the French editions by Seuil) is a straightforward French,[6] but a strained colloquial voice which seeks to cut itself down to oblique references; a supe-rior tone which captivates and eludes, making sometimes bizarre references in the midst of a narrative exposition of his systematic ideas. The primary alliance with Derrida's own theory of signs, as Derrida pointed out (Derrida 2004c, 48) is that for Lacan the sign is both a trace or mark, and a lack – dual from the beginning; and that for Lacan this is not merely a neurotic symptom, but a feature of all mentality, peculiar to human mental life from birth, although Lacan envisaged some sort of cure. As he saw it, structures for the subject, its language, or set of signs, do not simply refer, but slip, and mark absence. However, Lacan did not go so far as Derrida, and held on to what has been called a Heideggerian assumption, that truth has a locus which can be disclosed, and thus that the sign is not a pure trace, but ulti-mately does adhere to a referent.[7]

Following Lévi-Strauss, whose works continued to be produced at a steady rate through the 1950s and 60s, Lacan was to bring structuralism to greater predominance (he was known as the father-figure of structuralism), mixing psychoanalysis, Saussure, philosophy (mostly Heidegger) and charis-matic leadership. During the structuralist era the Unconscious enjoyed a new importance, since structures were based not on a mind or subject, but on self-subsistent language, and Lacan benefited (Dosse 1998a, 91). He said the Unconscious is the radical alterity of oneself, it is the Other.[8]

Lacan's influence grew, and improved the status of structuralism because he was both a great self-publicizer, and created a huge number of patients, bringing in the idea that short sessions of analysis were better for the patient and more lucrative for the analyst (Dosse 1998a, 25). He returned to the notion of the subject, speech and the road to the Unconscious, saying in 'The Insistence of the Letter in the Unconscious' (Lodge and Wood 2000, 75) that if Freud had known of Saussure he would have made use of him. The Unconscious has a linguistic structure – which meant that the mind could be demedicalized and debiologized. ' "Linguistics is surely the science on which the Unconscious is based". The letter supplants being,' noted Dosse (1998a, 125).

Although Lacan severely limited the power of signs and language to work as they have been supposed to work, he did so by describing signs *qua* signs which have, due to causes beyond our control, simply gone astray. That is, his theory does require a notion of a time in which signs may have worked properly. In the imperfect state in which the subject must function, the sign of lack holds the world together. The sign for the Thing which is Real referred essentially to a void (Dosse 1998a, 242).[9] In a simple dualism, there is simply an unknown void, and the signs which are supposed to work on it. In his *Four Fundamental Concepts of Psychoanalysis* (1964) the signifier occupies the place and site of the subject, replacing the subject, so that where once the Western sciences had seen an autonomous subjective mind, now they must see a system or chain of signs motivated by desire. But the subject is not thereby disappearing, but rather not-in-being, annulled, not ontologically graspable, just part of the void. The subject only makes itself intelligible with the signifying chain in which it is locked. For if desire or will or 'wish-fulfilment' was once the essence of the human, we must now see that desire and will are at the disposal of something external to the human, namely this chain of signs. Therefore, Lacan's attempts at cure, his seminars on practice, collected in that work of 1964, describe and prove that cure and illness depend upon language, while desire is unending, since it is generated by the absence at the heart of language and signs, which perpetually try to catch up with the thing-itself, but only ever find more signs, thus locked in desire. The absence gives birth to desire. It is notable that while Lacan's theory may be only tangentially close to reality and he does attempt to set it beside reality – as he does in his work on the Mirror stage (Lacan 2001, 1–8) with reference to the biological reality of the child – still, what convinces is not so much this useful appearance of his work matching up to empirical fact as that he put a great deal of effort into making his theory complete, without contradiction, and fully convincing by its own set of standards. His theory of desire relates to his other theories on signs, absence, time-delays in sign use, and so on. Psychoanalysis is required, since this chain of linguistic signs, constituting desire, does not dominate the conscious mind, as a great quantity of signs would do, by bearing down on the mind, but dominates, rather, in the Unconscious, where this chain of signs operates beyond control. The subject as non-existent thus becomes a go-between for the chain of desire in the Unconscious, and the 'everything' which escapes signification. Ultimately the imperative of matching sign to thing, of making the 'objet petit a' disappear, is something religious, with a teleological objective, ending in something like Hegel's Absolute Knowledge, which, again, made Derrida suspicious.

Lacan was in relative terms very old when he began to be recognized as the structuralist father-figure. Born in the first years of the century, by the time of the slow-down of structuralism in the 1970s he was an old man, but still asserting his right to lead. Despite Derrida's concern that he disseminate his reading of the Unconscious, he refused to do so, seeing that to let the signifying chain become pure 'trace' would be to let interpretation of its effects become infinite, which would make 'cure' impossible.

7
1967

In 1967 Derrida's second son, Jean, was born, and in the same year three major works were published, marking the culmination of years of work. These were followed by intensive 'deconstructive' campaigning in *Tel Quel*, and a multitude of public appearances, beginning in this year with a lecture in Brussels. Each foreign lecture would be in addition to his work at ENS, which he continued. However, his works were no overnight success, and their obscure character, limited to points of difficulty in an already difficult structuralist paradigm, left him with less fame than Lévi-Strauss, Foucault, Lacan, Althusser or Barthes, who were, in varying degrees, all publishing publicly well-received, even popular, books at the time. The three books were *Speech and Phenomena*, *Of Grammatology* and *Writing and Difference*, the last of which (Derrida 2003) was a collection of articles and conference papers, many of which we have already looked at. We have also already studied what Derrida had to say of Rousseau, Saussure and Lévi-Strauss in *Of Grammatology*. In this chapter we will examine the remainder of the year's products: *Speech and Phenomena* and the first part of *Of Grammatology*.

7.1 *Speech and Phenomena* [1967]

Speech and Phenomena is a late event in Derrida's Husserl studies. It is careful, the product of years, the product of a concentration of interest. It is succinct in a very specific and limited area, the product of a qualified scholar, but one also aware of what dangers the Western traditional side of Husserl held in reserve for linguistics and semiology. It is an act of distancing from Husserl, and in the ease with which it was written, the final flourish, totally out of character with the rest of the book, it has the aspect of something frivolous, and frivolous in the labour expended upon something so recondite. Moreover, the means by which Derrida attacks Husserl's system have an odd simplicity which somewhat undoes the extraordinary erudition and extensive knowledge. In effect Derrida says that if a self produces signs because it is in touch with itself, then it can be shown that, because a self is always not in touch with itself, and is already always dead at some level, then the signs cannot be produced in this way, or, if they are produced in this way, then they are dead signs, 'writing'. *Speech and Phenomena* leads carefully into the heart of the Husserlian science of science, the description of meanings as subject-constituted objects, constituted on the subject's self-expression, the subject's voice, its knowledge as a human product, for Western scientists.

Derrida's deconstruction attends to features of language or signs which are statements produced by the speaker. Particularly, Derrida explains Husserl's theory of statements which a speaker, or consciousness, makes when talking internally, that is, when he is 'thinking', talking to himself. Husserl categorizes these signs, sent from a mind to itself, as 'expressions'. What Derrida shows in his discussion is that statements produced by the subject, classed as 'expressions' by Husserl and described as originating in a present-to-self consciousness, are not actually possible, because of the problem of time; the 'I' is from the first and always a mortal and passing 'expression', and means essentially, each time it is used, that 'I am dead', because the sign 'I' and similar signs cannot be used in the present without destroying that immediacy.[1] With each inner *expression* of what 'I' am doing, 'I' have ceased to do it, and it thenceforth belongs to a past, dead, person. This problem is a real difficulty since Husserl's theory demands a self which is self-aware and immediately in touch with itself. Writing seems to be contemporaneous with the conception of the self as the first person singular which makes statements, from the self to the self, as 'expressions', which have no place in Husserl's scheme, unless they undermine it. For what purpose could 'I' expressions of the self to itself have, other than that of memorializing, inscribing, a set point in time, as all writing does? And if this is so, then at the heart of Husserl's present-to-self awareness there is a dead, non-present subject, using 'writing' and not voice.

Husserl, in using the notion of the self as present in time to itself, was using a pre-Heideggerian view of time. For him the essence of time is the 'now', the present moment (Derrida 1973, 63).[2] Derrida will now defend the very position which Husserl had sought to avoid. Signs as expressions are not useless in the self-relation, and he will show how signs can originate in a self which is talking to its dead ghostly self of the past or future. That non-presence and otherness are internal to presence strikes at the very root of the argument for the uselessness of signs in the self-relation (Derrida 1973, 66). What Derrida does not mention, to be fair to Husserl, is that immediately on completing the *Logical Investigations* Husserl started work on *The Phenomenology of the Consciousness of Internal Time*, which was to have an influence on Heidegger, and thus on Derrida's own scheme (Husserl 1991). However, Husserl's new recognition of time did not have any effect on his privileging the present moment in the impact of time on the system of language and signs, which meant that, overall, he remained blind to the implications (just as he did with regard to the place of writing in the history of science).

In Husserl's *Logical Investigations* scheme (Derrida 1973, 73), the third person present indicative of the verb 'to be' is the pure and irreducible core of expression (rather than the first person indicative). Expressions such as 'he is' are the ideal use of expressions regarding actual circumstances when signs are expressions produced by internal monologue. We have more trouble with first person present indicative uses such as 'I am'. Expressions such as 'I am at the window' present a problem in this scheme, and one which Husserl avoided, although he was aware of it. The said sentence, or sign, is in his account an expression which teaches nothing since the mind which uttered or thought it is also already aware of it, and the mind is thus indicating something to itself, which Husserl saw as a pointless gesture, and as we saw, it also indicates the subject's death. So the meaningful gesture would be 'I *was* at the window', which, while being an *expression* of memory, is also marked by temporality, so that expressions which refer the mind to itself are also always marked by a temporal absence or passing of that self. Such I-expressions are always aware of and structured by the passing of time, and they primordially accept the reality of time past, that is, they accept the diminution in importance of the immediate present. Husserl had always, up to the point of the *Investigations*, like Aristotle and Kant, recognized the essence of time to be this present moment in its immediacy, while expressions like this recognize, for the mind expressing itself to itself, the more essential dependence on time as the absence of immediacy, the absence of objects. I-expressions, and the self itself, therefore, are temporally structured in a manner which Husserl had failed to describe, and the mind always assigns meaning to itself as a thing of the past or future. The 'I', in fact, always recognizes itself as already dead, as already passed, as never, that is, finally present, and although there is, for Husserl, a fleeting glimpse of the consciousness by consciousness, this fleeting glimpse is a lure to something which exceeds his means of description. There can be no self-presence, so auto-affection is not self-identical, and at its heart is différance, which is also at the heart of pure transcendence, at the heart of the reduction of the voice to the expression, and expression to the idea. The self-presence of the soliloquy seems to be impossible, because whatever occurs in signs and meaning in the present is always deferred into the past.

7.2 *Of Grammatology* [1967]

In its first part *Of Grammatology* deals with Husserl, the thematic of writing, the voice, the ideal object, the whole Western tradition of logocentrism, or idealism; the second part deals with Lévi-Strauss, with Saussurean semiotics, and with Rousseau as a member of the Western tradition. This second part deals with these three much as the subjects of the papers and lectures of *Writing and Difference* are dealt with, and Derrida makes an effort in his later interviews to diminish the appearance of *Of Grammatology*'s being a systematic treatise by saying it should be inserted within a reading of *Writing and Difference*.[3]

Essentially Part One is a deconstruction of speech and writing colloquially understood, by means of a notion of archi-writing. But the result of this book is not the archi-writing itself, it is a more subtle, absent telos, namely the beginning of a type of thinking which has recognized that structures and systems on the subject of Being are always faulty.[4] The event of the first ninety pages of *Of Grammatology*, the first part of it, constitutes and summarizes the new and final conclusion of what Husserl meant to Derrida himself; it is a stage of the development of a Heideggerian progress, end, and overturning of the age of science, ontology and logocentric, systematic metaphysics. This had already been established in previous and contemporaneous texts. The new event announced in the book is the positing of a programme of research around archi-writing, which is based on différance as the basis of all oppositions. The archi-writing with which différance works is nicknamed 'the trace'. The means of setting out this vision of deferred Being will be 'thought', not metaphysics.

In Part One Derrida outlines his system of the trace by reference to Ferdinand de Saussure, who was arguably the first and leading structuralist thinker. The trace, or play of remains, overseen by différance itself (as opposed to presence itself) can determine the meaning of things and the meaning of writing as an originary and universal writing of differential traces, wherein everything is a trace. This is archi-writing, which appears to be a metaphorical change of things wherein, reduced to a differentiated system of signs to be read, writing first permits any meaning and any meta-physics at all, any psychiatry, science, any vulgarly understood writing. As the replacement and enhancement of the ideal core of meaning, this archi-writing is deeper than ideal entities. Différance irredeemably transforms a vision of the real world into a world of semi-darkness, in which the light of différance burns what it touches to ashes, and turns the human into the spectral, the book into a field of disseminated signs whose meaning can fall on arid ground, or good. Clearly what has occurred in this text is the pro-viding of the 'Other' to the Ideal (Derrida 1997b, 62). But deconstruction is never as simple as providing one system with its other. Quite the contrary, as Derrida said in 'Force and Signification' (Derrida 2003, 22).[5] The problem is to escape this duality.

The major breakthrough which has taken place concerns above all the sign. Today it has been generally noticed that the signified in the traditional scheme is itself a sign. There are only signs, and signs for signs. Nietzsche is supposed to have shaken the stability of the sign, despite his being part of the onto-theological tradition of thought. So to deconstitute the founding words of today's structuralism is also a task to be achieved to bring science into line with this revolution in thought which Nietzsche has announced, unheard until now (Derrida 1997b, 21). Even in Heidegger, Being is tied to the voice as a basis for signs, a sure place in which signifiers refer to signifieds. This is an onto-theological symptom, where God is the ultimate guarantor. And although the breakthrough is immediately linguistic, and affects the presence to self of the self, and is thus psychologistic, a task for psychoanalysis,[6] its major work must be undertaken by post-ontological metaphysics, thinking, the true ground, the Heideggerian thinking and questioning, not fully achieved by Heidegger himself, who was too hopeful that genuine words for Being could be spoken.

It is to Heidegger that Derrida aligns himself at the end of this part, when he announces, briefly, but significantly, the allegiance, with the reservation that:

Outside of the economic and strategic reference to the name that Heidegger justifies himself in giving to an analogous but never identical transgression of all philosophemes, thought is here for me a perfectly neutral name, the blank part of the text, the necessarily indeterminate index of a future epoch of différance. In a certain sense 'thought' means nothing. (Derrida 1997b, 93)

He proposes to follow and use this 'thought', in effect saying that it is the thought itself which matters in *Of Grammatology*, not the particular science of phenomenology or of grammatology which thought, in its attention and its reading, has been able to thematize.

8
Avant-garde Philosophy

8.1 May '68

Derrida, in 1968, began to give lectures in America: at Penn State, University Park; State College, Buffalo; Northwestern, Evanston; Yale; Long Island; and at New York University, Columbia. He taught and lectured outside France in Europe too, at Berlin, Zürich and London universities in this year. In France, meanwhile, occurred the momentous and bizarre revolt which brought the country to a standstill. May '68 was a student protest which turned into a general strike. There was total collapse of the state apparatus, and a strike involving nine million people, in which the managers were on strike alongside the traditional working class. But everything returned to normal on the surface within a month, and de Gaulle was re-elected. It was a flash in the pan, consisting of several weeks of anarchy, followed by an election in which the conservatives won after de Gaulle put his presidency up for referendum with Georges Pompidou.

May '68 was stronger on spectacle than on thought (Hanley and Kerr 1994, 5). In Germany the events of 1968, which were mirrored there, had a little more significance, since the stakes were a general overhaul of the system which had brought Nazism to power, but even in Germany the revolt failed. Since May '68 followed similar events in which intellectuals were openly involved, in which they had had beneficial results, such as the Dreyfus Affair, Stalinism, Eastern Europe, Algeria, and the Cold War, it called their actual necessity into doubt, because on this occasion the intellectuals played no part. Afterwards France was without intellectuals in the old sense in which Zola and Hugo had been public and authoritative figures.

Intellectuals once gave direction in abstract terms, sure of being heard and listened to, working on behalf of society. With the new movement of structuralism which had forced itself to prominence by turning Sartre out of his place,[1] such intellectual status was not an aim of the educated in those years. (In 1968 Sartre was imprisoned for selling an inflammatory journal, but de Gaulle released him, explaining that 'he is our Voltaire' (Hanley and Kerr 1994, 12).) It was a moment when the newly fashionable structuralism was found to be ineffectual and weak as a theoretical moment, and unable to control action. It led to the end of the fashion for scientific structures as descriptive of human experience. Lyotard was to say of intellectuals that they speak as the embodied voice of universals,[2] and yet in May of that year intellectuals, or 'philosophers', made no contribution, caused nothing to happen, and resolved nothing. They were out of step with society, and indifferent to it.

Responses to the events by the political class of revolutionaries who would once have welcomed it were in general those of fear, since they had not organized it, and by its nature it surprised everyone, including the revolutionaries themselves. If anything, it seemed to mean the bankruptcy of the revolutionary *idea*, the nervous response of an era to the demand to revolt, but no longer seeing any reason for doing so. The PCF was afraid that this revolution was going too fast, and tried to get solid results from it (Hanley and Kerr 1994, 19). The student portion of the revolutionaries, who had grievances which they could state, were in the main just play-acting, acting out a revolution without any heart, and certainly without any serious or reasoned motive. The causes of it have been examined and are numerous, besides the actual concerns of the students. The problem in understanding it is that these problems do not seem to have been enough to start the protest. So other factors must be included, such as that the students were afraid of growing up into the adult world (which Lyotard pointed to). France was turning to Europe, and the pace of progress and expansion was fearful. By turning to Europe, and losing its identity as the leader of the world, the land of revolution and equality – France – seemed to have become afraid of itself and of its future. Another factor was the government's hesitancy, and its reluctance to conciliate the protests, as it too was unsure of its new identity, treating the protesters rather as it had treated the Algerian uprising.

It was a revolution which feared revolution (Hanley 1994, 20), with no deaths, and, despite plans to storm various government buildings, a few riot-police and likelihood of some casualties undermined any concerted action. Again it seems to have been the point at which France was forced to recognize that its history of independence, revolution and colonialism had finally come to an end, and as a failed and irresponsible revolution it meant the end of the responsible, socialist and serious tradition of intellectual culture and critique, implicating structuralism, Derrida and the others in this failure of nerve and of authority.

The actual concerns of the students in the first place were: overcrowding, underfunding, failure rates at university, absence of contact between teachers and students, and the harshness of selection procedures. So the students did not protest for political reasons, for Vietnam, or Algeria, for example, but for mundane things, common problems of students (such as graduation difficulties, poor teaching quality, anxiety about jobs after graduation, and library access). These were also factors which worried the working class, that is, economic factors; for although France had turned to Europe, and was expanding and looking forward to an infinite progress in living standards, actual conditions were getting worse for this class, with longer hours, and lower wages.

Each of these factors means that the leadership of 'France' in intellectual matters, the reasoned edge of decision-making, had seemed to devolve elsewhere, into economic concerns rather than the concerns of truth and justice, or the concerns of art and philosophy. Marxist theorizing, intellectual debate, public idolization of thinkers and respect for learned people tended to diminish more and more following this year. Apart from anything else they no longer offered the reason for revolution, so that when it came at random, as a nervous response to change, a paradoxical conservatism, there was no leadership. It happened by accident, and the class of intellectuals, to which Derrida would once have belonged, comprehending the whole event with a glance and speaking for the most ideal and just perspective, were silent and appeared inept. What decided the event was the French government's decisive turn to Europe, the victory of de Gaulle in the election, and the fact that economic answers were offered to basically economic problems. This last, semi-socialist revolution, had been won by liberalism and capital, and no intellectual questioning or theorizing was required. After May '68 structuralism and Derrida became more and more confined to the lecture hall and the academic journal.

Derrida had spoken in 1966, at Baltimore, as if he had a plan and a leadership principle, something he believed in, but was this plan of any relevance to rioters and the mass of people? Derrida himself said later that he had found it difficult to feel any sympathy for the rioters and with the crowd, and did not like the way a feeling of community was inspiring their actions, rather than any distinct idea. Derrida's politics were never revolutionary. He was too cautious and preferred discrete changes, even if 'venturesome'. His dream of a truer Europe, living up to ideals already in place, a vision quite simply of an improved political entity, an improved discourse, may in fact match the ambitions of May '68. In May he was the one to organize the first general assembly at the ENS (Bennington 1999, 332) with the aim of thinking things through. He held frequent meetings with Maurice Blanchot during these weeks. A true follower of Heidegger, Derrida sought a revolution of the grasp of time and being, a turn towards the origin of things, rather than a change in behaviours. By July he was holding his first seminars at the University of Berlin, invited by Peter Szondi.

His work at Berlin was to produce *Glas*, when in 1973 he delivered lectures on Hegel, which he reworked into that book. Szondi had invited the still little-known and under-appreciated Frenchman to Berlin, as an admirer who became a close friend. He, Derrida and Celan would often meet in Berlin as well as in Paris, where Celan worked at the ENS alongside Derrida.

Derrida was, he says (2004a, 292), 'prevented from travelling by plane by an insurmountable fear' from 1969 to 1973. 'Whether it could be explained or not, it vanished in 1973. Between those years I did all my travelling by car, train, or boat, even the longest trips, for example to and from, and within, the US, in 1971 – of which there were many' (2004a, 292).

In 1971 he returned to Algeria for the first time since his family left in 1962, lecturing in Algiers. In a familiar pattern he now only visited foreign countries to lecture, yet these invitations to do so were frequently pretexts for him to travel and meet admirers. He also gave a short course of teaching at Oxford in 1971–72, plus teaching obligations in Baltimore in 1971, and Zürich in 1972. As well as this he gave individual lectures at Nice, Montreal, Strasbourg, Baltimore, Evanston, Yale, New Haven and New York in 1971; in Amsterdam, Leiden, Utrecht, Zürich and Cerisy-la-Salle (at a Nietzsche conference) in 1972 (see *Spurs*, below).

8.2 *Margins of Philosophy*

'Différance' was a paper given to the *Société français de philosophie* in 1968 which very much put Derrida's idea of différance (with an 'a') to the society, in the same terms as he had presented it in his work prior to 1967.[3] He insisted that différance precedes and generates philosophy by opening up the space for philosophy (Derrida 1982, 6). It is a steady repetition of the previous announcements on this transcendental non-concept which is intended to exceed all classical oppositions. It works in traces, or words which are not signs, not empirical, nor ontological things, nor ideal, but constitutive of an opening preceding a grasping of beings. However, différance is not a concept (Derrida 1982, 7) and does not function as a traditional transcendental substance, since its traces are divided, like a margin dividing two spaces, which, belonging to both sides of the division, is itself split. A trace is both a mark and a rift. To approach différance, we must follow traces since différance forms time, and puts itself off, aside. 'Différance' itself, as a word or trace, is itself not a sign, and has no proper meaning. It is the originary constitution of time and space, and hence beyond their frame of reference. It is the originary status of language, before such language becomes signsystem, meaning saturated, present/absent. Derrida makes différance understandable by saying that this, here, present as I now conceive it, is made up of non-present traces, governed by différance (Derrida 1982, 13) and it is this constitution of the present, as an 'originary' and irreducibly non-simple synthesis of marks, or traces, or retentions as 'protensions . . . that I propose to call archi-writing, archi-trace, or différance. Which (is) (simultaneously) spacing and temporalization' (Derrida 1982, 13). Hence it is the link and difference between space and time.

The sense of this restatement of his system in a more condescending tone than employed hitherto is that, to use a reference to another work, he had left Plato's cave, not to get to Ideas, but because the trace is neither sensible nor intelligible, something that the cave hid, and which Plato could not see either (Derrida 1998d, 178). Derrida's new Platonism calls one to leave the cave, and to come to a world as it is, and always will be, genuinely spectral and phantomatic. The ghost appears and disappears as it wants to, but is never localizable, never inhabits a place or time, but is between life and death, like their in-between, yet neither. Beings are not, and Being is not, either; there is only a sort of mixture of appearance/reality made up of their being repellent to each other. It is not a question, then, of using words of adequation. Our names and words can only cling to traces, not to the things themselves. 'There will be no new name' only following traces, he says, after calling Nietzsche and Heidegger to his aid (Derrida 1982, 27).

The subsequent collected pieces in *Margins*, a collection representative of his measured philosophical work of the late 1960s, are in general implementations of this theory, by using texts of German idealism both as proofs and as targets.[4] As différance regards, or defines itself, on the basis of time and space, its applications for historical metaphysics are manifold, like a universal solvent. Heidegger's note on Aristotle's and Hegel's view of time is approached and amended in 'Ousia and Gramme' in the perspective of Heidegger's critique of this view. Heidegger had made the footnote in *Being and Time* (Heidegger 1998a, 500) and Derrida intended to expand on it in view of the unwritten Second Part. Aristotle had held that time is a sequence of 'nows' based on the present moment. To question this ability to pin time down to the present is to question the possibility of philosophy itself (Derrida 1982, 39). The history of philosophy is permitted because of this linear, grammatical time, which permits something to be said of time, but inaccurately. By contrast the economy and the time of the trace cannot be mastered (Derrida 1982, 65).

'The Pit and the Pyramid' works similarly on Hegel's semiology, by imposing the economy of the trace on to conventional philosophical semiotics, in which signs are conceived of as tombs, monuments, shelters of meaning, like a (dead) body enclosing a soul (Derrida 1982, 82). For Hegel, the sign is dead and arbitrary, but the meaning lives. Being dead, the sign acts like a machine, and as a bridge. As Deborah Chaffin says, commenting on this essay: 'His various treatments of the sign work to show that the metaphysical tradition has always treated the sign as a transition or bridge between the sensible and the intelligible' (Chaffin 1989, 77). The essay shows Derrida's engrossing interest in Hegel, and his wide reading, referring to *The Encyclopaedia of the Philosophical Sciences* and the *Greater Logic* with a knowledge seemingly as thorough as his knowledge of Husserl had been. The sign is for Hegel a representation, a sign for a meaning [*Bedeutung*]. The sign encloses meaning, the soul within a body as it were, and this, of course, is outlined as part of the dialectic which begins with given types of thought and moves towards Hegelian Absolute Knowledge. In this way meaning embodied by the sign is constituted by opposition, since immediacy needs opposites as Hegel had shown in the *Science of Logic*. But then opposition has been for Derrida, for some time, not fundamental enough, and can be overcome by différance and the trace-economy, which is how the essay proceeds to undo the Hegelian dialectic, the history of metaphysics and Hegel's mastery of his subject matter.

Throughout his work Derrida had been pointing to the literary, rhetorical aspects of the works of philosophy. Often Derrida had precisely hit upon the most rhetorical tropological parts of a work, such as the image of madness in Descartes as read by Foucault, in which he said in a roundabout way that in the passage from Descartes the madness is not a genuine madness, but a part of Descartes' rhetoric, part of a collection of argumentative figures available for the writer in the seventeenth century. Derrida was to continue to deploy metaphors in his own work throughout his career as though he were not serious enough to settle for well-defined, rigorous concepts which are 'cold' as it were. During the 1970s, and starting with an essay collected in *Margins*, 'White Mythology', Derrida was to explain how this concern with metaphor was not simply a reading of weak, literary points in historical philosophy, but was part of a programme of a new sort of philosophy, in which the metaphor would be undone, a post-ontological writing, which he saw as both continuing a genuine Heideggerian thinking, and also as being an integral development of the theme of the trace. For him it seemed to answer the demand for a new language, and a language which is not constituted by its being a system of signs. 'White Mythology' was to be a first announcement of this, while, following some criticism of it by, amongst others, Paul Ricoeur, which Derrida saw as misjudged, he again described his theory of metaphor in philosophy, and developed it further, in 'The Retrait of Metaphor' (Derrida 1998d). The earlier work asks what sense is there in opposing the *concept* to the *metaphor* (Derrida 1982, 264). For example, how extraneous to Descartes' work is the metaphor of *lumen naturale*, since only with this guide can the discourse on the cogito take place, allowing the discourse to proceed. The natural light metaphor is never subjected to doubt. It allows Descartes to stay on the track of reason. 'Natural light' is the stable core of his thought. The metaphor, however, is not single, not a stock and sure metaphor, but by its nature is plural and unforeseeable, because 'natural light' means many things, an unknown quantity of things. So it gives rise to a syntax which is not exhausted by any one meaning, since metaphor is precisely not metonymic, and not a pure adequation to a given meaning. Philosophy would like to master the metaphor, as Descartes seems to have done with 'natural light', to interiorize it, and regularize it, into a canonical use in philosophy, but it cannot do so. Nietzsche himself had already said that in the beginning language and the basic traits of truth had been simply metaphorical, and over time, with erosion, metaphor had become normalized and its origins forgotten (Nietzsche 1980, 47) so that 'good' as a concept is originally a metaphor, for example. And so any text with metaphors in its argument, maybe all texts, have a meaning which is disseminated and has no original meaning and no destination. Derrida's later work in this direction was to be more radical; it would turn his new sort of language into metaphor, thus denying sure reference to it, and then further metaphorizing it, further removing or retracing it, so that language becomes a metaphor of metaphor in which meaning withdraws, and the writing itself becomes the withdrawal of the withdrawal of meaning, that is, a new, reversed meaning foundation.

8.3 *Dissemination* [1972]

Before making contact with de Man and America fully in the mid-1970s Derrida went through a severe working out of his ideas with *Tel Quel*, along with confirmed traditional Parisian revolutionary writers, Roland Barthes, Philippe Sollers, Julia Kristeva, and others. He was also to attend the 1972 Nietzsche Colloquium at Cerisy. The fruit of his work for *Tel Quel* was collected in *Dissemination* in 1972, the same year as *Margins*.

Dissemination, released in France in 1972, consisted of essays which are statements of how presence-based, and subject-based, expressions of mastery over existence by philosophy are simultaneously readable as absent, floundering in a lack of control or order. At the same time, these essays do not change order into disorder, but give a purified version of texts as degree-zero structures in which meaning is not lost, but found anew amongst the features of texts, in the mere giveness of textual concreteness, in the inscription of signs, the presence of blank spaces between letters, and in the self-referentiality of a text as the most sure thing to which a text or sign can refer.

Dissemination consists of an 'Outwork' or preface, and four separate articles which had been previously published in reviews during the late 1960s. (1) 'Plato's Pharmacy' seems to be a classic, due to its reading of Plato in a highly complex way but with simple reference points and brief, popularizing statements of the results of the reading. Plato's dual reliance on writing and his refusal to accord value to it is summed up in the fact that the word 'pharmakon', which is used to understand writing metaphorically, can be translated as either 'medicine' or as 'poison'. (2) 'The Double Session' considers Mallarmé's theory of writing and his ambiguous relation to it. He is seen to have been aware both of his dream of a pure Book containing pure undisseminated absolute knowledge, and just as surely aware that a book, or knowledge, must only in general give knowledge of itself, but not of anything outside the book. Finally, (3) 'Dissemination' is a review of a work by Philippe Sollers, originally published in *Critique* (261–2, 1969) with some further reference to Mallarmé's late poem *Un coup des dès*. Despite its being a collection of disparate productions, it is held together in an almost systematic way, with oblique references amongst essays to each other, and with a recognition that Mallarmé is the most recent forerunner to this critique of

absolute knowledge in written texts, while Plato is the most distant. Sollers'
Tel Quel is figured as the avant-garde hardening of this new science into an
anti-orthodoxy of the new age.

'Dissemination' is one of Derrida's most difficult, that is, intricate works
on the trace as writing. Its point is simple. Argumentation is slow, and highly
stylized. The layout of the text is theatrical, consciously an avant-garde,
slightly esoteric manual for advanced deconstruction. The matter of
Derrida's style could cause some embarrassment to admirers of Derrida who
wish to prove his value. His insights are not really so complex as to require
the lengthy, breathless yet painfully slow progress which they make. If
Nietzsche taught Derrida a lot, he has taught him nothing about using language in a rhetorical way, or at any rate, he forgot himself in *Dissemination*.
Condensation matters to Derrida insofar as he can create titles and catch-
words for his works and thoughts, but his idea of a fold in the text, for
example in Poe's 'Purloined Letter' (Derrida 1987a), due to which Poe's narrator is also part of the text and not outside of it, is an idea which could have
been stated easily in brief terms. Instead of doing this, Derrida questions the
multiple ways in which such a fold creates mirrors and reflections; he does
not stint in pointing out its ramifications for Lacan, for the reader, for Poe,
for analysis, for textual production, for Dupin, and for every other member
of the set of objects concerned. In short, Derrida leaves little to the imagination of the reader, but exhausts every avenue, aware that any one thing
involves most other things. (The more he says the less close to totality we
come.) This is the opposite of Nietzsche's heroic aphoristic 'grand style'
which Nietzsche learnt from Tacitus and Thucydides (Nietzsche 1968,
§428/9). Nietzsche repeatedly congratulates Thucydides for putting bold and
direct speeches into the mouths of his Athenians. Derrida's particular com-
pression and slogan-building, the construction of axioms, is not that of
Horace in which 'what oft was thought, but ne'er so well expressed' is the
rule, and in which normal words are given classical, dictionary-like treatment. Derrida tended to disfigure words, to change those already existing –
conducting a 'hand-to-hand struggle' with them (Derrida 2004c, 14). The
urge to transform current usages, classical French, to disfigure it and exhaust
it, was a motivation of his prose perhaps, which led him to go to such
extreme lengths in the search for a text which seems to say as much as possible on a given limited theme – to the extent that the object in question
becomes transformed. His French could not be further from Racine's or
Pascal's. But then, with his self-imposed pure diction, and his pure French
accent (1998e, 46), perhaps what alone distinguishes Derrida from classical

French writers, and from classicism/conservatism in general, is the pace of his writing, the slowness of his rhythm, his great and inordinate caution.

'Plato's Pharmacy' was published in *Tel Quel* (32–3, 1968) while 'The Double Session' was published in 1970 (41–2). Although 'Dissemination' was published in *Critique*, it discussed Sollers' *Nombres*. Publishing in *Tel Quel* at this time he was in touch with its circle of contributors: Julia Kristeva, Roland Barthes and Sollers, who held views very similar to his own. They were part of a set of literary structuralists, 'intellectuals', of which they were at the cutting edge, so that the esoteric quality of *Dissemination* was to be expected.

Tel Quel was a literary review with a strong Marxist/Maoist political bias. It had support from the French Communist Party since the PCF was trying to gain back some of its lost intellectual supporters. Despite being a literary review, its editorial board often rowed and split up because of politics. The style of Derrida's work in *Dissemination* reflects *Tel Quel*'s terrorist methods, its aim of staying ahead, not being surrounded, not being out of date, or allied to any other movement. This nervousness was again political, not literary.

Walter Brogan (1989) said of 'Plato's Pharmacy' that Derrida searches for the effaced originary archi-writing in Plato's text, which is prior to the definite meaning of the Platonic text. To this end *pharmakon* is found, as a metaphor, to mean either poison or remedy. 'The logic of Western philosophy requires the dismemberment and separation of the contradictory force of the word *pharmakon* into two opposing terms in order that the contradiction be exposed' (Brogan 1989, 9). 'For Plato neither the philosopher's written words, nor his logos, his own presence as a guarantee of the accurate interpretation of his words is sufficient since no discourse is capable of capturing the truth' (1989, 14–15). The *pharmakon* as a trace of this indecision appears at the start of the *Phaedrus* and at the end, in the first instance as a simile for writing, and in the second in the discussion of whether the hemlock will do Socrates good or evil.

Writing in fact has its appeal due to its lack of genuine reference and surety as to its meaning, and like Lacan's chain of signifiers which constitute desire, it is based on a lack of reference. This attraction leads Plato to write, though writing is a repetition of 'truth', not the truth itself. The truth itself is seen, is lived by a true thinker, in a disposition of the soul towards goodness. How could writing, or mere hearsay, match up to this conversion required for a true vision? This sight engenders, and it is this engendering power which Socrates says that he lacks, as if indeed he were also incapable of genuinely seeing the Truth, the Good, that true fire. Hence Plato is ambivalent about how much writing, like Socrates' discourse, may be necessary, though unregenerative. The unregenerative one, Socrates, is ideally suited to writing.[5]

Derrida has not reversed Plato, since Plato in this way reverses himself, ambivalent as to whether the *pharmakon* is good or bad, and hence whether writing is good or bad. Rather, the translators of Plato, who have not worried about this, the interpreters of Plato hitherto, are the real objects of Derrida's attack, as is the case with his work on *khora*, and indeed that of Heidegger on Plato's cave, in 'Plato's Doctrine of Truth' [1942] (Heidegger 1998b).

Derrida's literary preferences can be seen to belong with the most experimental sorts of texts, rather than with classical works of 'literature': with Artaud, Mallarmé, Ponge and others, sparse works of poetry, consciously *written* texts, quasi-dramas – Joyce, Kafka, Celan, Genet. Finally, they are poems for poets, and novels for novelists, works which describe how they were written, just as Hölderlin's were for Heidegger. The loose theme of *Dissemination* and of Derrida's work for *Tel Quel* is The Book [*Le Livre*] of Mallarmé, and the attempt to discover and then to reverse a book which was the final word in books, which would either contain everything in fact, or else contain everything by suggestion, using the limiting resources of writing which must be the means to absolute knowledge – a theme developed further in *Glas*. The 'Outwork' discusses the historical provenance of this project of a total knowledge and a written document, as well as the memorials of the effort, the actual written remnants of this always failing effort, of a memory machine which would know everything, and which needs writing to set itself into effect. Discussing Hegel, and Hegel's antecedents, as well as the medieval era of the book as a reflection of the divine mind and the divine creation, 'Dissemination' (an essay in the book of that title) proposes a writing which will *disseminate* and not gather, which has not the seed or sperm to originate such a book, not make a start on it and thus never complete it. The effort of making a start, a preface to it, is impossible (1981a, 3ff). Hegel (Derrida 1981a, 21) is seen to face the problem of the preface throughout his work, conscious that a preface cannot by its own logic do any good, almost aware that a start to the whole *Encyclopaedia* could not be made. The distinction between the anticipatory knowledge of the book's content and what it must achieve over a period of being written supposes a time delay, a discrepancy between the mind's certitude and the manifestation of truth in the book, be it *The Phenomenology of Spirit*, the *Greater Logic*, or the *Encyclopaedia*. The delay is in fact caused by the inconvenience of having to resort to writing, and to the communication of what is not immediately given. Hegel must unwittingly take a detour through writing. Time, writing and development are the essence of Hegel's system in which an initial potential idea of absolute knowledge is discovered and developed gradually and becomes substantial – even if over the period of a set of lectures or pages. 'Speculative philosophy thus proscribes the preface as empty form and as signifying precipitation; it prescribes it, on the other hand, insofar as it is in the preface that meaning *announces itself*, philosophy being always already engaged in the Book' (Derrida 1981a, 28–9).

9

America: Derrida as Literary Theory

9.1 The 1970s

In 1970 Aimé Derrida, Jacques' father, the 'travelling salesman', the one who had sacrificed himself for his family, and whose suffering was never sufficiently appreciated, died of cancer. Over the next three decades Derrida was to pursue his destiny as a teacher, and realize more and more with time that his efforts to deconstruct and bring a purer awakening to texts and events could answer to a deep need of the times. Derrida's ideal existence of things is not precisely 'ideal', or mentally, visually grasped, as it is in Plato, but is a real event, a genuine event, which, however, has been indefinitely deferred. The new directions expressing this were to be his literary-type works of avant-garde nature, roughly 1970 to 1980; his political and educational doctrinal expositions beginning with GREPH in the 1970s and on to his political works during the 90s; and his autobiographical works and theory, which peaked in the year 1990 with *Circumfession* and *Memoires of the Blind*. This late phase also saw the final revelation of what Nietzsche and Heidegger mean to philosophy and modern culture; we could consider the late Derrida as one of the peaks of the mountain range of the thinking of time and Being, in which the 'peaks' bring to a high level what the lowlands feel imperceptibly but thoroughly as the sway of Being.[1]

9.2 Travel

In his later work Derrida read and quoted Montaigne rather as Paul de Man admired Pascal in later life, doing so in *The Politics of Friendship* and his narrative in *Counterpath* (2004a). Montaigne, like the later Derrida, is frequently confessional and autobiographical, producing reflections on life rather than systematic philosophy. I believe that this type of theory-autobiography is also the appeal of Nietzsche, and indeed Derrida's work on Nietzsche in *Otobiographies*, and Derrida's seminar series in the late 70s on Nietzsche concentrates on this most fascinating aspect: that which persuades us to reread him; that point at which he made the science of life deeply involved in his own name and his own personal destiny. Central to that text and to Derrida's preoccupation with Nietzsche throughout the 70s is the notion that life and theory are porous. It is with the biography and the texts that we will be concerned in looking at this decade in the perspective of the frequently indistinguishable difference between the text and the experience of the philosopher, text and life, or death with life. The textual Derrida is equally the living one, if Derrida is conceived of as a 'spirit', or a ghost, and his objective will be to name his own-most self, his singularity, the purest individuality, a quest like the quest of Hölderlin, seeking all of Nature, and all of holiness, in the most humble and familiar place.

For Derrida the years of the 1970s and 80s were those of rather vagrant investigations, and endless wandering. He had made the destruction of logo-centrism in a terrorist sort of way for *Tel Quel*; it now became appropriate to build. This 'building' would be 'travelling' rather than Heideggerian 'dwelling'. The question of 'travelling with', raised in *Counterpath* (Derrida 2004a, 3), of travelling and living every moment with someone else, is, for Derrida, at its extreme, also the question of whether there is someone with whom you would die, with whom the philosopher who writes so as to secure remembrance, fame, influence, would share death, or allow it to be compromised, would allow his most intimate individuality to be compromised. Death, the method and moment of death, is the most personal moment and puts life into perspective, as total isolation for the most part, so that although it is said that one can live with another, is it so? For would you accept another right up to death, and sell your soul to duality as it were, or so that you could no longer maintain a sense of self, but were torn in half, open to another? Is this not impossible? Travel and 'travelling with' would therefore mean the most solitary behaviour, and the individual is always a traveller. The fact of death, or the end of one's time, of one's life, is something which Derrida disputed as the end of life, because he did not believe in the purest of isolations, the ultimate termination. The Other genuinely is desirable for the traveller, and is required as the only way in which one will ever be known properly. The Other sees what I cannot (as Caputo says when analysing *Memoires of the Blind*), because a pure and simple death would be one which one could experience, which, again, is impossible. The Other (which is a concept Derrida avoids by and large, for its 'fashionableness', though he always has it in mind) both ruins or depletes immediacy and self-presence, and yet also refuses to be wholly approachable itself, therefore rendering itself as an impediment, though not one to be overcome.

It is essential to Derrida's character that he does not need a spatial faithfulness, neither home state, nor a single 'home'. And is it even possible to share life with another, a community, for how else is the Other really other, unless it remains uncompromised (Derrida 2004a, 5)? Could you share your fate, and if not, can you have a home, or community? Everywhere one finds in Derrida this same impossible-of-resolution double-bind: on the one hand to let oneself die with another is desirable, and cannot be limited by any sense of selfishness: such is the discourse of Bataille's *Eroticism* (1987) in its extreme moments; on the other hand to do so is impracticable for a multitude of reasons, and in order to die as a self one must first be a self, in the infinite amount of responsibilities to oneself which this involves. Finally one cannot be a self without being recognized by an Other. For all of these reasons, Derrida's personality was a continuous struggle with notions of friendship, community, home, foreign lands, other languages, which could not be resolved, while his factual travelling is a reflection of this 'homelessness' beyond a conventional understanding of the *oikos*. It is a continual dialogue, and a mournful nostalgia, for what Roger Scruton has elaborated on in his recent patriotic works (2001 and 2005): the mourning, however, not only for a lost relationship to the land and the home, but also in the knowledge that such a home has never been, and will never become, a reality. Such became Derrida's concern, when he unravelled the economy of différance, as he travelled through the labyrinth of culture, in the coming years.

9.3 Life Death and the Other

As a life experience, Derrida's was one torn open for the Other, which is other because one is faced with, on our part, total isolation. Derrida's life experience was, in human terms, solitary; it was the fate of the wanderer, the traveller, who perhaps, by travelling, comes to know his home and himself essentially. The collection of quotations constituting *Counterpath*, with commentary by Malabou, and a commentary by Derrida himself, does much to analyse the absence at the heart of Bennington's 'Curriculum vitae' (in the appendix to his *Jacques Derrida* (Bennington 1999, 325–36)). Bennington had said that Derrida's later life is made up of extensive travelling and public speaking, teaching in various places and the like. Malabou's investigation into the nature of this travelling is of some value, and was of course endorsed by Derrida himself.

Derrida's travelling is recorded in Malabou's book as an appendix. One year of travel alone would show how various the locations and how restricted to work such travelling was. For example, in 1970 (a year during the period in which he was 'insurmountably afraid' of flying), he visited London, Oxford, Turin, Milan, Naples, Florence, Bologne, Rome, Brussels, Gent, Lîlle, and Strasbourg. This list in *Counterpath* was compiled by Derrida himself, from memory and from looking at the venues of published work. He says there that travel is for him a sort of misery (Derrida 2004a, 290), 'For believe me, there is someone in me who never would travel, at least never far from home, which is somewhere that I already feel as it were *moved* enough, more than necessary . . .' The experience of 'jet professors' is empty and pointless, making the teacher travel to his students rather than vice versa. Conferences are events at which the professor is 'seen' and makes an impact on a usually virgin audience with a new freshness and violence, like a singer at a live rock concert. For the professor himself such travelling consists of car journeys to airports, hotel rooms overnight, brief introductions to staff and students, and the general culture of waiting rooms. What redeems this existence is the promise of a truer life.

Given his isolation and the double-bind into which the Other puts him, Derrida theorized a sort of life which would be not authentic, that is, not circumscribed and limited by death, and also, not lived in the awareness of approaching death, that is, not lived in the immediate moment. He theorized or dreamt of *life death*, which meant life and death as one, so that death is not terrible, and life is not owned and enviously hoarded by the fearful instinct. This traveller, responding to most invitations, travelling wherever there was the invitation, was a believer in the absolute end, the absolute death, the very definition of an atheist (Derrida 2004a, 5), but when he wrote this, Derrida meant that while he believes in the absolute end, such an end is impossible. He also found death in reduced forms wherever he went, in whatever place, as a prefiguration of the final end, and as the residue of the gift of time, a gift with limited means, because, in fact, death is not absolute, but is dispersed here and there. He travelled so as both to follow this time which has been given, and also to find sanctuary on arrival in a strange place, that is, with the fear of death, and the hope of a living sanctuary, the peace of a melancholy sacredness, the feeling of being open to différance. Coming from isolation into a strange place, finding hospitality, is to find an empty and unfamiliar, but satisfying, welcome from the other person; in a strange place one finds home. The loneliness of the philosopher, of the subjective awareness, concerns itself, as a mood, with melancholy brooding on death, which is a real possibility, and seems to become as real as it promises to be, but here, and now, where it can be 'lived'. And the melancholy sacredness of a sanctuary, and welcome from strangers, has the appearance of offering an escape from death into a 'living on', since the memory of others ensures some sort of survival, an absolute life, and a lived death (Derrida 2004a, 5). What counts is neither life for itself, nor death for itself, not a good life and a good death (for these are impossible), but life death, or 'living on'. Somehow Derrida has managed to live the life of the Nietzsche who lived at large in southern France, Switzerland and Italy, a life of some danger which ended in madness for him, while also holding down his job at ENS and later at EHESS, and while married, and with his large number of friends and colleagues, so that if any resemblance to Nietzsche holds, it is his continual wandering, and freedom from place and time.

Travel is obviously crucial to this character and thus to this thought, to the thought of the person whose essence escapes him, this ghost-figure, this 'superman'. But it should not be our job to interpret travel, and its psychology, and then to transfer this on to the works. The biography only comes from the texts, if the biography is to make sense of Derrida, as a writer. What travel means in itself is neither here nor there, since there is no 'in itself', but travel is the bodily writing of Derrida's experience nonetheless. His avowals on the subject of travel match his understanding of what the matter of philosophy is. Travel: mere passing of space, new events, unforeseen things, going beyond of oneself, 'leaving the source', unnaturally, going beyond his self to fulfil dreams, and the rediscovery of the source (Derrida 2004a, 17) – is what occurs in the readings of metaphysics too. While the deconstructive reading exhausts the possibilities of metaphysics so as to reveal a higher possibility, travel is Derrida's own desire to exhaust himself and reveal the catastrophic, sacred solace, and death which, when travel could just as easily reveal literal death, is also feared. By exposing oneself to the otherness of the world and its chances, one is also exposed to the chance of being known and seen and recognized by the Other. In travel and in deconstructive reading, literal and metaphoric death are made to come, and are called, simply, if they are called by any name – *l'avenir*.

Blanchot and others were astonished by the awkward behaviour of this travelling, this hectic restlessness, the signs of one who does not have a core, or a soul, although they were especially offended that he took his work, his excellent research, out of Paris and abroad (Derrida 2001b, 94). It was leaving the city of Paris, the familiar friends, which offended them most. But he travelled for other people, for the Other, who invited him to this adventure, and demanded the risk of catastrophe and death, and if it were up to him he would not leave. In this he was like the poet Hölderlin, who followed, or was moved by 'divine' desire, which uprooted him, but which drove him to song because being uprooted gave him a better vision of the true time and nature of his 'roots'. Maybe the Other is the one which offers solace, and is also feared, like death. At no point can one say, or did he say, or, by definition is it possible to say, whether the Other is not *malign*. One just dreams of a death which is also life.

The Other, which is encountered in travel, and in certain readings of philosophy under the guise of *Khora*, or the delay of time between religion and philosophy in Hegel, is also the Other who expelled him from the French school in his childhood. It is the death which comes by chance across any life, and the Other who could imprison him and take his liberty as it did in Prague. The Other, that is to say, is bad also. But it can also be good, like a good community, one blessed by a god, hence one's hope for the coming of the good, of justice. This is why, in general, Derrida's is not a normal politics, and in its similarity to Hölderlinian poetics, it is a tragic position. The Other cannot be contained, cannot be used, is not at our disposal to programme or command, or integrate into a set of laws or a policy, to use for a leftist end. It has to be hoped that the Other will come as justice, and if one must negotiate with the chances of the Other, we must do so with justice as our guide, always, when responding to necessity. It is because Derrida also has simultaneously to welcome the evil chance from 'the coming' [leavened] that he also has a sort of superhuman hope, a Nietzschean pessimism. Derrida himself was aware that Nietzsche's pessimism, his 'Dionysian pessimism' (Nietzsche 1968, §95) – knowledge that the evil must be as necessary as the good, that evil is as likely to come as the good – were also invitations for Nazi interpretation. Derrida himself, with his openness to a future and a coming which one cannot really control, was to lend himself to such coming Nazisms. This is the occasion, however, of a true responsibility in reading, and in deciding, in interpreting. For the Other, or God, does not give the law, but gives only a sense of justice. It is we, or those entrusted with power, who make the laws, and laws must be framed responsibly according to the justice which stands beyond them. This responsibility and the eye for it, this knowledge of what is good, is all that one can decide upon, not in despair, but in lucidity, regardless of whether our outlook is optimistic or pessimistic, with a sense of hope that, as Goethe had it, and as Nietzsche pointed out – all things are good in the end.[2]

So Derrida's experience is both to find and to speak of the Other, and to suffer its chances as it comes in the future, exactly as Nietzsche did. Unlike Nietzsche, who despised the modern city, he loves the people and cities he finds,[3] and unlike Nietzsche he dislikes the landscapes and the solitary places which reflect only himself (he finds the desert horrific).[4]

In the previous chapters it was a matter of discovering in what way Derrida had developed in Algeria and France, while in this, we examine his adult life of teaching and research into philosophy, in both France and in America. He sought himself in the Other everywhere, and sought to question structures and hegemonies by invoking the Other. In America it is particularly prevalent, in the wider history of that nation, and in his view its activity there is, as deconstruction of history, native to that country, a country of development and of opposites and contrasts, a synthetic Europe. This is a reference to the pragmatic, justice-and-change-seeking side of America perhaps, the side of America for which what works, what is tradition, is also 'true'. It is the land of the American 'dream', where the impossible can occur. For Derrida, in the 1970s and 80s, 'America is deconstruction'.

9.4 America

Derrida's own experience of America was one of teaching and conversing, a multitude of meetings, conferences, interviews, alliances and quarrels. The Baltimore Conference of 1966, already mentioned, was his second trip to the US, the first time being in 1956, which he spent at Harvard. Later milestones would be similarly academic, reflecting Derrida's fantastic reception by the foreignness of that continent and its ways of thinking. But then, Derrida had, since childhood, considered the US, 'America', to be his second home, or even his ideal 'home' in the absence of a true home. He would first be received by the American academic establishment as a literary writer, or one who had something to say on what literature is. Paul de Man was crucial to this, campaigning on behalf of American deconstruction for the rest of his life. A brief survey of Derrida's activity there shows a widening of his influence. In 1975 de Man secured for him a visiting professorship at Yale where he lived up to teaching obligations thereafter until 1986, giving seminars either in the spring or autumn; 1978, a session at Berkeley; in 1982 he was named Andrew D. White Professor at Large at Cornell University; in 1987 he gave lectures at Dartmouth College, Hanover, and began teaching regularly at Irvine into the year 2000; and in 1986 he began teaching at the various schools and universities in New York, specifically CUNY, every autumn until 1991. From 1992 onwards he was contracted to teach at New York University, New School for Social Research, Cardozo School of Law, every autumn term, and he fulfilled the obligation until his last years.

Derrida explains his experience in America, and his view of it, in *Memoires: For Paul de Man*. Because de Man was more than usually aware of the delaying feature of time, and wrote on it in the full awareness of its currency in France, as Derrida his friend thought of it, he formed with him an alliance which was distant, and already marked from the first by death and absence. We must concentrate for some time on this critic and philosopher, who introduced Derrida to America in many ways. Paul de Man died of cancer on 21 December 1983, in his early sixties, writing and thinking into his last days. The three lectures in *Memoires* were written three weeks after his death, between January and February 1984, and delivered in French at Yale in March, and then at the University of California, Irvine, as Derrida explains in his preface. By December, Derrida had prepared them for publication.

Derrida was unable to give any story of de Man's relationship with himself, though he later had to do so in 1987 when the storm broke over de Man's long withheld involvement in the Nazi occupation of Belgium. In this 1984 lecture Derrida said that de Man was 'deconstruction in America', and also 'Hölderlin in America', meaning both that his work brought deconstruction to light in its native land, and that he must be considered the mad, and most sensitive awareness of existence, as Hölderlin was, the awareness that the unity of things and divine otherness threatens the subject always, and makes poets by tormenting them with the impossibility of accurate speech about the true way of life, death and nature. These themes are explained throughout. It is remarkable that de Man is one of the few explicit allies in deconstruction, and Derrida here discusses the name and the movement, and uses it in regard to Paul de Man, who was fascinated by it, as something larger than himself, at work outside of his own personal texts. It was the way things and texts escape cognitive judgement, evaluation, statement, and control because of time, and the way it limits human existence. Derrida says of this term, 'deconstruction', that it works by accumulating the forces which oppose it, using them, without totalizing them, or putting them to profit. It is a phenomenon in progress, and no narrative story can account for it. Deconstruction is wrongly perceived to be of European origin. It is a French/US hybrid, and perhaps marks the origins of Derrida himself, whose roots were in the early globalizing culture of the USA.

This is an example of the way in which a philosopher cannot espouse a system or a name for a system unless he is utterly sure of it, while the literary critic, in this case de Man, somewhat requires a methodology and system, and in his case the more vague it is, the more amenable to adaptation and occasion, the better. It is often said of Paul de Man that America did not really see the type of person that he was insofar as he belonged to a different age, as well as to a different land, being an immigrant from Belgium (Jameson goes so far as to call him an avatar of the eighteenth-century materialist). His ascetic temper, his strictness as to whether to say whatever he thought was right, or whether it was better to let it be subjected to a deeper thinking, is a case in point. De Man's ascetic temper is the same sort of thing as F. R. Leavis found in Ludwig Wittgenstein who befriended Leavis at Cambridge, a religious obligation without any rational or orthodox explanation.

An Umberto Eco article of August 1983 on American deconstruction (*Liberation*, 1983 August 20–1) says that deconstruction is a sort of hybrid growth, bringing many disparate theorems into a discourse or a school, which was only finally brought into a thing, *qua* deconstruction, when it was so named in America, where it was received more readily than in France and Europe. There it was a way of life rather than a reaction to structures. Basically, in this discussion of de Man as the other side of deconstruction, with de Man as the occasion for outlining what deconstruction had been, Derrida said that deconstruction cannot be captured by social sciences (structuralist thinking), as it questions the notion of science itself. It is the end of the naïve possibility of sciences. It has in any case too many aspects – religious, technical, academic, ethical – all of which, being Enlightenment categories, are of no use. And as Derrida says elsewhere, to name it is to exhaust it, something he does not wish to do. *In fine*, he is not able to tell the story of deconstruction because it is against the grain of deconstruction to create narratives, he says. The lectures revert back to not being able to tell a story, a theme also found in interviews. Derrida (1995b, 118–19) himself reflects on his style of random but loose projects, and hints at something which could result in a personal writing, something resonating with his own life alone, with a language capable of voicing the impossibly intimate.

But this avowal in *Memoires: For Paul de Man* of not being able to tell a story is disingenuous in some registers. It is possible to see Derrida as the historian of philosophy, the one who tells its story from a new angle, from the perspective of justice and injustice. What Derrida means is multiply interpretable. In the first instance he means he is not able to create a piece of truth, as Wittgenstein regretted that he had never created a work of truth about himself, of clarity (Monk 1990, 282), a continuous narrative of the sort which settles things about what is true and clear (Wittgenstein also had a very high estimation of the *Confessions*, like Derrida). On the other hand, he means he cannot structure a set of facts, make a system from them. If he ever had done so he could himself have been subjected to deconstruction. (On this matter I refer the reader to Bernasconi (1992, 161–2), who says that occasions provide the ethical imperative to deconstruct, and yet the ethical starting point is still selected and formed in Derrida's own mind, rather than having been pre-supplied.)

Again, 'America' would be the title of a new novel of the history of deconstruction. All of America's features and history would be required to explain it, especially, again, its youth, its dreams and its welcome. As an immigrant, or exile in America, from the Europe which had developed the theory of deconstruction, de Man is central to a study which follows Derrida in America. Without de Man, deconstruction in America would have been nothing, or something different. It would not have been conscious of itself as the self-destroying structure which is perpetually open and closed at once to the Other's existence and its coming. He, coming from Europe, and France, originally from Belgium, was its centre of articulation, or the ally of Derrida in the furthering of its clarification, and by pointing to its obscuring effects.

The name 'deconstruction' may have been exported to the USA, but it is native there (Derrida 2004a, 222). The USA is the historical space for all the themes and effects of deconstruction (Derrida 1986b, 17–18). The US is deconstruction in effect, it is what happens today (Derrida 2004a, 225). All of this is so because America is the place at which the West's tradition of exclusion is currently being undone and continued, the place at which the West of Europe has created both a satellite and a master for itself, an external mirror, which, like a simulacrum, is nonessential, and also as real as the original. Finally, the USA is at the cutting edge of what the European tradition has sought to exclude and change itself into. At times it seemed that Derrida preferred America to Europe. By the time of his final years Derrida had turned once more to Europe as the future of the global community, ashamed of American arrogance and its lack of roots, its lack of a restraining, balancing memory of history and religious tolerance. Above all, its lack of tolerance.

9.5 De Man's Response to Derrida's *Of Grammatology*

Bernasconi's essay (1992, 137–66) was motivated by the feeling that, as he puts it, Derrida seems to be impervious to criticism, and yet de Man seems to have made some sort of impact in his early essay on Derrida's *Of Grammatology*. Derrida's fault has to do with the extent to which he creates stories and then deconstructs them, thus giving the impression that he has made an effect on pre-established structures, which are in fact structures which he himself creates. That is, Derrida is 'literary'. As a discussion of de Man and Derrida together, and as a deep, close reading of their interrelationship as regards Rousseau, Bernasconi's is a very faithful and valuable text.

We know that de Man responded to Derrida's 1967 work *Of Grammatology* in *Blindness and Insight* in its 1972 edition in the seventh chapter – 'The Rhetoric of Blindness'. This was one of the first in English to make a study of Derrida's work. De Man, as the elder, was the one to patronize Derrida. It was, after all, he who introduced Derrida to the USA, being installed there himself already, and he who directed the USA to read Derrida. He was not a disciple either, and never really learnt anything from Derrida, although he did take the name 'deconstruction' as his own. This is important because it sometimes seems that Derrida did more for de Man than the latter did for him.

De Man avoided the entire first part of *Of Grammatology* in his study, that is, its theory, and also the introduction to Part Two, concentrating exclusively on the sections dealing with Rousseau's *Origin of Languages*. He brings out the law of the supplement which is outlined there, as a counter to the law of identity which Rousseau did not follow. Apparent contradictions in Rousseau's text are resolved by the law of supplementarity. As is well known, de Man insists that Derrida misread Rousseau, that Derrida is a 'blind' thinker, and that Rousseau is one of the few non-blind thinkers, totally aware of his blindness as he was, ironic always from the first, and creating history, instituting historical narrative, always with a sense that he was merely creating literature because the true nature of life or Being is something which retreats.

Derrida is more literary than he himself imagines, and Derrida's thought relies through and through on stories, de Man said. What Derrida meant in his lecture 'Memoires' when he says 'I have never been able to tell a story' (Bernasconi 1992, 159) is that de Man had said that he wrote 'histories' and narratives which he then deconstructed in a dramatic way. Derrida was aware of this critique of him by de Man, and wished to rebut it in a kind way in that memorial lecture. However, it is clear enough that de Man was right about the nature of Derrida's work: it is literary in quality and in its general point, even though its argumentation is conventionally philosophical in its details, and is adept at discovering non-empirical, metaphysical facts. That it was written as philosophy does not mean that de Man could not describe it in general, and due to its blindness, as a species of literature.

9.6 Derrida and the Literary

What then is literature? This question was the first question which Derrida attempted to answer, prior to his investigations of language and the word with Saussure and Husserl. For de Man the literary is a language which escapes the logocentric fallacy of believing itself capable of capturing events and things perfectly. Literature is that discourse which plays with its own status as fiction, and is incapable of truth. The literary, which Rousseau never ceased to create, and of whose status in his texts he was always aware, is that which 'explicitly or implicitly signifies its own rhetorical mode and prefigures its own misunderstanding as the correlative of its rhetorical nature' (Bernasconi 1992, 154). A genuinely literary text will thus only set up oppositions and binary concepts because it is playing with them, and is aware of how it cannot fully capture reality. It is thus not part of any logocentric tradition. And it is this of which Derrida is not aware as he discusses the 'history of Western metaphysics'. In *Of Grammatology*, Derrida's main mistake, or lack of self-awareness, is his belief in the motif of 'the history of metaphysics', a history which has only been written by himself and a few other thinkers, and which beyond that written history has not genuinely occurred. This history is a great, and alluring, supremely interesting myth, a literary device, a marvellous story which Derrida has conjured up.

Bernasconi concludes that 'Derrida would be invulnerable precisely for occupying such a position of total control', in total control precisely because his arguments deal with literary fictions, not factual conditions. One does not really argue with literature, and the mastery which Rousseau held, as a

literary philosopher, one who was aware that his work was only a rhetorical strategy, a dramatic work, is the mastery which belongs to Derrida,
whether he knew it or not. Of course as Bernasconi knows, Derrida later
came to question whether the object of deconstruction – 'the logocentric
tradition' or the 'history of metaphysics' (Derrida 1998e, *passim*) – really
existed. But this is not to say that Derrida did not go on to continue to invent
new stories. The economy of Derrida's texts is outlined as (1) parasiting on
texts, and never inventing actual positions of his own, rather creating narrative readings of them, and (2) only admitting to telling such stories, and
actually creating them *ex nihilo*, as it were, in the name of ethics, as for
example when he was forced to tell of de Man and himself on the invitation
of *Critical Inquiry*, for whom he wrote 'Paul de Man's War'. As inventions of
his own, these themselves would leave Derrida open to criticism of the sort
he is not usually open to.

Derrida's definitive response to critics of de Man and himself over the
latter's war record was his 'Paul de Man's War'. This article by Derrida refers
to twenty-five essays and articles which de Man had contributed during the
war. In an article following its publication, John Wiener, a historian of such
crises in the European conscience, attacked Derrida for not taking de Man's
collaboration seriously, for talking of responsibility without using any ethical
terms or getting involved in any ethical discussion. In his own article Derrida
had said that de Man's later attitude is present in the young de Man, and
accuses de Man's *New York Times* attackers of being 'full of hatred'. He thinks
those attacking de Man are totalitarian, and must be deconstructed (Wiener
1989, 802).

Finally Bernasconi points out that not taking a stand of its own (as it had
not done up to that time), Derridean deconstruction had no real power. He
speculates that only with Levinas had Derrida found an unimpeachable ally,
and that he may in future go on to follow Levinas in his ethics of the Other
in more concrete terms if he is to overcome this powerlessness – which in
general is what occurred.[5] By doing so he is forced to create his own sort of
gathering, his own hegemonizing alliances, which naturally, not being conceived as fictions and rhetoric, will be open to attack as every other discourse
is.[6] As a voice for justice with power to create stories of injustice, but never
to give concrete examples of justice (it is always 'to come') he is impreg-
nable, and not very open, like, indeed, a false justice, something beyond
scrutiny. For this reason his efforts at justice and ethics can seem deceiving,
and although the reactions of Wolin and Fried (Fried 2000, 199–245;
Wolin 1993, 283–94) and others are not to be trusted as being genuine and

unmotivated, their anger and jealousy, their misguided criticisms, somewhat reflect this annoyance that Derrida is, by being literary, beyond any critique or any justice himself.

9.7 Tel Quel

1971, the year Derrida returned to Algeria, lecturing in Algiers and revisiting the old garden where he had lived and been formed (Bennington 1999, 248), also saw a conference in Montreal, at which Derrida delivered 'Signature, Event, Context' (subsequently published in 1972, in *Margins of Philosophy* (1982)), a paper which was to resurface when John Searle published a critical account of its content in 1977, and which marked a growing antagonism between the continental, rather provincial, late-structuralism, and the English-speaking sort of thinking, both of which were linguistic philosophies.

Meanwhile in France, in 1972, came the definitive rupture with Sollers and *Tel Quel*. Despite the proximity and solidarity from 1965 to 1969, Derrida had never been a part of the review, and had never ceased to show his independence, which was badly received by his partners there, notably because of their theoretical-political orientation, their dogmatic Marxism, and their zeal for the French Communist Party (PCF) which lasted until 1969, and because of their Maoist dogmatism afterwards. To Bennington, Derrida explained this distance by pointing to the actual essays he wrote for *Tel Quel* at the time which were avidly taken up by the journal, but which were, it seems, not part of *Tel Quel*'s overall political programme as Derrida saw them. None are extreme, all are politically balanced, even neutral (Bennington 1999, 333).

On 12 September 1969, the newspaper of the PCF, *L'Humanité*, published an article by Jean-Pierre Faye entitled 'Le Camarade Mallarmé'. Ideological differences had forced Faye to found his own journal and to leave *Tel Quel*. He attacked *Tel Quel* in the article for *L'Humanité*, referring to Derrida, though not by name, when he alleged that the journal was taking on Nazi ideological themes because it studied and followed Heidegger. A language of the German extreme Right was being used by the Parisian intelligentsia, he said, and the agent of this collaboration with the enemy was implied to be Derrida. An exchange followed in which Sollers defended Derrida in *Tel Quel* while party officials responded in *L'Humanité*. The exchange lasted for some time.

Later in 1971 *Tel Quel* broke with the PCF definitively, and declared itself Maoist. It, too, then attacked Derrida on politico-theoretical grounds, notably because of his reserve towards Marxism.

9.8 1972

For Derrida, as we have seen, 1972 was the year of the second 'biblioblitz', or the publication of several high-quality works within the space of a single year, as if with the intention of making an overwhelming show of force. The third publication of the year was *Positions* (Derrida 1981b), a collection of three interviews, quite technical in nature, and restricted to questions of theory, and of Derrida's new 'deconstruction'. After this release of works, Derrida seems to have emptied himself of content, and now settled down into a more formal period of lecturing and international appointments at different universities. There had been a five-year pause since 1967, and there was another pause until *Glas* [1974], followed by publications randomly and prolifically thereafter, often in the form of bulky texts, collections and sets of lectures. He began to consider joining and forming new organizations, different from those standard political groups with which he had been in contact in earlier years. At the Cerisy-la-Salle conference in July 1972 most of his generation met to discuss their great precursor and idol – Nietzsche. It was on this occasion that he delivered his charismatic performance on Nietzsche entitled 'Spurs'. Prior to Heidegger's critique in the mid-1930s, Nietzsche had not been thought of as a philosopher, but as a literary, poetic writer with odd and anarchic ideas, who had a destiny culminating in a bizarre madness typical of romantic German poets. From the perspective of his followers in the late twentieth century Heidegger's view had to be disqualified somewhat, and Nietzsche could again be seen as the poet and imaginative critic of 'everything', the philosopher beyond philosophy, but with the advantage of having foreseen the end of the normal truth-based metaphysical enquiry in which a thinker intends to set forth absolute truth, and is expected to achieve this.

9.9 *Spurs*, Nietzsche at Cerisy [1972]

In this paper Heidegger and Nietzsche are dealt with as old familiar friends of those attending the conference, and as old friends of Derrida. Heidegger could not theorize Being, he says, because where beings come from, the proper, which makes them the property of something, is an enigma:

> Because they constitute the process of propriation, the giving of the gift can be construed neither in the boundaries of Being's horizon nor from the vantage point of its truth, its meaning. . . . There is no such thing as the gift of Being from which there might be apprehended and opposed to it something like a determined gift . . . (Derrida 1979, 121)

Which is to say that while a gift seems to have been given to a definite land or race, we are mistaken, for Being, if it gives, gives everything which it has to all, not being able to divide itself up as a thing distinct from what it gives.

Nietzsche resides in the same place, of the abyss, in which the gift of life has an impersonal, random giver, and he weighs anchor in a sea without owner. Women too have been seen to be at home there, in the abyss, but have got used to it and have enjoyed appearance, Nietzsche wrote (Derrida 1979, 85). In this sea, upon which women are ships and on whose imaginary shores the idealist stands, nothing can be decided, nothing can be assigned as certain, whether man is woman or woman man, or who gives and who receives, whether Being gives, or whether there is no Gift and no Being. So what, asks Derrida, in this history of thinking the abyss and the sea, is actually going on in writing, except metaphor and style?

This leads to the question of style. For what is certain alone in Nietzsche's work is that there is writing, although what is written cannot be *certainly* deciphered. No question of Nietzsche interpretation, nor the methods of interpretations, nor the presuppositions for any method, can be settled as firm matters, even though Nietzsche is certainly a philosopher of the nature of things metaphysically. In the annunciation of a way of reading Nietzsche, and as an interpretation of Nietzsche, this paper is a stylish, learned, elegant and pointed masterpiece in the assertion of deconstruction. It also has the potential to irk even the most Nietzschean and sceptical of Nietzscheans. It both sets up a sort of writing which derives from him, dealing with Being and the metaphysical unity of all discrete things according to a law, and also undoes any attempt to make him a part of a heritage and a school. How could an orthodoxy be set up on these bases?

To whatever lengths one might carry a conscientious interpretation, the hypothesis that the totality of Nietzsche's text, in some monstrous way, might well be of the type 'I have forgotten my umbrella' cannot be denied [this statement in quotes was a note on a scrap of paper gathered together amidst more meaningful notes and aphorisms in Nietzsche's *Nachlass*]. Which is tantamount to saying that there is no 'totality of Nietzsche's text', not even a fragmentary aphoristic one. There is evidence here to expose one, roofless and unprotected by a lightning rod as he is, to the thunder and lightning of an enormous clap of laughter. (1979, 135)

But all is not as it seems immediately. This statement does not mean that there just is no possible interpretation of any work, but rather that language addressed to the Other, such as Nietzsche's is, is dangerous. Against critics of Derrida who were beginning to say that such deconstruction permitted a reading with any result at all, Christopher Norris defended Derrida some years later, when the *Spurs* lecture was more widely available. There is no licence for limitless interpretation in the *Spurs* contribution to the Cerisy conference, he says. Rather *Spurs* shows why it is that Nietzsche obliges us to think the risk of lending our ear to the Other (Norris 1986, 64), a theme which Derrida took up again in *Otobiographies* (see below).

Lyotard and Deleuze were at Cerisy, and here Derrida probably got to know them for the first time, although Lyotard's contribution at the conference was a decidedly straightforward interpretation of Nietzsche of the sort which Derrida 'deconstructed'. Lyotard aligned Nietzsche to the 'hippies' and other social drop-outs then abandoning Europe's living culture. Of Deleuze he was to say that with him he had an absolute closeness of strategy all of his life (Derrida 2001b, 192). He made it clear to Deleuze that he disliked the idea of philosophy as the creation of concepts (something Deleuze and Guattari developed as late as *What is Philosophy?*) but their ideas of absolute difference, and of simulacra, are the same. So too their critique of capital, a theme as it were crossed out in Derrida's texts, in part due to his not wishing to get involved in French Marxism, which would have made the inattentive believe that he was an opponent of it. That Derrida found the critique of capital to be so central, that he made this avowal in *Work of Mourning*, and yet does not express it in his works directly, is something worthy of more consideration when we assess Derrida's politics. Only later in life did he speak openly of it, and never in terms actually of 'Capital' in its connotations of restricted economy, socio-political space within the liberal state, or the reality of labour and exchange. If ever he did make a critique of capitalism *per se*, it would have to have been in terms of globalization, 'globalatinization' and the mediatization/militarization of the public and private spaces (in Derrida 2001a, 194–5). But one wonders just how near or far Deleuze was to the *Tel Quel* group and his other friends of the Left. Derrida and he also shared the hatred of the closed space of literature, the closed space of politics, the closed space of jurisprudence, and all such 'closed' departments in academic and worldly things, all specialisms, which are actually, or more properly, the confinement which experts wish to keep in order to exert more influence with less interference. Derrida and Deleuze saw this result as effected by TV, newspapers and the developments of the technological age. They had the same enemies. It was friendship (Derrida 2001b, 193).

At the Nietzsche colloquium were also Pierre Klossowski, Sarah Kofman, Philippe Lacoue-Labarthe and Jean-Luc Nancy, amongst others. As for Lyotard, Derrida said of him (Derrida 2001b, 214) that he was one of his closest friends, for forty or more years and that, as a sign of their ethical and amicable proximity, Derrida said that he was then, in 1998, living in Lyotard's old house. Lyotard was the driving force of the *Collège international de philosophie*, an organization which Derrida set up in the early 1980s, and which we will discuss shortly.

In the meantime, his friendship with Foucault ceased abruptly, and remained in suspension until 1982, the break arising from the postscript to *Madness and Civilization* in 1972, when it was reissued. From neither Foucault, Lyotard, Lacan, Deleuze, Levinas, or even Heidegger (who was still alive in 1972), could Derrida withhold his real thoughts and opinions on their respective ideas.

10
Glas

The major work of the early 1970s for Derrida was to be his *Glas* [1974]. This book is a work of passage from the Derrida of *Tel Quel* and anti-structuralism, to the Derridean practice of questioning genuine philosophical problems: the nation, the family and God amongst them. In 1973 Derrida took up a teaching role at the University of Berlin where he presented the series of lectures which make up the left-hand column of this book. As already mentioned he was invited by Peter Szondi.

This remarkable book, Derrida's eighth, deserves in-depth treatment. In the final years of Heidegger's life, here is Derrida producing, on behalf of the future of thought and the 'destiny' of Being, the Echo [*Anklang*] of the Other Origin within the corpus of the greatest logocentric modern philosophy.[1] One could assume that it had been worked on for several years, and one can speculate, indeed it is certain that it is a sort of culmination of a great deal of thought; but then the style is not laboured or precise, and often the work on Hegel seems to have been lifted from lectures Derrida had delivered. Possibly it has the strangest format of any philosophical work ever published in book form, with its double columns, split by an empty space on the page, and using several fonts and print sizes, interspersed by bits and pieces of quotes and references, notes, and other heterogeneous things, and then, finally, in a number of styles of composition, and with a number of authors (insofar as it is a tissue of quotations). It exercises the privileges of writing, and forces the reader to swallow a pure writing, without any presence, single meaning, or, in other words, without any determinate meaning. Derrida refuses it any theme. Resistance to any meaning in *Glas* is both well known and difficult not to struggle with. For example, David Farrell Krell's 'Note' in *Derrida and Difference* (Wood and Bernasconi 1985, 11–16), which asserts that not only is writing the repressed element of language in the history of philosophy, but that the pure voice has also been repressed in that history, since the pure voice is a power of engorging, and of loss of rational control, loss of mastery *vis à vis* rational communication. Descartes nestled beside his fireplace, writing his *Meditations*, was neither speaking nor writing, but something in between, and repressing both the voice and the letter, both of which *Glas* revives. But in this assertion Krell has made an interpretation of Derrida's intent, and of the text's meaning, though it could be shown to have no such meaning.

Glas is clearly aimed at a highly educated group, or a set of associates, particularly the psychoanalytic establishment who had learnt something from Jacques Lacan's theory of the transference of desire on to signs. The machinery of sign formation became itself the desired object for them, without any final transcendental, possibly present, signified object. Psychoanalysis had been referred to in *Of Grammatology* as a potential agency of the grammatological revolution, since grammatology and psychoanalysis concern an alteration in the subjectivity of the subject. Derrida had, seemingly, decided to undertake this programme of grammatological psychoanalysis for himself.

Différance only operates by the agency of the 'subject' between, as it were, the difference between Being and beings. This place is written in *The Question of Being* (Heidegger 1959) as ~~Being~~ (see Silverman 1989, 154–68). The question of what Derrida intends to do when he writes, who to, and for what reason he makes these unusual and innovative gestures, could be answered by looking at his contemporaries. *Glas* is innovative in form, but in its ideas, in its critique of the author, the person, the body, and of writing, it is more of an exercise in then-dominant and revolutionary ideas – along Marxist or intellectual Left lines. The way in which Derrida stands out and makes for himself a name in revolutionary thinking is a matter for history to decide, therefore for us. But his principal ideas are not his own, deriving rather from others of the tradition, and from his colleagues, working for a new 'uncon-cealment' of the West and France.

What is new about *Glas* concerns its stylistic conventions, since printing, font, grammatical, significatory and semiotic conventions are the first targets of this obviously antagonistic performance, specifically Saussurean linguistics of the structuralist sort, which is subject-centred. All of these antagonistic effects are only possible by means of writing. The next immediate feature is the book's apparent dullness mixed with its fireworks. It is dull because, though it seeks to cover the subject of what a book can be, it is really a discourse on Hegel, so that those interested in books and simplistic rebellion against tradition will not find much to interest them, but rather a lecture course on the family and God in Hegel. It has been pointed out by a recent biographer of D. A. F. de Sade (Plessix Gray 1999, 269) that dullness can be aggressive, and sadistic. The pleasure, if there is any, in the reading, which is not 'erotic', in de Sade's *120 Days of Sodom* (1992) is violence against the reader, as scene after scene unfolds across the pages of the book, each scene of sexuality lacking any genuine desire or love, reducing the bodies of the characters down to dehumanized machinality intent on hurt and death. Each scene, colourless and lacking sympathy, also lacks any reader-writer complicity, in a mimetic portrayal of Sade's fantasies and his philosophy, which crushed his mind and his desire, confined to the Bastille as he was. Sade was treating his reader to a form of sodomy by asking him to read this repetitive high-frequency horror, which is, eventually, boring.

The composition of the book was, it seems, quite as haphazard as it looks on the surface to have been. A lecture on Hegel (and one which is erudite, original and certainly not 'dull') has been completed first, followed by the insights and conclusions which it produced. Next, Derrida, noticed that these conclusions involved matters of family, sexuality, God and the personal lives of writers, so he opposed to the original lecture-text one which is its direct opposite in these terms, namely the text of Jean Genet, the novelist, playwright, homosexual and compulsive burglar. The text to which Derrida returns there is the very beautiful first work of Genet's, *Le miracle de la rose* (Genet 1993), although Derrida also reads and reports on most of Genet's work, his novels, and plays, and even refers to this writer as one of his correspondents. At the time, in France, Genet was well known amongst intellectuals and public, having been released from prison on the petition of a group of writers led by Sartre, who recognized his genius as a poet. He was a homosexual as well as an atheist writer, who abused aspects of religion to produce aesthetic effects. He was also, for Derrida's purposes, obsessed by the fake, and the 'kitsch'. Derrida put the parts of these two texts which made them both most vulnerable in their logic of production, namely voice-production and textual production, to the forefront, by embellishing the whole mixture with notes on what combines all writing and voice-based logic into one single process, mostly the problem of self, family, the truth, corporeality, the scatological, death and remains, or 'tombs'. At the very height of the text, the title 'Glas' finished off the whole composition by making the ultimate theme of this book not Hegel, not Hegel and Genet, and not voice or written text, but the sound of the knell, the simple sign or sound, which, without origin, and like all of our language, seemingly created from nothing, acts like a machine, or is a machine of textual production, involving death and life in one. The privileged sound of the knell which Derrida chose was the 'gl' sound. This language machine, which we receive, and make use of, and which makes use of the writer and thinker, is given as a gift which only something like Being could have given. Because it was gifted, the 'glas' machine interrupts without warning, and in an unforeseen way. It attempts to be a 'pure' gift, not a Hegelian, German and local one.

Derrida provides in his Hegel lecture a running commentary on Hegel's view of marriage and the family in the early theological writings and in the later *Philosophy of Right*. Everything is regulated by the dialectic, according to this commentary; and it is this law of dialectic which is continually being interrupted by the gift. It is because it has this gift as its object that the text seems to have come from nowhere, to be unrelated to the very sober works of the previous years. It burst into the literary scene and the academic culture with an unforeseen energy, with its motives carefully concealed. Many of his critics and followers base their idea of Derrida as a thinker on this work, though others, who think of him as a transcendental philosopher, tend totally to disregard it.[2] Richard Rorty belongs to the first group, Rodolph Gasché to the latter. *Glas* was once thought of as a highly complex and mature work of Derrida's, distinctive of a late style of developed deconstruction. In hindsight it appears to be in fact an early work, not merely because prior to it Derrida had published only a small percentage of his total output, but because its style and theme, lacking any overt politics, confined to the treatment of texts alone, rather than to the facts of current history, and the nervous, highly complex and self-consciously obscure tone, are features of his early work, not of his later, more confessional work. *Glas* has all the features of being the work of a beginner, one seeking to impress his own name on the history of philosophy by making a great impression, by going all out to bring forward a new idea. However, the question of family, blood-ties, marriage, friendship and ethics (Kantian or Hegelian), as well as nationality, become enduring themes and problems.

10.2 Psychoanalysis in *Glas*

In his introduction to the *Glassary* (1986), Derrida expresses his intentions in the 1974 text as having been to make a non-phonocentric book, a book which depends on writing more than on speech (one cannot speak two simultaneous texts at once, while one can make an effort at reading with an eye on each column). 'Glas' itself is a non-word. It is a phoneme, or even letters which are variously inserted into an assortment of written words/signs. The glas can mean essentially the ray of sun on a column which Hegel described as the occasion of the first speech in man and religion. The ray of light on the column is a sound without noise, and leads on to spoken worship or culture.

Ultimately *Glas* is a book of anti-paternalism, anti-philosophy and anti-Western philosophical values. It is a book of thefts, rather than of creation. It is full of quotations and graftings, and it is a kind of writing which clings to itself and to things, rather than dividing, ordering, obeying law. In an accompanying interview, Derrida expresses the book's intentions in terms of *cramponnement*, which is an activity which both holds things together, and makes a breach in their common fabric (Derrida 1995b, 5–29). It is homosexual and womanish rather than paternal and providing. Again in contrast to rational discourse, this one uses ambiguities throughout, basing itself on them, but so as to form two or three discourses, rather than simply causing amusement (although this is also the intention). In general the Hegel text comes first and was written first, and the Genet-Freud text comments on it, disrupts, mocks.

Ulmer says (Leavey and Ulmer 1986, 23) that it is not as eccentric as it may first appear, and it has a rationale and a methodology. The first principle is that it was written as the surrealists and concrete poets wrote, using automatic procedures. Such automatic writing was intended to produce or find parts of the Unconscious, to find the properties of words, if left to themselves, and this is what *Glas* does to philosophical concepts and literature. It is psychoanalysis at work on the classical subjectivity and the classical Hegelian tropes, expressing its repressed desire and its repressed unconscious, its erased text. It understands that a speaker or writer of phonetic writing can never exhaust or saturate his words with intended meaning, so that there is always a hidden core to words in which the Unconscious finds itself. Insofar as this text announces this, it also performs it, making of words a network not of absolute knowledge as Hegel's text did, but of hidden resonance, secret and powerful influences, constantly at work in the overtly innocent and proper concepts of philosophy, specifically in the discourse of familial relatives, and the triune God. In this way Derrida refers back to his work in *Margins of Philosophy*, particularly 'Signature, Event, Context' of 1971, and forward to the same position which he defended against Searle in

1977. In some circumstances, interpreted correctly, with a proper analytic, nonsense can become sense. Hence the rule of logic and the dialogical book is overturned, especially by the ambiguity of speech itself. The logic of this text is rather the logic of dreams, of simultaneity and synchrony, of hidden and private meanings of words: words which sound alike, and are taken to be alike.

The point of the two columns is to allow this analysis of the psyche of philosophy and literature to take place, with the result that between the two columns a new discourse, a discourse without words, a mere bell, the light on the column, is created and suspended, ringing out. The sound 'glas' represents, and is, if anything, the sucking sound of the throat prior to speech, the open throat, which in the context of the mother discourse, rather than the Freudian father discourse (taking it as read that the father has ruled the West's classical metaphysical description of truth and knowledge) is most often associated with the sound or feeling of the mouth on the mother's breast, clinging, stopped with breast milk, the sleepy, dreamy state of the baby on the breast, and the state of mind in which Joyce demands his reader to be in *Finnegans Wake*. The 'Gl' sound is neither in the throat, for the sound opens the throat up, nor is it outside the throat – since it is not a word.[3] This sound is the between of the two columns.[4] For Derrida, in his search for some power, gift, or language which could voice the voiceless, the most pure originality, it was always the 'between', the line of difference which yielded some hope.

11
GREPH

11.1 GREPH

Derrida formed a friendship with Sarah Kofman, Jean-Luc Nancy and Phillipe Lacoue-Labarthe in 1974 which was to lead to the foundation, in 1975, of the Research Group on the Teaching of Philosophy (*Groupe de recherche sur l'enseignement philosophique* – GREPH), a project which was to have a generally unsuccessful history in terms of its achievements, as Derrida saw them, but was nonetheless worth the effort. In 1974 he began discussing this project, which was to become an open organization based on rue d'Ulm at ENS and centred on the research by delegated researchers into the history and conditions of, as well as the present potential for teaching and the propagation of, philosophy. In 1974 he also set up the *La philosophie en effet* series with the other members of GREPH, with Editions Galilée, with the aim of publishing works by GREPH, or works with its imprimatur. The new series was set up with Lacoue-Labarthe and Jean-Luc Nancy, after Editions Galilée had recently been refounded by Michel Delorme, who acquired it after a period with Aubier-Flammarion. A preliminary conference for GREPH was held in June 1974 with interested academics, colleagues and students. A programme of regulations and objectives, drafted and signed at that date, with the intention of putting the group on to an operational footing in summer 1975, was written.

Derrida's preferred method of political action tended, in the succeeding three decades, to be that of initiating new groups in concert with interested others, from scratch, and then raising an appeal to the wider educated minority for support and interest. Groups of this sort have included GREPH itself, the International College of Philosophy (founded on the request of the Minister of Education in 1981), the Estates General for Philosophy of 1980, and numerous more directly political organizations over which he had less influence, such as the Cities of Asylum organization, and the group which supported Nelson Mandela.[1] In his last decade Derrida took more and more interest in patronizing UNESCO too, sponsoring events in Paris via the International College of Philosophy (CIP).

The same year of GREPH's foundation, a term which is used loosely (for the group was constituted by members who expressed an interest in its project, but from whom nothing substantial was required) saw the first of the collective GREPH texts, signed, like the initial draft of a constitution and programme, by collectivity. GREPH was at that time involved in promoting philosophy at secondary level in schools. In an interview of the 1980s (Derrida 1995b, 88), Derrida describes it as bringing together teachers, high school and university students who wanted to analyse and change the educational system, and in particular the philosophical institution, first of all through the extension of teaching of philosophy to all grades where the other so-called 'basic' disciplines are taught. Derrida there recalls that President Mitterand had made very precise commitments in that direction to him at that time after his election in 1981. 'We are delighted. The problems will not go away and neither will those who are fully aware of their seriousness and who have to deal with them.'

The Estates General for Philosophy, mentioned above, was held in the Great Amphitheatre of the Sorbonne, following the Haby Proposal, in 1979. This large meeting was organized by GREPH. It assembled many philosophy teachers opposed to a government reform that would have curtailed significantly the teaching of philosophy in secondary schools. The Haby Proposal, which produced a very bleak situation, was described in *Un tableau noir*, collectively signed by The Estates General committee (Derrida 1990, 273–9). The proposal had put an end to any future recruiting of philosophy teachers for the secondary level, and the shifting of philosophy professors to other departments, only in order to avoid outright dismissal of them. The recruiting of philosophy teachers had taken off in the 1960s in the era of structuralism, further extended in the aftermath of May '68 when Vincennes was founded (the psychology department was set up with Derrida's oversight. Foucault was selected as head by him – in despite of Lacan, who was the natural choice). In the late 1970s, philosophy, following structuralism, was again in decline, and the government set about allocating time to 'useful' disciplines.

The Estates General of 1979 is an example of Derrida's political engagement, which is direct, and thus displays the side of Derrida which is genuinely political, rather than the side of this thinker as a theorist of a
'democracy to come'. In fact, as we shall see, in *The Right to Philosophy from
the Cosmopolitical Point of View*, the two are linked, since the right to philosophy is of significance, and cannot be done without, if such a democracy is to
be allowed to come. Nevertheless, this engagement stands out from the
theory of democracy, in that it does not involve writing books, or writing in
the usual way, but rather, the canvassing of government to make direct
changes. The Estates General for Philosophy simply desired to turn back the
clock, as it were, a measure of Derrida's political conservatism perhaps, his
belonging to the old guard. His later linking of philosophy to democracy is
not congruous with the dependence of a totalitarian vision of socialism
inflated by philosophy in the 1960s prior to the lost illusions of 1974.
Derrida, like other anti-liberals, was to embrace democracy, and yet to
lament the loss of philosophy's prestige which democracy brings with it,
because democracy is rule by the mass, rather than by an intellectual elite
such as the Russian revolutionary model afforded, or by representation,
such as the English model affords.

11.2 The Estates General for Philosophy

The Estates General for Philosophy, which again was not entirely Derrida's
idea, but which he believed in firmly, was an intervention in government
policy. Its name, *Les États Généraux*, was itself an intended reference to the
early post-1789 revolutionary councils in which class distinctions were dis-
regarded, and emergency meetings convened to formulate plans to deal with
the new situation. Derrida's and his colleagues' own concerns over the
phasing out of philosophy from the syllabus in secondary and *lycée*-level
education required such a meeting to attend to a crisis, in a revolutionary
mood.[2]

Later in life, in a more speculative mood, Derrida said that government
alone could save thinking and philosophy from the stasis which affects
Western universities which, by policy, exclude foreign influences from the
teaching or reproduction of the standard 'positivistic', analytic philosophy,
which had invaded France recently, after putting an end to speculation
already in Great Britain, Germany and America.[3] Governmental or
political involvement in philosophy teaching is necessary if the regenerative

production of philosophers, all exactly alike, and confined to a servile relationship to positivism, is to be suspended.[4] The kind of democracy of which
Derrida speaks is not the English representative, territorial kind, where 'mass'
sentiments cannot always shift policy (as they can in non-English democracy), nor the kind where representatives have no duty actually to represent
a definite body of voters, but he is thinking of, and confronting, the rather
insidious sort of European democracy, which does suffer from an absence of
loyalties, and is governed by a rootless law and totalitarian perspective, upheld
by bureaucrat ministers such as we feel have the power in the European
Parliament. Such a democracy does indeed require amendment, but the UK
style of democracy is ailing too, and is being replaced by international bodies,
which prescribe its laws for it, and tear up the old, organically produced 'law
of the land'. It is this European Parliament, and the international law, to
which Derrida is looking, both because it is the future, and will bring peace,
and also because it is corrupt, unjust, and needs philosopher-overseers.

In another episode of his continuing involvement in education policy in
France, Derrida was commissioned to write a survey of requirements for
philosophy teaching. The 'Commission on Philosophy and Epistemology'
outlines his views on its teaching in the early 1980s (Derrida 1990, 619–59).
He stressed at the time that his report was largely voluntary, but was also
requested by the Mitterand government, which had been elected in 1981. It
became apparent with the years that Mitterand had been humouring
Derrida somewhat, and was, as the first socialist President with a majority
government since the end of the war, in need of as much support as possible. Still, Derrida was sincere about his concern for the sidelining of philosophy in modern France, and was himself an opportunist in his political
activity. British philosophy departments do produce and hire analytic
philosophers, who are of little creative value in terms of the use of democracy. They are not literary or daring enough. Of course, American and
German departments are the same, as discussion at the occasion of the *Right
to Philosophy from a Cosmopolitan View* had it (in 1991). Problems of the irresponsibility of native cultures to behave in their own interest in 'late capitalism' in terms of human rights and the education policy of populations had
been brought to heel in the West by such rules as the International
Declaration of Human Rights. Such a ruling may have to be imposed on
culture to restrain the uninhibited 'dumbing down' of modern culture, especially at universities, he seems to suggest.

In his report to the Mitterand government, Derrida wanted three decisive
steps in philosophy teaching: an in-depth study period at university level; an

intense training period at sixth form, or the *lycée* period; and an initiation training period at secondary level. More than a thousand extra teachers would be required for stage three, or the secondary level. He demanded this in his report for Mitterand and continued to do so through the 1980s. Only with extra teachers and more study would things improve (Derrida 1995b, 331).

When Mitterand was elected the situation seemed to be on the verge of improving significantly, but the new government, in any case, intended to reduce the hours allotted to philosophy in schools. Derrida's report says that class sizes must be reduced, and that the number of classes taught by individual teachers must also be reduced, while time allocated to philosophy must be maintained at current levels, which logically implies extra teachers. Philosophy must be studied from an earlier age, because the basis of it is neglected if learning is not begun early enough. It takes, his report says, months for people even to see what philosophy is about. Finally, many students want to study philosophy at secondary and at *lycée* level, and despite what may be imagined, students find philosophy not too difficult even when fairly young. He proposes an oral examination at baccalaureate level rather than a dissertation, since at baccalaureate level students are still not sufficiently learned to be able to express themselves on philosophy. His proposals are surprisingly practical and get down to concrete situations of education. Research was carried out by GREPH to show that ten- to twelve-year-old children can read and comprehend the essentials of difficult philosophical texts.

12
Yale

12.1 After *Glas*

1975 was a slow year for Derrida. It was the year of crisis for French political and structural theory when, with revelations of Soviet injustice arriving
in France, the urgency of having to reorientate was felt by the structuralists,
by Derrida himself, and by the public at large. Everyone suddenly realized
that democracy was worth defending, and that individual persons, rather
than structures and ideologies, needed respect. Derrida began to concentrate
on the immediate precursors of structuralism, and gradually he also began
to approach a position from which he could discuss the Other and ethics. At
first this new direction expressed itself in a study of the fine arts, and a turn
to the land of justice and liberty – America. From America he received Joe
Riddel's *Inverted Bell*, which has been called the first American deconstructive work (Derrida 2001b, 125), and he sent a letter to the author. Derrida
was doing work with Valerio Adami, writing the pamphlet for an exhibition
of his drawings, later published in 1978 in *The Truth in Painting* (Derrida
1987b).

The next year, 1976, Derrida showed his continuing agreement and collaboration with Luc-Nancy and GREPH by giving a collective interview with
them on how literature and philosophy are not distinct or separable. This
collaboration, seemingly more intense at this time, shows perhaps to whom
the works *Glas* and *The Post Card*, and other 'middle period' texts, were
addressed, or on behalf of what cause they were developed. Interviews are
given, including the apology for *Glas*, published as 'Between Brackets' in
Diagraphe, 8 April edition. *Spurs* (Derrida 1979) was published in France, on

Nietzsche's styles; he was speaking in public, and at ENS, on the work
Nietzsche with increasing frequency and fluency.

Of Grammatology was translated and published in English in 1976, 1
event signalling the demand for Derrida's work in the English-speak
countries, particularly in US universities. In these years only the *Trutl*
Painting and *The Post Card* were published in France as books. All the sa
though we mention his excessive writing of articles and essays, with
much substantial writing of works (the two texts just mentioned are coll
tions of essays and articles), these texts maintained his momentum.

Derrida's stand-alone lectures in the last years of the 1970s were delive
at a variety of places: Princeton, Venice, Virginia, Charlottesville and SU
Stony Brook in 1976; at Columbia, New York the following year; and U.
Irvine, Columbia in 1977; Cornell and Geneva in 1978. In 1979 Derrida v
at Oxford, London and Edinburgh universities, where he was composing
'post cards' collected in 1980.

After *Glas* Derrida became internationally renowned and began to be as
ciated publicly with the already famous but now declining French structu
ists, thinkers of human behaviour and society as a strict science, and especia
in America's strong literary studies culture at its universities, with literat
and 'Theory'. He began to teach some seminars at Yale in 1975, with Paul
Man and Hillis Miller (whom he had met in 1968 and whom he followed
Irvine in California when Miller left Yale in 1986). This year saw the beg
ning of that which was called the Yale School, gathering Harold Bloom, P
de Man, Derrida, Geoffrey Hartman and J. Hillis Miller. It also saw the beg
ning of the debates and wars over the invasion of 'deconstruction in Ameri

12.2 Yale

Yale University, where de Man taught, had a prominent and famous p
gramme of literary studies, perhaps the best in North America. In 1975 Derri
began teaching for several weeks each year at Yale alongside Hillis Miller a
de Man. 'The Yale School', as the group of literature and philosophy teach
at this university came to be known, was characterized by using non-litera
terms to explain literature, a characteristic which de Man taught them
refine into a more precise semiological, post-structuralist analysis. The sch
was most itself by being different from the prevailing American New Critici
and Formalism, which read meanings and structures in texts, and had deriv
from, and remained largely homogeneous from the time of, T. S. Eliot's ea

criticism of poetry. At Yale, in contrast to this traditional modernism, Harold Bloom read 'genius' in works, Hartman read materialism, and Miller saw the workings of consciousness. Later, Fredric Jameson, brought to Yale by de Man, became part of it too, but was less of a literary critic, and tended thus to show how little of a School or movement there really was at Yale.

The Yale School, formed from the nucleus of the two European deconstructionists and the native Americans Hillis Miller and Geoffrey Hartman, as well as Bloom, was first announced around 1975, when Hillis Miller, in the *New Republic* in November, and in the *Georgia Review* in 1976, stated that de Man, Bloom, Hartman and Derrida 'come together in the way the criticism of each is uncanny, cannot be encompassed in a rational or logical formulation and resists the intelligence of its readers'.

Like most schools or movements, it found occasion to be born as a consequence of another movement which was getting long in the tooth. 1957 was the high point of the New Criticism and literary modernism in America. Northop Frye published his *Anatomy of Criticism*, giving a scientific purpose and appearance to literary criticism. Note the scientific pretensions for poetry as early as 1917 in T. S. Eliot's 'Tradition and the Individual Talent', and in Ezra Pound, and finally I. A. Richards, with his Basic English programme, in which English poetry was to be of most value as an instrument of pedagogy. American and English critics after Pound, Eliot and Richards believed their criticism was far superior to that of the Continent, and superior to any other type hitherto. It was a movement given confidence by religious conviction as well as by the ambition of becoming a science. It sought to dignify criticism by making it useful, a dignity which the new Theory and the members of the Yale School denied it.

New Criticism's key notion was the study of the poetic symbol or metaphor, characteristics of true 'poetry', which T. S. Eliot discovered and imitated in his own work as the method of his criticism and poetry. There was the conviction that a symbol or word, or sentence, or finally a poem, could, if it were properly crafted, fully approximate to the thing itself, the Real world, and realize and perfect the world itself by liberating the language, purifying it, producing a semi-mystical state of insight and communion. The science of 'Tradition and the Individual Talent' was a science of disorientation, of producing magical effects by use of word combinations, which could be given a scientific, predictable function. Regardless of the imprecision of the words, by virtue of a mystic passivity to literature, they could meet reality head on, and change that reality into a literary place. This view saw poetry as the possibility of changing the essence of the world, and perfecting it. It is religious in impetus. Naturally, Rousseau, who doubted this power of language ever to *mean* in this perfect way, and who valued subjectivity alone, was despised by New Criticism and its modernist poets Eliot, Pound and the like. So too the philosophical extravagance of Byron and Shelley, or the non-literary faith-poetry of Milton, whose work seemed barbaric, was despised.[1] The autonomy of texts, the irrelevance of any extraneous factors for the text, including the thought which went into it, which New Criticism espoused, took away most of Rousseau's interesting features. T. S. Eliot's dislike of the Romantic poets is very famous, while de Man's interest in them exclusively is exemplary of how little Eliot and he were alike, and of how new the Yale School appeared.[2]

12.3 Paul De Man, *Memoires*

Originally, de Man, like Derrida, had been Husserlian. The objective world, since it is finite and unknown in itself, must, he thought, be known only to exist as something meaningful because of the subject's own intentional structure, or the transcendental structure of consciousness. One does not know the world, but one can know the subject. Both Derrida and de Man retain the transcendence, but jettison the semi-religious idealism of Husserl, the belief in the immediacy and value of consciousness as a sure reference for meaning. They jettison consciousness but retain the transcendental feature, which is language.

In the *Memoires* lectures Derrida pays homage to de Man by recreating his friend's philosophy of remembrance. Following the thread or the void in which there are still languages, traces, without reference perhaps, the human faculties emerge – the soul, the memory, and so on, and make themselves known against the backdrop of the void. The memory of de Man lives after his death, just as, because he escaped valid signification in life, memory had always survived him, had created an image of him. Even while they were together, the lecture says, de Man was little more than a memory to Derrida. The sadness of failing expectations, the way that time defeats even the most simple wish for intimacy, trust, or the immediacy of a confession of friendship, is denied us. This tone of mourning which, being sure in its pessimism, is not so harsh or pathetic, pervades the sentences of the two foremost deconstructionists when the one who survives speaks of the other. Even while alive, the living thing is really already dead for the faculty of remembrance. It is in this sense also that the other person is totally other to knowledge, and being other, it may be completely and overflowingly alive, but for memory and knowledge it is just dead. What survives of him, and this otherness, is just the image of him, what is called memory, in what is called 'the soul'. Before his death he lived or existed as a memory, like a written trace of himself, as though dead (Derrida 1986b, 29). We mourn, truly, always for the missing presence of our friends. My inside, de Man posited, was the result of having to make up for the absence 'outside me', for there would be no use for self-consciousness and interiority if it were not for there being an absence needing to be filled without. I am only a person or a soul insofar as I am called to becoming so by another person, for the soul is the place for creating the image of the other, for remembering. This inside only exists so as to remember the dead, the always distant Other. And though Derrida and de Man may speak of the other person, their words are destined to speak only of an image. These words are allegories.

So the recalled Other, this remembered other self, in this case de Man, recalled by Derrida, is an image, a made-up one, a soul invented, recalled, an allegory, a set of words and meanings which mean something different from what their literal sense and appearance seems to be. This recalled person is a fiction, an empty image inside my own soul, signifying not the other person. It, the misdirected image (Derrida 1986b, 34), is the origin of the power to fictionalize. Not being able to mourn the living-dead one, we make an image or allegory of it, unrelated to reality, or the thing itself, mourning a substitute. As when one dies, and the other remembers him, and he lives only as image or memory after that death, so it is before the one's factual death. The self is a creation, the constant subject of literature; and the self of literature always is a self-confession, an autobiography in which the writer misses himself but confesses himself nonetheless. Such was the basis of Derrida and de Man's 'deconstruction in America'.

12.4 *Limited Inc.* [1977]

In 1977 the theory of iteration, the rereading of traces and texts ad infini-tum, never to find a central meaning or truth, which Derrida had formu-lated and de Man embraced, was to be received in the American- and English-speaking world, as Derrida's texts were translated, and contested with growing frequency. The text *Limited Inc.* records such an exchange, for Derrida was to reply to contestations of his ideas. *The Post Card* records another, and originated in 1977 in the analytic-philosophical heartland of

Oxford. In *Limited Inc.* (Derrida 1988) Derrida attempts to show John R. Searle, who had written a quite predictable essay on 'Signature, Event, Context' in 1977, that Searle is more of a 'continental' philosopher than himself, and more like Rousseau than he suspects. Derrida's point of view records Searle's naïvety, and the innocent echoes of Rousseau which he makes, doing so in a creative way.

Later, Derrida was to say that, since everything today has to go *via* America for authorization in the current state of the world, analytic philosophy has total control over philosophical matters, because it alone is an authorized philosophy. This is not due only to its being American but because, by its nature, the analytic approach is imperialistic (Derrida 2002b, 29). It is also to say that Derrida has no hope of converting anyone to his way of seeing things by virtue of his writing alone. For analytic philosophy, and for that matter, for continental philosophy, his life, his writing, his life as writing, may as well not have occurred, because analysis is a prejudice. The only effect has perhaps been within and amongst his friends – at Yale, Irvine, and amongst a few examples of the New International who admired Nietzsche and Heidegger too. This might also explain the style of *Limited Inc.*, which is lazily sarcastic and ironic. Derrida's response to Searle, particularly the SARL remarks, which alerted him to the several authors who had contributed to Searle's text, replacing Searle with a corporation of writers (hence the title, 'Limited Inc.'), was very hurtful to Searle, who was not accustomed to this personal level of argument. Derrida meant to damage and inhibit Searle from making further attacks. He succeeded in that Searle was reported as never having recovered from it (Dosse 1998b, 40). Derrida remarks that the situation in US universities is somewhat worse than in Europe, and requires real government intervention if philosophy is to exist there at all. For, Derrida points out, because America's tradition of philosophy is imported, and was imported fairly recently, there is no tradition of reproducing philosophers, down even to the details of commonplace reproduction of 'types' of philosophers, within departments. US universities do not produce conventional types of philosophers or teachers, and individual thinkers are therefore freaks of the process, unintended by-products.[3] Moreover, the closing of ranks against the speculative philosophy, which is an instinctive exclusion, more or less ensures that any development of a native philosophy is most unlikely.[4] The major problem with this is that philosophy, which in America has the role of legitimating the US government and the scientific enterprise, takes no notice of literature and the arts, and culture in general, and no notice of the problems of the Other, and so on (Derrida 2002b, 29).

It also takes no notice of things which cannot be verified or predicted, such as the future, statements on the total character of the world, the strengthening of culture, or even high culture itself.

It is also unable perhaps to make even a start on dealing with subjectivity, or liberty, democracy, choice, and other emotive things which 'literary studies' must, in consequence, take care of. It is a problem of internal constraints supposed by analysis itself. Analysis cannot produce, or justify, the production of language. Even its major thinkers, such as Wittgenstein, had determinedly tried to put an end to creativity in philosophy of Hegel's type.[5] Wittgenstein, for example, also tended, while taking away philosophical problems, or 'curing' those who ask them, therapeutically, to reduce the creativity and the independence of all who followed him. He told intimates to give up philosophy and take up something useful and better for the soul (see Monk 1990). Something similar happens to all analytic philosophers who follow the method and teaching of the *Tractatus Logico-Philosophicus* or the *Logical Investigations*: they give up philosophy once they learn that there are no philosophical problems, or in other words, once they see that their language is insufficient. Monk (1990) points out that Schopenhauer was Wittgenstein's favourite philosopher, and that Wittgenstein admired Kierkegaard, and Nietzsche's *Antichrist*, as well as St Augustine. Wittgenstein never read much history of philosophy. This list of Kierkegaard, Schopenhauer and Nietzsche is more or less exhaustive of the anti-Hegelian thinkers of the nineteenth century, showing that while Wittgenstein had not read Hegel, he saw no justification for Hegel's type of thought, that is *thought*, not propositional logic. Perhaps too much credit is given to Wittgenstein, even by those who tinker with his brand of Aristotelian logic, and have resituated themselves with regard to him. Schopenhauer himself desired to put an end to philosophy so as to make way for artistic contemplation and saintliness, an ethical turning of the soul towards 'Platonic' Ideas. By and large, so did Wittgenstein. The good conscience of academic philosophy departments, and the recent turn to medieval-logic-without-God-the-creator, is no doubt of a piece with Wittgenstein's turn to the piety of silence and wonder, that Schopenhauerian desire to silence genuine philosophical wonder and questioning, which bizarrely erupted in Berlin at the turn of the nineteenth century, when the English were studying Indian history and its long-dead culture. Analytic philosophy, one suspects, has as its telos the establishment of a universal culture for a static, totalitarian universal civilization. There is nothing dead or machinal about Derrida's alternative, however: his messianic faith, and the Heideggerian questioning.

13

The Post Card

13.1 Derrida and the Post/*Geschick*

Derrida faced the dual challenges of meeting increased work and teaching commitments, and also the increased responsibilities of fame, in the later 1970s. But at the age of forty-seven he turned inwards for one of the few times in his life as a writer, and composed two pieces of literature: 'The Book of Elie' (subsequently worked up into *Circumfession*), and certain 'post cards', which he began to create in 1977 while at Oxford. With 'The Book of Elie', which was created out of the desire to name the 'real' Jacques, rather than the one who resembles me or you, we deal later. The 'post cards', collected in 1980 amongst lectures on psychoanalysis, we will look at now.

The first half of *The Post Card: From Socrates to Freud and Beyond* (1987a), the part which for the first time introduced Derrida's personal life to us, is a set of post cards, compiled in date order, but subject to random erasures of certain parts. Each one is supposedly written on the reverse of a post card bought in a gift shop next to the Bodleian Library in Oxford, which shows Socrates sitting writing at a desk while Plato leans over his shoulder, as if telling him what to write. The artist, who was medieval, and was illustrating a book on fortune telling, has probably made an error in his labelling of the two philosophers.

The drawing of Socrates and Plato illustrates that the chance of failure, of error, in destination, is always a chance, for this writing has missed its destination, and here Plato precedes Socrates. Derrida concludes, with a subtle appropriation of Heidegger's late thinking of 'destiny' and destining, that writing is emitted by something like, metaphysically speaking, a postal network, and as in such a network of relays and addresses, any error or catastrophe or stroke of luck can occur, during a sending from one to the other. His 'metaphor' explains time facing backwards, intentional errors, effects explaining and preceding causes, the end before the beginning, neither end nor beginning when once such a network has been deconstructed, and shown to be as impure as it is. Poetry and philosophy, which are part of the postal system of sent and received messages, have no proper time. Knowledge is overturned, it is certainly undone by the potential for error in a postal system. The end of time will come when the post card is read properly and finally (Derrida 2004a, 125, Derrida 1987a, 115), because only with the end of time will meanings and the reception of meaning be certain and 'fully-present'. That is, positivism, as the scientific pinnacle of the knowledge-system, is deconstructed, along with psycho-analysis. The aim of these post cards is to deconstruct analytic philosophy, based in Oxford, using an alliance with J. L. Austin as its strength, for they are written in the performative mode, a tissue of biographical reference, anecdote and semi-diaristic accounts, like, in fact, the writing on the reverse of a post card:

> The day before then, seminar (at Balliol, around *La différance*, ten years after the lecture I had given right here, if you only had seen the embarrassed silence, the injured politesse, and the faces of Ryle, Ayer, and Strawson, okay + 'philosophy and literature. [. . .] I write you the letters of a travelling salesman, hoping that you hear the laughter and the song[)]. (Derrida 1987a, 14)

Knowledge is undone, by psychoanalysis in fact, by the Other, by what is beyond the aporia which various positivistic axioms or presuppositions produce of themselves – such as: that speakers have intentions which fully saturate their utterances with meaning, that these intentions are fully present to themselves; that events have strict causes and effects; that an addressee either does or does not receive a message, and either does or does not understand it. Which means in fact that the psychological status of reception, understanding a message, and so on, is at stake.[1]

One could call Derrida's description of the 'sending' of the meaning of events and the 'delivery' of traces, a metaphor, or a metaphysical description, in metaphor, of the sending of Being. This however is not exactly the case. The 'postal system of meanings and meaningful signs' uses a metaphor apparently, in an attempt to describe what 'meaning' is. A metaphor uses an established thing, here the post, in order to understand something not known, in this case 'meaning'. But what if, Derrida asks, with reference to Heidegger (in 'The Retrait of Metaphor' (Derrida 1998d)), this supposedly well-known 'postal system' only gained its own meaning as postal network when once Meaning itself had been understood? Then, 'postal system' would have to be understood according to what 'meaning' means; and what if 'meaning' can only be understood if metaphors are used to describe it? Before 'postal system' can be called metaphor in this case, 'meaning' would need to be explained. But Derrida holds that it cannot be explained without use of terms such as 'postal system', in which case it is more than a metaphor. It is a traced explanation, one waiting for a full meaning. For what does 'postal system' mean, what does the written trace 'post' mean, and is it ever anything? It is in this way that all of Derrida's work in *The Post Card* is a withdrawn, retreating, trace-metaphor, a sort of withdrawal of the withdrawn value of metaphor.

13.2 The Postal System

The lectures making up the second half of *The Post Card* were delivered in the 1970s, based on Nietzsche in part, for the most part on a discussion of Jacques Lacan's psychoanalytic theory, and Freud's speculations in his worrying *Beyond the Pleasure Principle*. The aim is the disruption of the psychological description of the self as a working postal system of messages between the self wherein, as Lacan has it, one always is in touch with oneself, in a circuit of messages sent from the Unconscious to the conscious. The point of this postal system of messages affirmed by Lacan, and derived from Freud's system of the Unconscious versus the conscious mind, is that such signs and meanings which operate in the conscious, and emerge from the Unconscious, arrive at their addressed destination, or in other words, they actually work *qua* signs and meanings; his is a postal system which never fails. Again, we are dealing with whether messages and signs are always full of intended meaning and with nothing else, which Derrida had disputed with the theory of the sign as a trace, and meaning as an effect of mere repetition. The Freudian-Lacanian scheme describes a circle of self-possession by a subject in control of his own comings and goings. Lacan rather renewed a discredited Freud, but in a linguistic way, rather than reading him literally, as a natural scientist. Using him as an authority in this way he was antagonized by members of the psychoanalytic community who found it more decent to read Freud as a quasi-biologist than as a linguist. For Lacan therefore, Freud was being used and read as a text of theory somewhat between literature and philosophy, and read at face value, not as a science. It is with this literary and philosophical Freud that Derrida was interested himself, conscious that this Freud was, like Nietzsche, Heidegger and the rest, not quite an authority, or the figure in whom the world had any great faith. Similarly Freud is read as 'literature', or as a great novelist, by Harold Bloom in *The Western Canon* (1995).

The question of whether what is sent is received also raises the matter of the sending of the Law of Being by Being.[2] Heidegger perhaps never went to the end of his expedition following the *Geschick*, by which Being gifts itself to Germany with a gift sent from the 'essential sway' to presence, and he never managed to think this *envoi* as 'postal principle' (Derrida 2004a, 152). The postal principle is for Derrida the way in which meanings, traced upon Being, are dispersed. Events in themselves, of course, are not sent, there are no such physical gifts in themselves, as gifted in any explicable sense, only the traces of what they mean for us, the traces of the meaning we give to such gifts. A trace may never become a meaning. Heidegger may have found 'the post' too machinal for his liking as a description of how Being gives its law and its meanings, its signs, but again, Derrida differs from Heidegger in accepting writing machines, the machinality of traces, and their liability to failure. The post for him is simply a relay. This scheme, this technics of events and meanings of what is, which undoes what is by reducing it to trace, is set forward in *The Post Card*. This theme is not limited to that text, since trace, différance, sending, absence of origin, and so on, are familiar. *The Post Card* just gathers, or sets it all in motion, and for this reason, despite its obscurity, it is a major text of deconstruction.

'To Speculate – On Freud' discovers the various sendings of Freud, and the institution of psychoanalysis. His grandson, the pleasure which takes a detour through pain, and the sending of Freud's authority to an institution of psychoanalysis, are described according to the 'postal system'. Nietzsche too is seen to work by posting things, and writing in a rhythm of sending things from 'here' to 'there', and back [*fort:da*], in what Heidegger called 'the ring', by which things are the locus of 'the four', and by which the will to will owns what it rules over (by means of the Eternal Return):

> Third return of Nietzsche. Third circular recourse before leaving again. This seminar will have played the fort:da of Nietzsche.
> Which is rhythm.
> Pleasure is a kind of rhythm, says a fragment of 1884.

> Is what we have retained from *Beyond* . . . anything other than a rhythm, the rhythm of a step which always comes back, which again has just left? (Derrida 1987a, 405)

'The Purveyor of Truth' (*Le facteur de la verité*) which deals specifically with Lacan, also deals with the giving out or sending of something which is expected to return to a proper place, in this case a letter which returns after having been stolen, and which the psychoanalyst knows how to find, knowing that a letter has its true place in the Unconscious. Such a letter has a circular path of going and returning to self, of going and staying *as the same*, but with the detour as something to be cured. Lacan gives a reading of Poe's 'The Purloined Letter', a reading which Derrida questions:

> Not that the letter never arrives at its destination, but it belongs to the structure of the letter to be capable, always, of not arriving. (. . .) Here dissemination threatens the law of the signifier and of castration [the law of signs] as the contract of truth. It broaches, breaches the unity of the signifier, that is, of the phallus. (Derrida 1987a, 444)

Derrida made this remark while composing *Dissemination* and *Glas* in which the unity of the phallus, even the unity of the phallic column of a written page, were breached. The point is that the relationship of signs to signifiers, for Lacan, is a unified complex which, for the subjective mind, takes a detour, wherein the sign floats off, and breaches this unity, only to return. Derrida splits up this simple unity.

14
Nietzsche and Heidegger

14.1 A Late Start

From 1975 to 1990, Derrida released several publications of completed texts such as *Limited Inc.* [1977], *The Truth in Painting* [1978], *The Post Card* [1980], *Otobiographies* [1982], *Memoires: For Paul de Man* [1984], *Of Spirit* [1987], and others. Shorter works of this period, such as the work on academic politics and teaching, were released in two large volumes. The academic work of this nature was released in 1990 as *Du droit à la philosophie*, while the occasional and relatively short essays on diverse subjects were collected under the title *Psyche* in 1987. Neither of these collections is systematic, and the volumes, which are collections of lectures, discussions and literary improvisations for the most part, are indicative of how little time Derrida spent on actual work in private, or, as it were, on his own.

The work which Derrida had done, the reading which he had done, was reading in public, and was concerned with what in the 'Roundtable on Deconstruction' (Caputo 1997a, 3–28) Derrida called 'the major works of the metaphysical tradition', what in this day may be called the 'Dead White Male European' tradition. Derrida went so far as to say that he does not like to read or write on 'Living Female Extra-European' writers, but that this is a personal choice, and cannot be justified in a language which eschews value judgements. Hegel, Heidegger, Nietzsche and Freud were consistently and almost exclusively the objects of Derrida's reading, much as the English and German Romantic poets and critics were Paul de Man's objects of study. Contemporaneously with this heightening of pure reading and of making a place for the White-European-Male writer (if we use these misleading terms for simplicity), Derrida also began to refer to himself with greater and greater frequency, in interviews, and discussions, and in references to himself in his lectures as he grew more celebrated. A genuine interest in his own self, and, by transference, the ownmost self of every other person, became an issue. In contradistinction to Lacan, he believed in a healthy psychosis, a relationship with the self and the Other which was not understood in signs alone, and which could dream, and not be at one with itself. But then, with a thought which is a multi-valenced type of reading of the world and experience *qua* archi-writing, reading of the metaphysical tradition, reading of history as temporalized into the present, and other nuances of the mode of existence 'reading', it is natural perhaps that the person of the reader is himself the next source of interest.

In the late 1970s and the 1980s Derrida's ENS seminars covered Nietzsche and Heidegger to a surprising extent and we will now subject these published works to some scrutiny. Why had Derrida waited so long to speak on these two, turning to them only in middle-age, when it is, their being so well established, easy to teach them and question them? His study of them somewhat resembles his early study of Husserl. It is lengthy, resulted in valuable works, but attended to minor matters, obscure points, as *Spurs* does, or the text on Trakl covered in *Of Spirit*. *Psyche* [1987], the collection of lectures and occasional pieces from the 1980s, includes at least four major essays on Heidegger of the twenty collected. Two of these are edited versions of the *Geschlecht* series of seminars on 'Nationalism and Nationality in Philosophy'. This seminar series ran into double figures, and only the first two sessions were collected in the 1987 book. The study of Heidegger, was, as we will see later, also a project in which acquaintances of his were involved, and constitutes a first study of Heidegger's politics in France.

Overall however there is only one major thread guiding Derrida's belated study of Heidegger, except an undercurrent of a new ontology in which Being does not give a Law, but rather is insubstantial and self-deferring, a study which maybe required of him in his later maturity. The subjects dealt with in regard to Heidegger in the 1980s are sexual difference ('Geschlecht 1'), the determinative factor of nationality in philosophy ('Geschlecht 2'), metaphorics in Heidegger's text ('Retrait de la metaphor'), religion (*Of Spirit*), and the theme of representation and translation as the guiding force of the modern era's approach to Being ('Representation', in *Psyche*). In this last essay Derrida gives an indication of why he read Heidegger at the XVIIth conference for Philosophy, at which it was delivered, and at which Derrida was the opening speaker. He makes sustained reference to Heidegger, he says, at a French conference, because Heidegger had done so much of the questioning of representation, and had already covered most of the ground. Prior to his public study of Heidegger, Derrida had already made use of a central aspect of Heidegger's thought in his motivating of the trace by means of the 'Post', in *The Post Card*. It is not then so much that Derrida wishes to teach something new about Heidegger, but that he wants to make use of his work and to continue its momentum and its tradition. In this sense, Derrida believes in the myth of the end of metaphysics, and continues the unfolding of its turn into a new origin in Europe and in the 'Lands of the Centre' to come. Like his teaching, publishing and speaking, Derrida's reading of Heidegger reveals the metaphysical substrate of things, called différance, and not called Being. Différance had come about as an idea because Being is essentially, and inexplicably, different from beings. His thinking echoes Heidegger's fundamental ontology, and Nietzsche's doctrine of the superman, but with a heightened sensitivity to the nefarious effects of a conservative revolutionary philosophy upon 'mankind's' destiny.

14.2 *Given Time*

The first half of *Given Time* is a study of Heidegger's late essay 'On Time and Being' (1962). Its movement was to distance Derrida further from the master, by showing again what was obvious, but which he felt needed to be said over and over again in various voices: that Heidegger was part of the 'great transcendentalist tradition' (Derrida 1993b, 53). Heidegger had revolutionized the German term and activity 'thinking' which he had inherited, into an activity combining thinking and thanking, thanking Being for having given itself as philosophy, and thanking it by thinking upon it. Such a stance, a comportment, was the earthy and revolutionary destruction of idealistic thinking into something other, something which was seen by him as a truer and more attuned thought. But this thought is not abandoned to the totality of things without an anchor. Its anchor is in what Heidegger termed the 'Origin', the factual conditions of Ancient Greece; the 'Other Origin' is in the factual historical situation of Germany or Europe, it *is* Germany. The Being in question is the collection of beings which constitute Europe and the Greek–German axis, the places to which Being gives with most care, and the thought of whose people should be filled with the most thanks and meditation of the gift they have received from Being.

But if Being gives/*gibt*, then it gives, Heidegger says, on the condition that the Greeks alone really receive, and that they reciprocate. They receive because they alone are able to think/thank. From this nation-centred giving by Being which determines the shape of thinking, and which is naturally limitless and self-originating, and which Heidegger interprets as a conditioned gift, Derrida takes away the certainty, since he is concerned that determining the unknown like this is dangerous and ille-gitimate, as it forces transcendental limits to it, signing a pact with the unknown to safeguard it and to control its power within known limits (Derrida 1993b, 53; Caputo 1997b, 167). The circle of control, of history, of Greece giving to Germany, and of spiritual Being giving to both, in an event of *Ereignis* which thought can control and master by its labour, is a circle which, Derrida says, cannot contain Being itself, since Being as the giving power sets the circle in motion, and yet must also contain it, neither as interiority nor exteriority (Derrida 1993b, 30).[1] Paul de Man had made the same point in an essay on Hölderlin's 'Andenken' in his *Blindness and Insight* (1983).

In plain terms, a circle of exchange cannot be set in motion and continue in motion without an absence, for otherwise time would not function. But such an absence cannot be Being *qua* giver which is fully known, present and grasped by thoughtful thanks, as Heidegger has it, for then it should be present. Hence the gift of Being, that is, the gift of spiritual life, must be undeterminable, and, giving without return, and without the knowledge or wish for return, without thanks, it is just pure giving. In this way, by describing or playing with the beneficent nature of Being when it gives philosophy, Derrida has shown that Being cannot give, or be determined to give to one place and time alone, to Germany or Greece, and must be governed by chance, and be subject more to dissemination than to gather-ing. Heidegger's thinking also had it that the poet and philosopher 'hear' the words of Being, which are always speaking, but rarely heard, but Derrida's theory holds to the opposite conclusion to Heidegger's: the lan-guage of Being is not exclusively ancient Greek, or modern German. Despite the appearance of having been a nihilist thinker with the attitude that the West must be pulled apart and its disciplines mixed together, Derrida had begun to show himself to be working conscientiously on crucial thinkers with the aim of showing how their nationalism and total-izing attributes could be undone for the benefit of the modern Western states. He also clearly had a single motif in mind, quite other than a mere random destruction of things.

14.3 *Living On: Borderlines*

'~~Being~~': this symbol or 'trace' appears first in *Zur Seinsfrage* [1955] (Heidegger 1959), which may be the most important pre-Derridean decon-structive text. *Zur Seinsfrage* or *The Question of Being*, as it was translated, was a letter written to Ernst Jünger concerning the latter's *Über die Linie*, in which Jünger had presented a way of stepping out of the era of Nihilism into a better age. The text is important for Derrida since Heidegger puts a line between Being and beings, and, at the crossing of them, on the line, he posits something else, namely 'Being', crossed out. This sign, which signs nothing, is the gap in which Being and beings meet, the trace of the différance of Being and beings. Being relates to beings here, in an absent place which is also the place held by Dasein. Therefore instead of the classical mind or subject, Heidegger has brought to light a trace, a sort of writing, neither a thing, nor the origin of things. It is the opening of writing, which he puts in place of the subjective logocentric mind. This central point of crossing is called by Heidegger *Ereignis*.[2] That meant for him the point at which things occur[3] and things occur or are 'en-owned': through *Ereignis* Being, or Germany, welcomes thought, and thought opens Germany up to be seen and lived in. 'The line between what it is and what it is not, between its being and its relation to Being is the very line of differance, the line whose event of occurrence is *Ereignis* itself' (Silverman 1989, 160).

Poets, says Heidegger, have felt the loss of the ground, making the poet find himself in an abyss. Gods could have aided the difference, but they had gone. Rilke, Heidegger noted in 'Wozu Dichter', or 'What Are Poets For?' (1946) (Heidegger 1950; 1975, 89–142), could appropriate the line, and demarcate the difference, on a firm ground. Noticing the difference between beings and Being, or rather, Being and Nihilism, means everything here.

Derrida discusses this line, or crossing of borders between two realms, in *Living On: Borderlines*, a text framed in terms more familiar to Derrida, who tended to speak, in the 1970s, of *life* and *death* rather than Nihilism and Being. Here, in his discussion of Shelley for a memorial volume for Jacques Ehrmann, formerly of Yale University, he discusses the demarcating line between life and death in Shelley's 'Triumph of Life'. The collection was *Deconstruction and Criticism* (1979), an important text of the time for the Yale School, close on the heels of the 1976 English edition of *Of Grammatology*. It also included 'Shelley Disfigured' by de Man. The volume established the School, as it was intended to do. As Derrida saw Shelley's poem, which each of the contributors had to concentrate on, triumphing over life, death is on its other side, it is the excess of life, excess of life is death. 'Living itself can only be a theme in a text, but between the texts, as in Heidegger's ontico-ontological difference, the disclosure of living itself comes alive' (Silverman 1989, 163), just as Being reigns [*ereignet*] on that line of difference. So while the difference of Being and beings is ~~Being~~, so the difference of life and death is living on, or *life death* and a language which is crossed out. In Silverman's view, Derrida reads the edges of texts, the barriers, so as to mark these differences and so as to bring out a new meaning (repeated in *Of Spirit* and elsewhere – *Glas* for example, and *Otobiographies*). The new meaning does not have 'life' for its theme, but actually is purest deferred life.

Living On (partially collected by Peggy Kamuf in *Between the Blinds*) was later collected again along with 'Pas', 'The Law of Genre', and 'Title, to be specified' as *Parages* [1986]. Shelley's 'Triumph' recounts the endless passage of life (Shelley 1945) regardless of us, chaining us, especially Shelley himself, who in his last days seems to have had a vision of his life's blindness and futility. The Roman 'triumph' takes place at the battle's conclusion back in Rome. So the full celebration of life's battle against humans takes place after the victory, 'For in the battle they and life did wage She remained the conqueror' (1945, 'Triumph of Life', ll. 239–40). Life celebrates its victory beyond life, in death. The excess of life is death, or, just maybe, the excess is *life death*. The poem is a classic example of how literature refers to itself, folds on to itself, is hymenized, and without external or internal borders. This means it has a sort of infinity, and a machine-like indifference to any intention of its author.

Derrida mentions in passing that 'The Triumph of Life' is a poem, a bounded piece of work which 'it is not my intention to discuss here' (Derrida 1991, 258), but rather he shows how living on is possible for a life which is a trace of itself since, if 'There is no "first" trace' (Derrida 1991, 265) for the work of literature, and the trace possessed the author, then there will be no final trace for the author either, but he will always be possessed by this trace-system. What has no original exemplar or 'first' moment, also has no 'last' moment. Shelley's text is the work neither of a living man nor of a dead one – which means that in it he still lives on. Textually Shelley is alive in this work, for as its author, he was never alive to begin with. They never could, at any rate, have made any reference to its absolute 'Other' namely the world or its author, except under very exceptional circumstances. Rather the text of poetry, the story, the piece of literature is always folded upon itself, and self-enclosed. It did not have an author, which is to say that its author can never have died. On the other hand, these internal margins, these folds, are themselves traces to read, that is, to deconstruct. It may be possible to trace out the living on of the author, the 'Other', for, beyond the non-living, non-dying text and its author, there is, perhaps, a most complete and pure life:

> The apparently outer edge of an enclosure, far from being simple, simply external and circular, in accordance with the philosophical representation of philosophy, makes no sign beyond itself, toward what is utterly other, without becoming double or dual, re-marked within this enclosure, at least in what the structure produces as an effect of interiority. But it is precisely this structure-effect that is being deconstructed here. (Derrida 1991, 268)

That is, there is a chance that, with deconstruction, the absolutely Other could become a referent, in the time reserved for it. This thematic of life and death as 'living on', and the consequent justice owed to the dead and the as yet unborn, is explicitly and clearly remarked on in *Spectres of Marx* in the introduction, for when one 'lives on', one also must care for those others who live beyond life, the not-yet alive, and the dead (Derrida 1994, xx). This completely mysterious individuality of the dead poet could, just once, become the content of a poem.

14.4 *The Truth in Painting*

Various essays on Heidegger and Kant were collected in *The Truth in Painting* in 1978, along with several other works on drawing and the visual arts. The collection included an essay on Van Gogh's shoes and on Heidegger's view of it (in his 'The Origin of the Work of Art'),[4] on the notion of frames and lattices, and the Heideggerian notion of technology as 'enframing' [*Gestell*].[5] Next to this, and an essay on Kant's notion of the sublime in his *Third Critique*, were a couple of essays which were the result of collaboration with visual artists, Titus Carmel and Valerio Adami, for whom Derrida wrote exhibition catalogues, considering them as deconstructive artists. In these catalogues he is again dealing with precisely where the frame of an artwork is, if 'art' does indeed have a difference from 'life'. Derrida was to become involved in visual art again in 1990 in arranging an exhibition (memorialized in *Memoires of the Blind*) and he was to maintain a friendship and working collaboration with Peter Eisenmann, the American, New York-based architect (although the 'art' of architecture is something, admittedly, quite different, and Derrida was no architectural designer). The plotting of a city is, on the other hand, crucial to a sense of place, and is related to Being insofar as the city is the place of 'dwelling', and part of the act of 'building'.[6]

The *enframing* power of technology, which Heidegger considered its essence, and which Nietzsche indicated could be turned into art, was in his later works seen by him as a potentially redeeming force in technology itself, since art too enframes in a way, and technology could be turned into art if technology were properly harnessed. In his removal of borders from 'art-works' Derrida was considering this possibility of refining the distinction between art and technology, and of thereby redeeming technology in the interests of taking responsibility for it, and instituting a culture of genuine work, in the sense that art is the most genuine species of work. But Derrida would not allow art to reveal a 'true' world by representing it. Such a truth would be indefinitely concealed in another time, and the 'art-work' would be a spectral version of this truth.

14.5 *Otobiographies*

Derrida's text *Otobiographies*, of 1979 (Derrida 1985), delivered at a colloquium in Montreal (published in French 1982) followed several years of study and teaching of Nietzsche at the ENS. That Nietzsche-based work was published in part in *The Post Card* ('Legs de Freud'), which relates Nietzsche to other thinkers by thinking 'the ring'. The purpose of *Otobiographies* seems to have been mostly, by way of treating Nietzsche as a person, to show that since all that we have of him are his printed works, then one cannot know this mind, this present-to-self-existence, which he was once, if indeed he ever was present-to-himself. Therefore, and this is the point, it was not incorrect of the Nazis to align him to themselves, even though we must reappropriate him. Aschheim (1994, 232–71) says that Nietzsche was used by the Nazis and thought of as a National Socialist well before they came to power. His *Zarathustra* was set beside *The Myth of C20th* and *Mein Kampf* in the memorial to victory over Russia in the First World War and the curators of his Archive, led by his anti-Semitic sister, were overjoyed. His works and slogans were repeated everywhere in journals, posters, and in common talk in the Third Reich. The reason for this, however, was that his sister and the others were not 'good philologists'. This is the question of *Sec* which had been discussed with Searle in the previous years, in which it is said that context determines the event-quality of a text's meaning. A nearly identical thesis had been upheld about Nietzsche in *Spurs*. In the end, Derrida's pre-occupation is again nationalism in philosophy.

At the same time as writing this paper and giving the seminars at the ENS, Derrida was also writing his 'Book of Elie'. So, naturally, Derrida was interested in theory of biography and autobiography in Nietzsche and in general.

An autobiography is not a life-story, neither in Nietzsche nor Derrida. Writing is the writing of a dead man, and in the text the writer is dead, leaving the text absent of author. So the text is not the life of the author, though it refers to its author: it is *life death*. Signing his name on life, Nietzsche gave it death, and became death as life. In Derrida's view, a text is dead, like a machine, and because it exists as the product of a living man, but is always working while away from him, and even after his death, it is the sign that he is dead already. The person 'Nietzsche' was not ever present to himself, or never was a complete person at any moment insofar as philosophy cannot appropriate the self, or as Derrida liked to say, it is obsessed by and troubled by the aporia of 'the proper'. Hence his self-reflection is always incapable of encapsulating him, and could not be described. So *genuine* autobiography is neither writing, nor yet the silence of the bodily fate (the voice).

Now in autobiographical reflection, genuinely so-called, one is between textual production, or death, and self-presence, or life. Autobiography is between text and body, between life and death. An 'autobiography' has a life as its theme, but never embodies that life, or really makes it as personal as the life really was. This means that one cannot ever genuinely know what the person 'Nietzsche' meant to say in his texts since he was neither the body of 'Nietzsche' nor the text of 'Nietzsche', and he may or may not have been a Nazi. Between life and death is the space of archi-writing, the line, making both of them different from each other, rather than a unity; the line itself is no solid, self-identical thing either, but is split and different from itself, being the line both for the one, and for the other. At this line may be read the truer life.

In his *Ecce Homo* (Nietzsche 1979, 37) Nietzsche indicated this midpoint of plethoric harmony with himself as the 'Noontide', the point at which auto-biography is both written and erased. There, the self has the slimmest of chances of actually being written. To an extent autobiography is possible, but is disseminated everywhere. Of course every philosophy is an unconscious self-confession, which means that every philosophical work is already auto-biographical and includes its author's life. 'We no longer consider the bio-graphy of a "philosopher" as a corpus of empirical accidents that leaves both a name and a signature outside a system which would be offered up to an immanent philosophical meaning' (Derrida 1985, 5), which is to say that a philosophy is never free of its author. But the body is, on the other hand, the text's other, and is not included in it.

De Man in 'Shelley Disfigured' expressed a view similar to Derrida's in *Otobiographies*. Because 'The Triumph of Life' is a fragmentary poem, due to its author's death, during the time of its composition, in a boating accident, Shelley's fate or biography forms this text, and lies on its external border, and is integral to the interpretation of the poem. Even though strictly a text is simply writing and does not include anything of its author, our interpretation of it includes that fate. The poet's life and death are in the poem when we interpret it (see McQuillan 2001, 71), and it is written at the division of natural life, and textual artefact. Again, on their margin, their difference, is a trace of their unity – *life death*. This is where *Ecce Homo* as truest self-revelation is written, halfway between Nietzsche the man and Nietzsche the text. The writing faded with the body, with the actuality of Nietzsche.

Only the name will inherit the credit which Nietzsche deserved. Hence Nietzsche the person gained nothing, and the name was inflated in value, but not he himself. But Derrida insists that Nietzsche did accrue some credit or interest, which returns to him in the time of the autobiography, a time not of normal time, but of *life death*. We never do own anything, never fully receive what we hope for, but only at the border between death and life where 'we' properly are, in the future time, or a past one when we recognize our differential nature, but never here.

> You will not understand anything of his life, nor of his life and works, until you hear the thought of the 'yes, yes' given to this shadowless gift at the ripening high noon, *beneath that division whose borders are inundated by sunlight*, the overflowing cup of the sun. Listen again to the overture of *Zarathustra* [my italics]. (Derrida 1985, 13)

But this means also that Nietzsche's most pure individuality is not in his autobiography as such. Autobiography cannot be written fully; it is just everywhere in life and texts, but nowhere in particular. It is the difference between them, the traced unity on the borderline between the two types, or the purity spoiled by the universalizing agency of language. His personal life gets lost in the moment of writing, is lost in différance, deferred by the effects of death and writing as temporal phenomena. Incidentally, this means his texts and his personal inclinations are lost, so that we have no means of aligning them to himself. Even Nazis or the like can appropriate his personal life and make him one of theirs – without any way of irreversibly showing that this is correct or not. *Otobiographies* is typical of Derrida's work. It propounds a *theory* of writing, but masks it beneath a temporary argument, in this case rescuing Nietzsche from a political commitment.

The theory of autobiography given in *Otobiographies*, according to Berezdvin (1989, 92–107), is that the Nietzschean autobiography was written for readers who would only know of him when he was already dead (or mentally so, insane).[7] Because it was written for the future, for a future 'famous Nietzsche', on borrowed credit, a narrative to be read by future admirers of a new famous Nietzsche, it was a dual self which composed *Ecce Homo*. It is then open to those who receive him as famous/recognized, though these future receptions are not certain, because they may not occur, and because the meaning may not be grasped in the absence of the writer himself. The return of credit to the dead man may be intercepted, since the meaning of self-confession is not sure of its own meaning, having been written for another, and not for a self-present self. By its nature, a confession opens up for another what we ourselves find impossible to decipher.

Nietzsche's way of writing himself, in recollection, in order to revalue it, and make it better, was made of a lived pathos which he transformed into an ethos containing a judgement, something which redeemed it, blessed it. This is linked by Berezdvin (1989, 101) to the Eternal Return, which revalues a life by recollecting it. Reviving traces of a past life, a dead life, the writing is a deathless dying. The force and pathos (by which he means the most pure individuality) are revived like traces, and given meaning, an ethos (or a universal expression, applicable to all people). A real text is a living-dying. And giving this writing to the future and the other, this writing is a living trace of a dead man, hence a *life death*. Reading, we reactivate, defy time's passage, in a drawn-out life death (1989, 107).[8]

15
The 1980s

15.1 Influence and Opposition

In 1980 Derrida received his first honorary doctorate – from Columbia, New York; he also submitted his work for the *doctorat d'État* at the Sorbonne, concerning which there was much trouble, but which he finally received. The award of *doctorat d'État* usually requires that the candidate should already hold a position at a university, have given papers and lectures, and have published research of an original kind, all of which qualified Derrida for the award. Bennington has pointed out that Derrida had faced problems throughout his career, and at the age of fifty was still finding his way difficult because certain forces, aware that Derrida was an excellent teacher, hated him. The French establishment seemed to dislike his approach, his ideas, his method of reading and his very creativity, that is, his energy. But he was not really alone in suffering this blocking. His students and colleagues suffered the same treatment at the hands of the academic establishment. The occasion of his submitting his work for the award of the doctorate was the vacancy of Ricoeur's chair at Nanterre. Associates had advised Derrida to put himself forward, which he did, but found as soon as he did so that the appointment was no longer on offer, having been blocked by the Minister for Education, A. Saulnier-Seite. Following this he was invited to apply for another chair by a panel of judges who were mostly colleagues, but when he applied he was rejected by the panel, which also consisted of government members. A few years later he was to accept the position as Director of Studies at the *École des Hautes Études en Sciences Sociales*, after being elected at the end of 1983. At the ENS he had been an assistant, with, it must be said, many overseas teaching positions. The position of Director of Studies was the position held by Althusser back in the days when Derrida was still a student, familiarly known under the title 'caïman'.

The thesis, which he had meditated back in 1957 as 'The Ideality of the Literary Object', was ultimately submitted and defended on the basis of the works of the years 1967 and 1972. He explained, in his defence of this work to the panel of judges, what deconstruction was, and how his work had been badly received by both his admirers and detractors. It had been misinterpreted, especially insofar as he was not really a metaphysician of 'différance' or the trace.

'Deconstruction is not, he says "primarily a matter of philosophical contents, themes, or theses, philosophemes, poems, theologemes, or ideologemes, but especially and inseparably [of] meaningful frames, institutional structures, pedagogical or rhetorical norms, the possibilities of law, of authority, of representation in terms of its very market." ' (Norris 1987, 14)

Derrida explained at the time that his work was originally literary, a questioning of the literary object, and an investigation into the effects of the institution, which is always written, of literature.

In the very same year the *Decade de Cerisy* was held, entitled *À partir du travail de Jacques Derrida*, organized by his GREPH associates Lacoue-Labarthe and Nancy, and attended by a large number of important French thinkers who had decided to attend out of admiration for Derrida, who based their own contributions around his work, signalling how integral Derrida had become to French cultural life.

15.2 Levinas

As has been noticed already, Derrida changed with the decline of structuralism. The early 1980s were the years of the definite end of that movement, for during these years its proponents all died, more or less. According to Edith Wyschogrod, in the early 1980s Derrida suffered a sort of conversion to Levinas and the 'other person', the Other as person, with a reading of Blanchot and Levinas. 'Levinas believes that the recourse to the alterity of the other person who resists incorporation into the totality offers a way for transcending the structures of totalization' (Wyschogrod 1989, 182). The main species of totalization was always Heideggerian Being. There are three texts marking this conversion made by Derrida away from scientific studies towards the reception of the personal and the ethical:[1] 'Violence and Metaphysics' [1964], 'At This Very Moment Here I Am . . .' [1980] and 'On An Apocalyptic Tone' [1980]. In the key text 'At This Very Moment', Derrida follows the description of Being, the *il y a* in Levinas as the first violence, the violence of Being-in-General against the individual (Levinas 1969). 'Consciousness cannot get rid of itself, the weight of its unending presence is experienced as engulfment by the *il y a*' (Wyschogrod 1989, 184). Levinas says the *il y a* is worshipped in despite of this, in Paganism and by peasant communities, cultures like Nazism. The *il y a*, or existence in general, swallowed up the Holocaust. The better stage of culture would then be a transcendental position above the *il y a*, and finally a recognition of the (empirical) face of the Other. The archi-writing, consisting of faces as traces of the Other, writes itself outside the framework of the logos which dealt with *il y a*. All philosophy and metaphysics has so far ignored this transcendental tracing of the face. Derrida became aware of this 'trace' whilst he was preparing publication of the first version of 'Violence and Metaphysics', since Levinas was in 1964 just announcing it. Derrida included footnotes in his first draft for the *Revue de métaphysique et de morale*, but was dismissive of this idea of a language of traces outside of metaphysics. Though the trace was beyond ontology, its expression was ontological. Derrida questioned whether an infinite face, such as God's, and such as the genuine Other's, could be dissociated from finitude and metaphysical discourses of finitude (Wood and Bernasconi 1985, 32). By 1968, when he gave the 'Différance' lecture for the French Philosophical Society, he included Levinas as one of five modern thinkers who had resorted to the use of the non-ontological event of traces, signalling that he approved of this development.

When in 1980 Derrida contributed to a *Festschrift* for Levinas (Derrida 1991, 403), Derrida insisted, as he did in 1964, that the language of Levinas is both spoken (privilege being given to the voice in the expression of the face) and the language of the 'same', so that Levinas' project fails. What has changed is that Derrida is less in need of enemies and more in need of new ventures after the absolute end of structuralism. In 'At This Very Moment' Derrida shows that the other is thematized in Levinas' work, with a fine ethical intention, but is yet not able to be presented in the language he is using. The core intent of Derrida's work is to show that by talking as himself, to another person, just as Levinas tries to do, he is appealing from within himself to an Other, at 'this very moment'. But since writing and speech are subject to repetition, are universal, and compel the individual to be generally understood, they are lost in the process of being re-signed, of using a language of the Same which is a violent, unethical knowledge, the sort which logocentrism always applied (Derrida 1991, 403). The lengthy discourse deals with the singularity of the name 'Levinas' and yet with the possibility of the substitution which writing foists upon that name (1991, 411). Ideally Levinas would never write a work, but the Work, not this work here, but a work of the pure transcendental Other from the voice of the face of himself, rather than with a language subject to the operations of machination and violence:

> How then does he write? How does what he writes make a work, and make the Work in the work? For instance, and most especially, what does he do when he writes in the present, in the grammatical form of the present, to say what cannot be nor ever will have been present, the present said only presenting itself in the name of a Saying that overflows it infinitely within and without, like a sort of absolute anachrony of the wholly other . . . (Derrida 1991, 412)

15.3 'Of an Apocalyptic Tone' [1980]

Derrida concluded the conference devoted to himself at Cerisy in 1980 with some explanation and justification of the apocalyptic tone which he had assumed in recent years, or was to assume more and more, no doubt mindful that it was doing him personally no good at all to have such a view on the world and thought in academic circles. He is thinking of his work on Levinas, and actually of Levinas, speaking for him. It apologizes for thinkers very like himself who, then still living and working, were religious and yet not orthodox, like Blanchot, Levinas and, to a more limited extent, Lyotard, and his associates Nancy and Labarthe, as well, maybe, as Ricoeur. Such thinking hears the call of the Other, what would once have been called God, and makes itself ready for the Hebraic coming of the Other from without time which is recognized as coming only on the condition that it does not come in time at all. His work on Heidegger in *Given Time* and *Living On* could be seen to be apocalyptic or calling on an unknown Other in this way. In this way it is also a critique of the *Book of Revelation* of St John in which an improbable coming reign of justice founds a world-view. It is contemporaneous with another essay of a similar theme showing that this preoccupation, while being inherent in Derrida's thought of what is ghostly and not yet 'here', was actually something of a discovery for him – namely *Psyche: Inventions of the Other*. The revelation in question is a waiting for a higher truth of reality, which unconceals the real nature of the truth, in a time when Christ will come again, or the Messiah will finally come. But true to the non-occurrence of the event, Derrida's and Blanchot's Messiah, the 'Other' who is the object of this new religion, will not come, and there is no truth to be revealed, or no justice at a stroke which one would have expected on such a day. Rather, the devotee must always *pretend* that it would come on a normal day, knowing that it will not really; or if not pretend, then he understands that normal time is not the time of justice, but one must still act as if it were coming. Time and presence are not the horizon in which the most serious things occur.

'Of an Apocalyptic Tone' recognizes that those who organized the conference and those who submitted papers had assumed a semi-religious response to the crisis of the West (which was a crisis for France too), and it looked at this crisis in the perspective of modern times since Kant. The paper's title refers to Kant's 'On a Newly Arisen Superior Tone in Philosophy' which asked for Enlightenment values in philosophy, and refused to depend on religious visions and religious discourse to settle philosophical questions (Caputo 1997b, 88). Such a refusal was good in Kant's day, but must be tempered today, Derrida implies, in the name of the Other, which is something which Kant would have scorned, but which today, when religion seems to be making a timely revival in the West, must be discussed by philosophy, to temper the excesses of rationalism. Derrida does not mean to abandon the Old Enlightenment whose philosopher Kant is, but to allow some faith to apply in philosophy. The demystification must be careful, and some leniency be given to the religious tone of voice, so that the place of religion as a necessity can be found. The apocalyptic discourse is a discourse on the secret, the non-known, which in itself is not in any case unphilosophical, and in keeping with Kant's religion within the bounds of reason alone, simply recognizes the secret which impassions thinking. The crisis of course is the dangerous conservative politics and capitalization of the West, which gets stronger in all Western democracies with the years, bringing the disavowal of all that is not useful, all that is still shrouded in darkness, and the secret, which Lyotard again was another to have discussed over and over again.

The apocalyptic tone is a call to the Other without hope of answer in this time, in these times. But in this time it must be made all the same, and there is reason for it too, such that it should be given a hearing, even though Kant once damned those who spoiled rational discourse with obscure gestures and threats, arguments and tones of voice, which were inappropriate at that time. Whatever exists is opened up by a call from the Other, in the sense that language and speech are from the first devoted to a promise for the Other, and the Other comes first before the word. Existence is first from something prior to personal or objective existence. Nevertheless, Derrida's is a religious assumption, or an ungrounded one, which presumes to know the coming of something as yet unseen by the Enlightenment values, the price for which is that nothing can be said about it. What comes and what one asks to come, cannot be controlled, and more importantly, what the thinker of the Other says, is that the Other cannot be revealed by his textual revelation.

15.4 'Psyche: Inventions of the Other'

Another text of the Other, fixing it firmly at the centre of his view of thinking, is 'Psyche'. The text 'Psyche', collected only in 1987 (Derrida 1987c) as the lead essay of the collection of that name, is a lengthy essay on the subject of the Other in multiple aspects, in terms of literature, religion, the subject, and so on. It has the appearance of a treatise, and that indeed is what it is. The basis of this treatise on the Other is to redefine this Lacanian and in general traditionally French theme, so as to delimit how much it is possible to say about it, and even, how much it is desirable to say about it. In effect Derrida says that it is neither possible nor desirable to say anything about it, nor to do anything positive to welcome it, yet to expect it, and to notice its coming in its surprising effects. The proper stance for the Other is that of waiting, passion and readiness for the future from which the Other comes, for it never comes from the present. Whatever occurs in fact is not the Other. In this tone of waiting and readiness Derrida echoes his early text 'Structure, Sign and Play', which ends with the famous lines on the coming of something monstrous, and the command that we become Nietzscheanly stronger so as to bear it, and to love it, whatever shape the event of the future assumes. The Other comes as a disaster, always a disaster for Blanchot, regardless of whether it is good or bad, for in its coming it is too strange for reality to bear. As such it is the counterpart to the earlier 'On an Apocalyptic Tone' essay, and shows with what new boldness Derrida has begun to outline what was concealed in vague terms at the conclusion of 'Structure, Sign and Play'.

15.5 The Early 1980s

As we have already pointed out, in the first half of the 1980s the major structuralists, Foucault, Althusser, Barthes and Lacan, either died, or ceased to write. In some cases they even closed down all operations. De Man also died in this period. Derrida had depended on these figures as collaborators and as rivals. So to some extent Derrida was to lose his power to create in this time; his coherence and motivation were lost. The backlash against structures came along apace. One could see the early 1980s as a crisis in his writing, if not in his life as such. It was also a time when he was happiest with government. The bibliography was, in terms of interviews and articles, translations and occasional pieces, never so large, but the actual products in terms of genuine texts or concerted effort were at their nadir. One could doubt whether Derrida were to recover from this period.

In 1980 Roland Barthes,[2] with whom Derrida had collaborated in *Tel Quel* and whose work had been influenced by Derrida's own, died. Derrida began rereading Barthes' books, especially the first and last ones (Derrida 2001b, 36). He contributed to *Poétique* in 1981 with 'The Deaths of Roland Barthes', one of his first reminiscences of the dead of his generation. The article, subsequently published in *Psyche*, is a sort of deconstruction of the idea of the photograph.

Why did Derrida have to work on architecture, on photography, on drawing, as well as on literature and philosophy in the 1980s? His involvement in other aspects of culture is unprecedented in the history of canonical philosophers. Between 1982 and 1987 he was involved in three films: in 1982 in a film by Ken McMullen called *Ghost Dance*, in which he appeared; again in 1986 he collaborated with J.-Ch. Rose on a film about Caryl Chessman; and in 1987 he played a part in a work by Gary Hill called *Disturbance* (Bennington 1999, 334–5). Is this involvement in the fine arts part of the mixing, rejoining of disciplines; that is, is it done on purpose but without heart, or is it a development of traditional aesthetics? Finally, was Derrida just rather aimless and homeless at this point? His literature work is largely from this period, collected in *Acts of Literature* (1992c). The literary work tends towards being on people who knew him and whom he knew, like Celan, Genet, Ponge, as well as on modernists Joyce, and Mallarmé, in particular. The early 1980s became for Derrida an exciting time in which, due to the fame of his thinking and writing in America, which had become a new 'ism', and his enjoyment of publicizing deconstruction, he was able to work on a multitude of new things, and he showed no inclination of limiting his interests.[3]

In 1981, with the election of a socialist government in France, Derrida began to become more politically active himself, and with Vernant, the structuralist historian, and some friends, he founded the Jan Hus association to aid dissident or persecuted Czech intellectuals, of which he became vice-president. Jan Hus was, in the words of Roger Scruton, one of its English members, an 'underground university'. 'Our desire was to help our Czech and Slovak colleagues to continue teaching and learning in private after losing their university positions and being reduced to menial jobs' (Scruton 2001, 125). The first Jan Hus was an English project, known as The Jan Hus Educational Foundation, and was founded as a charity, becoming an autonomous institution based only on the agreement that intellectual freedom was intrinsically valuable. The French Jan Hus was founded, by Vernant and Derrida, on the prompting of Scruton and others, but received its funding from the government.

So in 1981, Derrida again travelled to Prague with the aim of furthering the cause of Jan Hus. It was on this trip that he was arrested by the Czech authorities for his work for the dissidents, but on trumped-up charges, namely that he was smuggling drugs. The drugs had, he says, been planted on him by the Czech authorities, and so he spent twenty-four hours in legal custody. Protests and help from French intellectuals were joined by Michel Foucault, and were based on a signature campaign. He met Foucault on his return, on 1 January 1982, after a period of not speaking which had lasted ten years. In the end the French government and President Mitterand intervened and Derrida was 'expelled' from Czechoslovakia (Bennington 1999, 334). While in prison he underwent an eight-hour interrogation by state officials, whom he pitied, but which was terrifying. He says that all involved knew that it was a trap and why, and so it became a play of nerves, in comic complicity. He was then working on Kafka and 'Before the Law' (Derrida 1992c, 181–220). Kafka was of course a Czech citizen. Derrida said in an interview that it was probably while he visited Kafka's grave that the drugs were planted in his valise (Derrida 1995b, 128). His Czech lawyer gestured to him that it was like a Kafka story, smiling. There was nudity, photographs, near violence, and the prison uniform. He only tells the story, he said in the interview, so as to capture some sense of the absolute singularity of himself, a singularity which signs him alone, as those silk worms did which in youth he had seen emerge from their cocoons.

Derrida had some celebrity after this episode, but was uncomfortable with it. He was televised in Germany on the train home, but the TV interview unsettled him by forcing him to talk in a half-restrained way, and he found himself uttering platitudes, or afraid to say, so publicly, what was secret and close to him. He said, two years later, recalling it, that he wanted to get back to his obscurity again, to write. His dwelling upon the person and the subject, and the repeated turning to autobiography at this time, first seen in *The Post Card*, and ending perhaps in the work with Bennington in *Circumfession*, is the keynote of this period of his work, which is also a recuperation from the impersonality of structuralism.

Derrida participated in the organization of an exhibition of 'Art Against Apartheid', and initiatives in view of creating the 'Cultural Foundation against Apartheid', as well as the 'Committee of Writers for Nelson Mandela' in the early 1980s. A large number of interviews were given: on the new International College of Philosophy, on his own autobiographical project, and one entitled 'Yet another Derridean interview' (in *On the Beach*, Australia, autumn 1983). There was a great demand upon him to appear in journals and newspapers talking about his work, but it seems that he refused to talk on present-day politics, or anything of that kind, although this reserve was only to last until the early 1990s.

In December of 1983 Paul de Man died of cancer, and Derrida delivered a funeral oration for him. 'In Memoriam, of the Soul: for Paul de Man' was delivered on 18 January, at a ceremony at Yale. In this text, which has already been mentioned, and which was published in *Memoires* (Derrida 1986b), Derrida discusses openly what deconstruction is, and what it was for Paul de Man. It dwells on 'Deconstruction in America', and on perceptions of de Man, as 'Hölderlin in America'. Derrida says there that he had never disagreed with de Man openly. In April 1984, a de Man lecture was delivered at Irvine, where he met Riddel whom he had written to many times before. The year after de Man's death saw the death of Michel Foucault on 15 June, one of the first Western victims of the AIDS virus.

15.6 Literature, Aesthetics and Politics

In the late interview with Roudinesco in which Derrida recounts his teaching activity he again turns to what was his first question, 'What is literature?'. Literature, he held in his maturity, is 'the right to say everything' (2004c, 127). For him, and this became more explicit with the years, literature is essential for democracy for it has the privilege of saying whatever it likes, while normal speech is severely restricted as to what it can suggest, what it can do or dream of. The laws of the state play the role of restricting non-literature, so that the difference between literature and non-literature has to be adjudicated, and it will be harder to decide with coming years as the power of the state becomes greater with advances in technology. The law and the juridical authority will have to decide what literature is, but within literature anything can be said. The way in which literature is the 'right to say everything' is the prosaic way in which the author of literature can disclaim any personal responsibility for the utterances contained in his work: 'In the fictional world, a narrator, the character in a novel or a theatrical work, can say anything at all' (Derrida 2004c, 129). The distinguishing feature is that the author cannot be punished by law for what he says – if his utterance or dreaming is literary.

Such 'literature' as an institution has not always been given the right to say anything at all. The threat it faces is that which the stage faced in the Jacobean era, as opposed to the liberty it had in the Elizabethan. Literature not only opposes the law of the possible and the permissible, but the law of God, a drama of opposition, guilt and punishment which Joyce in *The Portrait of the Artist* seems to have felt internally to a high degree. Half of Joyce's fun, his inspiration, seems to have been in finding this liberation-by-literature from pious sentiments and religious usage. His early idol was Henrik Ibsen whose plays famously scandalized playgoers and the public with their portrayal of nihilists, single and immoral women, and scandals in public life, wherein literature plays freely with the iron necessity of ordinary life.

Why should Derrida associate punishment with literature, indeed define it as the risk of punishment? Hölderlin, cited by Heidegger, wrote: 'the free imitation of art is a terrible but divine dream' (Heidegger 2000b, 136), because the possible becomes actual in art, and the real becomes ideal. Derrida's view of literature, the future, risk and democracy is also, however, quite consciously faced with the era and the orientation to literature which belongs also to the early twentieth century, particularly to the Weimar and Nazi era in Germany during which art and literature blended with life and political activity. Derrida often takes a basically Heideggerian-Conservative Revolutionary work as representative of the most prominent tradition, and the one of which he approves – with reservation. Literature is associated with the risk of punishment because, for Derrida, most of what literature proposes should neither be said nor carried out. Carrying out literary dreams amounts in Derrida's favoured authors, like Kafka and Joyce, to something of a nightmare. It is thus that he both likes and dislikes the way in which

Joyce tries to catch every aspect of normal life in one book, and in which, perhaps, Stephen Daedalus' statement that history is a nightmare from which he is trying to escape, applies to a novel of this sort (as T. S. Eliot seemed to feel on reading *Ulysses*).

What Lacoue-Labarthe seems to suggest (Lacoue-Labarthe 1990) is that in Alfred Rosenberg's *Myth of the Twentieth Century* and in other expressions of Nazi ideals (lambasted in particular in Syberberg's *Hitler: A Film from Germany* (1977)) the Nazi thinkers and policy makers entered into myth, acted out illegal, punishable literary dreams, turning literature first into myth, and then into policy. In the film, and quoting Hitler's inner clique, one of the puppets depicting the Nazi leaders rouses the members of the movement by telling them that one day they will be depicted in a great film, and memorialized as heroes if they act grandly and *as if* they were literary, mythic heroes (Syberberg 1977). Thomas Mann (1949) in *Dr Faustus* implies also that a sickness of the artist was the sickness of Germany as a whole, and that his artist-protagonist, Adrian Leverkühn, suffers from a deficiency in his grasp of reality as distinct from his imagination, so that his final religious composition takes place amidst what he sees as an actual dream of final revelation by Satan. Nietzsche too was not unaware that in turn-of-the-century Germany and in modern Europe the sensibility and the way of life of the artist has become the ideal, the ideal type of man. He considered this to be dangerous and sickly, for artists had hitherto been the 'chandala' and the accursed and outcast. Now they were in a position to run society with their fantastic dreams and boundless immorality, their free-thinking (Nietzsche 1968, §116). Nazis believed they could avoid the punishment due to criminals because they lost control of the distinction between literary and non-literary fact, as well as the distinction between themselves and figures from history and literature. They entered myth. In this way Derrida is situating himself alongside them in this key area of his thinking, but with a great delimitation.

Derrida does not insist that literature is always fictional, but as a more general definition, it is writing which is conscious of its status as writing. A diary for example is also literature and, as such, permitted by this institution of 'literature' to say anything and everything. De Man held that Derrida was a literary writer, a teller of a great story, though the story was not true (de Man 1983, 'The Rhetoric of Blindness'). In this way certain sorts of utterance or artworks are not properly literature. Homer's heroes desire to be memorialized, and desire only glory – a lesson given to the reader who is also intended by Homer to admire and imitate these aristocrats. So

Homer's intention is not to express his ideas, dreams or freedom, but to fulfil a social and religious role (although this religious role may only be *different* from the current democratic role). Modernism has a similarly dim view of all epic poets and myth-makers from the time of the origin of Christendom, singers who praised the murderous egoistic rapine of their masters, feudal and barbarian warlords. Eliot, who in this seems to agree in principle with Derrida, said that Virgil, not Homer, was literary, or, as he put it, is a 'classic' (*What is a Classic?*: Eliot 1974). Wagner, who was idolized at the time of Europe's great 'auto-immunitary' crisis, did admire these Dark Age epics for their social and religious function, basing *Parsifal*, *Tristan* and the *Ring* on such non-literary, mythical narratives as those of von Eschenbach, and von Strasburg, and the poet of the *Niebelungenlied*. (Wagner is quite extensively committed to this praise and mythicization of warlords and feudal rulers. His *Meistersinger*, though not a tragedy or a version of an epic, deals with German lyrical poets from before the Reformation. Wagner thus represents the growing cult of the totalitarian writing, Myth, as opposed to Literature.) One could see a parting of the ways on this question, a division within the European sensibility which hung around the Second World War, as one of its causes, between those who believe in literature as a right to be free, and those who see it as an expression of a law of behaviour. Tacitus' mythical narrative about the Germans in the *Germania*, and the genocidal, fratricidal vision of them in the *Niebelungenlied*, became the last word in German self-image throughout the nineteenth century, and blossomed back into 'life' with a decision to choose the hero in the 1930s, where the hero became the race- and family-obsessed epic barbarian.

Paul de Man's last works and lectures on 'Aesthetic Ideology' are of relevance here. De Man sought to show that the signifier is, like the referent, material, and hence, as a set of mere marks and inscriptions, should not be taken to be something which should immediately, without reflection, guide action. That is, the sign 'Aryan' could mislead one into thinking that there really is an 'Aryan' race, when in fact the materiality of persons and their distinctions cannot, except without great violence, be associated with the linguistic division of persons into separate races according to linguistic, mental signs. G. C. Spivak, Derrida's translator, and one of de Man's students at Yale, makes this point with reference to the term 'Aryan' in her work on post-colonialism (McQuillan 2001, 118). The material signifier in literature means nothing, but it invites us to dream and to become aware of the reality of reality.

15.7 The International College of Philosophy

Jean-Pierre Chevènement was the new socialist government's Minister for Education, and one who, by and large, followed the policies of the previous conservative minister, M. Savary. His policy was in favour of the 'old-school' education, and he attended to the public feeling that educational innovations had gone too far. He did not see the need for innovation, but for return. At the time when Savary was minister, public opinion had it that a primary school teacher taught nothing because he was not allowed to teach anything. Education was too lax (Hanley and Kerr 1994, 38). Change was needed, but teachers were to do it by taking back their traditional role, and should be relied on to do it. There were to be fewer innovative restrictions, but on the other hand philosophy was to suffer a reduction of time allowance since it was seen as the innovation-element, even though Chevènement had said that he supported Derrida's work for philosophy in schools.

The CIP, commissioned by Chevènement, opened its doors on 10 October 1983 (Caputo 1997a, 63), with Derrida serving a one-year term as its first elected Director, after which he was succeeded by Lyotard (Caputo 1997a, 68). He had been commissioned, along with F. Chatelet, J. P. Faye (an old rival from the *Tel Quel* days) and D. Lecourt, to found the College. Chevènement had commissioned a study to be headed by Derrida that led directly to the establishment of the CIP. Derrida's report[4] set out general categories for research: telecommunications, the life sciences, problems of medical sciences (genetics, transplants, etc.), smart weapons, and so on. In the first year of the college there was a seminar on philosophical problems surrounding hospital autopsies. Although Derrida had advised that philosophy should play a positive role in these areas, as the guide and teacher in how to tackle issues of relevance, he rarely thought on these matters himself. He was to do so with more openness in late interviews and dialogues which reflect EHESS seminars, and was also to give a more Derridean view of the role of philosophers in the coming years, when in 2004 he said that the role of philosophers in a reconstructed cosmopolitan world might profitably be that of observing and supervising the formation of laws passed by government, concentrating on the applicability of justice in individual cases.

John D. Caputo, of Villanova University, said that Derrida stressed research as his objective, and as the ideal objective of philosophy today. Of this research aspect of philosophy, and its contrast to the actual philosophical work of Derrida's generation, we may perhaps find something when Derrida's EHESS seminars are edited and published.

Unlike GREPH, the CIP was to have a long history, and even up to 2000 was still sponsoring events organized by UNESCO in France, and was hearing papers from Derrida. The CIP was after all a government-funded project.

15.8 The Mid-1980s

In 1984 Derrida's publishing output per annum expanded by three times its size during the 1970s and was consistent for ten years, until it tailed off again in the 1990s. One could say that this overexertion marked his reception fully into public life, and the way in which he now began to campaign, to prac- tise deconstruction in the public sphere, and in general culture, as well as in philosophy. Campaigning for philosophy during the 1980s, he became a radical. He also became adept at giving interviews as well as becoming self- consciously the founder of deconstruction, moving away from the Paris circle towards 'the world'. 1984, the year of this liberation, and the begin- ning of a massive output in articles, interviews and papers, was also the year in which he finished at the ENS, and moved to the *École des Hautes Études en Science Sociales* as Director of Studies, having been elected to that position by the school's members. It marked the end of a period in which he worked as a professor at one of the most prestigious institutions in France, but where he had held more recently an unworthily humble position. The history of the ENS in the twentieth century has yet to be written, although its place in cultural and political events would require a history invoking almost every event and major personality of the intellectual and cultural twentieth century. By and large the ENS had lost status by the period after the war, for while it had once been the breeding ground for the nation's political elite, this status was lost gradually to the ENA, the school of administration, during the 1940s and 50s. Simultaneously, however, its cultural place grew inordinately. It was the centre of structuralism, the base for Althusser, Lacan and Derrida. After structuralism, academic life settled down to a dispersed research amongst larger groups or teams rather than these solitary 'monsters'.

In 1984 Derrida travelled to Japan for a second time and spoke in Frankfurt at a conference with Jürgen Habermas.[5] He attended the opening conference for a colloquium on Joyce at Frankfurt, again, and delivered 'Ulysses Gramophone' (Derrida 1992c, 253–309). Derrida had read Joyce first at Harvard and, Caputo says (1997a, 181), had been at work on Joyce since the start, most of his work being done in the light of Joyce. Even the 'Origin of Geometry' as he studied it has been subjected to Joyceanism. In origin the overall aim of his work is, Caputo says, to expose what we call 'meaning' and 'ideality', science and philosophy, to this Joycean operation; to hold the feet of the identity and ideality of meaning 'to the fire of differance' (Caputo 1997a, 185). Derrida interrupted Husserl with Joyce, but did not thereby accept Joyce wholeheartedly. For being like Hegel, Joyce is like the German thinkers of cohesion, absolute knowledge and metaphysics, so that in Joyce we encounter a logic of Heideggerian 'gathering'.

In 1985 Derrida gave a paper in Israel, just preceding the Palestinian uprising. 'The Eyes of Language' (Derrida 2001a, 189–227), deals with a letter by G. Scholem, and discusses the renewal and use of the Hebrew language in Israel as the national language. This was the first time Derrida had visited Israel, the paper is the sign of a new vocal concern with Religion. The third such visit saw him deliver 'Interpretations at War' (Derrida 2001a, 135–88).

'The Eyes of Language' deals with Israeli culture and politics, and also expresses Derrida's desire to have a say on Israel in public. In private he sympathized with the Palestinians, but whether he took sides is another matter; he clearly did not, having given lectures in Israel. His expressed opinion at the turn of the century was that, since Israel existed, it was irreversible and its right to exist could not be controverted (Derrida 2004c, 119). His reaction to the US response to the 9/11 episode shows that he both disliked the deaths of the thousands there, and feared the irrationality of the US government, although he did not take sides as it were. He in general only took sides in matters where injustice was easy to distinguish, such as when speaking and acting as regards the death penalty in the US, Apartheid in South Africa, or the immigration policy of France in the 1990s.

Chirac replaced Mitterand in the spring of 1986, a Right-wing elected government; a bill for university reforms was in preparation. There were student protests against a bill which would allow universities more self-government on account of the removal of restrictions, which included those which kept fees down, determined admittance of students, and guaranteed degrees at the end of the course.

15.9 'Khora'

'Khora' [1987] is a simple text in its meaning, written by Derrida for a memorial volume for Jean-Pierre Vernant, the structuralist historian of

Greece, who had travelled to Baltimore in 1966, and co-founded the French Jan Hus with him. It was commissioned for a collection published by EHESS where Derrida was then working. *Khora*, as a word, appears in the *Timaeus* (Plato 1966), part of the trilogy also including *The Republic* (Plato 1977), found in a section dealing with cosmology and the origins of the universe, and of individual beings and forms. The khora is Plato's means of joining the sensible with the intelligible, but, as a receptacle, the khora seems to spill into the whole dialogue, because it is an empty spot, which cannot be contained, but which tends to contain. Derrida takes his time, repeating after Plato as he described it, situating it both in Plato's scheme and as it has been received by the scholars. *The Timaeus* covers everything, but halfway through it is found this 'Khora', an open chasm in the middle of the book (Derrida 1998d, 242). He decides that 'Platonism' itself is just an effect, an after-thought, since there is no Platonic text which could contain khora, no sure Platonism, but something infected by khora which interpreters have been anxious to pin down, to translate, to convert into a Platonic concept, in order to make Plato's work into a Platonic teaching. Aristotle himself characterized khora as 'matter' (Derrida 1998d, 259), but the translators and scholars of Plato must be more cautious, Derrida says, since it is clear that the Platonic texts contain elements which undo the text and a Platonic system, and which the text cannot master. The 'khora' is such a place of instability, which the Platonic text has no chance of subjugating. The desire to bring the West's memories back and to inherit some of them, good or bad, was this year to open up amidst deconstruction's own texts and members in a very mediatic way too.

16

1987–90, Deconstruction and National Socialism

16.1 Crisis in the Politics of Deconstruction

Since the beginning of the 1980s Derrida had tasted some success and acclaim from the French reading and academic public. He had travelled in South America and met Borges, he had worked with architects in New York, been elected Director of Studies at the EHESS, been the friend and associate of Mitterand and his Education Minister, and had found some celebrity after his imprisonment in an Eastern European state. He had also received regular teaching posts in Europe and America, being named A. D. White Professor at Large at Cornell University in 1982, for example. He had given a multitude of conference papers and lectures around the globe, beginning in Europe and North America in the 1970s, moving on to include Japan, Israel and South America, and his works were being translated continuously into other European languages as quickly as he was writing them. He had begun to campaign politically, and had generally entered public life, while remaining the thinker of an austere doctrine and an essential and smart new school of thinking with colleagues in the US and in France. In 1987 he received his second honorary doctorate – this time from the University of Essex, followed by another from Palermo University in 1988. By the late 1980s therefore there were groups of people inside the academic community who wished to diminish this Algerian-born Frenchman, whose ethical statements on behalf of the Other seemed to be impeccable, whose background, and devotion to philosophy, were beyond reproach, but whose 'patriotism' was suspect.

The later years of the decade saw the end of Derrida's inter-disciplinary, extra-university effervescence, and gave way to a more single-minded attention to a limited sphere, more serious and sedate, namely politics and ethics. These years also saw several scandals and demonstrations of open hatred towards Derrida and deconstruction. The charges brought against him were brought up in unorthodox ways, generally involving the use of media in a way which Derrida saw as unscrupulous, and usually by qualified people who were exploiting the public media and lowering the tone of their usual discourse. These charges tended to accuse his philosophy of being anti-Semitic in its origins on the Continent, and then ultramodern and multi-ethnic as well as 'obscurantist' and sham-philosophy, in the UK and America.

In retrospect there was a lot of fear in the motives of his attackers: fear concerning the territorial losses to be suffered by analytic philosophy, and jealousy because Derrida's star rose so high, and his powers and his range were so effective. Derrida's seminars at the EHESS show that he was both very mindful of racial and national questions, and that he was dealing with problems which were realist and relevant, rather than obscurantist. His courses included 'Nation, Nationality, Nationalism' (1983–84), 'Nomos, Logos, Topos' (1984–85), 'Kant, the Jew, the German' (1986–87), 'Eating the Other' (1987–88), and 'The Politics of Friendship' (1988–89), which was a seminar that week after week interpreted the phrase, attributed by Diogenes Laertius to Aristotle, 'O my friends, there is no friend'. The relevance of these courses was, however, mostly to Europe's future, something which UK and US readers may have missed or else despised, even though Derrida was in some sense trying to 'Americanize' Europe's future, and so the attacks on an apparently 'charlatan' Derrida began in Anglo-Saxon countries.

Indications that the accusations of Nazi sympathies and Right-wing proclivity were part of a general trend and not particular to Derrida were seen in the first murmurings found in *La Pensée 68* (Ferry and Renaut 1990), which was issued in 1986 and which condemned most of the structuralists, accusing them of being French versions of supposedly German Right-wing thinkers. Derrida was 'the French Heidegger'. Clearly this renewed dispute over fascism was part of a backlash against structuralism in general, the last remnant of which was Derrida.

1987 saw the beginning of these disasters and crises, plus his response, which was being undertaken without external pressure seemingly, but no doubt opportunistically and in self-defence. Generally speaking, the year of *The Heidegger Controversy* [1990] (Wolin 1993) marks the beginning of Derrida's turn to overt political statement and the beginning of what John

D. Caputo has popularized as Derrida's messianism which, being more of a coherent philosophical stand, his first 'system' since *Of Grammatology*, seemed to lend to Derrida's work something of an authority. Siding with Heidegger, by taking Heidegger's rectoral work seriously, and pointing out how it can be redeemed, Derrida from then on seemed always to be in Heidegger's position in 1933, announcing the Other in a straightforward way in each domain of culture, religion and politics. His personal life gradually came to the fore too, becoming something of a cult for himself and for interviewers alike, as noted by Bennington in his *Jacques Derrida*, 'Curriculum vitae' (Bennington 1999, 325–36).

In 1987 Derrida played in the work *Disturbance* by video-artist Gary Hill, and read *Feu la cendre* with Carol Bouquet for *La bibliothèque des voix*. More seriously, his messianism also developed in the *Of Spirit* lecture of 1987. That it had not been overt before does not mean that he had not meditated on religion and politics before, yet the concrete statement of it, as opposed to the hints and gestures towards it in early works, means that Derrida developed his messianism in public, in his lectures, gradually admitting to it with the confidence which comes of trying it out.

Derrida had a responsibility to explain his alignment to Heidegger after 1987. This too had not been something previously latent and suddenly bursting forth. Derrida had always been close to Heidegger, and had followed him, as a descendant in the tradition of an academic thinking which attempted to revolutionize the academic institution and the nation at large. Both Heidegger and Derrida used a style of thinking which faces the mystery of Being, just like philosophy hitherto, but without setting out 'results' of thought which could be learnt and methodized. With his messianism, his deconstruction primarily of the history of metaphysics, the last great figure of which was Heidegger himself, Derrida was ultimately critiquing and following Heidegger most of all. The purpose of the 1987 *Of Spirit* lecture (Derrida 1989) was to offer discrete alterations to Heidegger's *oeuvre* in its religious bias, its political statements and position, its influence as a force of centralization, and the Greco-Latinization of the West's thinking, which in Heidegger means the founding of philosophy in a thinking of the German homeland.

In practical terms, Derrida took away what made Heidegger a Nazi thinker, he denied the power of a present, appropriating Being; he made time into the gift of the Other, rather than the gift of meaning to a nation. This Other, as became clear with *Circumfession* in 1990 (Bennington 1999), was something called God – and its name remains undefined with the search of years – and Derrida's thought, especially after *Spectres*, also makes use of this religious coming of God in the perspective of socialist and Marxist politics, going so far as to place the theory of the Other at the heart of decrepit Marxist theory, so as to give Marxism a revival, under a deconstructive guise. In some degree, the passion for the Other and the coming of better things, in which one must have faith, things of a Marxist colour, is a structural politics (of passion not knowledge) which, Derrida says, he has always followed in favour of Marxism, and by implication, it is good enough to replace Marxism itself. Derrida finally announced a system in these years, which takes a political position.

Derrida is the more likely to have some influence and rightness in his minor changes of Heidegger and Marx, the Heidegger of politics and national language, national socialism and European German-Greek history, because he has not simply turned away from the catastrophic injustice and suicidal proclivity of the West, but has engaged it, in all of its evil and its triumph. By turning Heidegger's type of faithful, pious questioning of the world as a religious event, a miracle of its occurring, into one in which the same feeling and piety exists, but in a more passive, faithful, ethical and absolutely welcoming and limitless thinking, not based on any events or origins in the West, Derrida has taken his place as one of the points at which philosophy continues today to fulfil something like its old role. Rather than speak in a Rectoral Address affirming the national spirit of a new awakening in the present day, on behalf of a revolution in government and a *Volk*, Derrida had suspended such things for the moment, but he nevertheless looked to a deeper time to sort out the injustice or the lack of attunement to the nature of things in modern culture and politics. As a thinker and academic who did not get involved in a catastrophe, and maintained his balance, Derrida continued to speak on international politics into the 1990s, on religion, education and the personal existence of the subject.

16.2 *Of Spirit* [1987]

Derrida's *Of Spirit* tends to be Jewish and not Christian, aleatory and differential rather than gathering, hearing the call of the Other, not that of Being. It delivered thought from the Greek moment of a Being, which gives only to Germany and Greece, and turns towards a cosmopolitan future.

The text was a lecture delivered at the International College of Philosophy in 1987 at a conference entitled 'Heidegger: Open Questions'. Derrida's contribution, at the conclusion of the conference, attempts to show that Heidegger's work and thought is Christian, and that, despite Heidegger's supposed intentions, his thought on Spirit can even be seen to be Judaic, and, further, Derrida thinks, this is better. This is a very simple theme, and so it is a powerful lecture. If Spirit as 'fire' is specifically a German metaphysical result, how can it also be Judaic, or Abrahamic? But the obviousness of the fact that Heidegger never really treated of the religions of the Book, never placed himself explicitly in this context, never gave expression to what he owed to them, is something which one usually simply sees beyond, and does not speak of, or think of. Derrida therefore remedies a defect, and also makes a very obvious and bold statement. His lecture will also, Derrida says, look at Heidegger's politics, which Lacoue-Labarthe had first raised as a problem in his work on Heidegger in the mid-1980s (Lacoue-Labarthe 1990).

Geist,[1] after the Rectorate, became for Heidegger that which protects the piety of thinking, saving it from technics. Questioning rests on Spirit. In this emphasis on Spirit, a religious concept, which Heidegger refused to use in *Being and Time* for that reason, Heidegger had fallen into an old habit of German philosophy, namely to rethink and revitalize religion, or rather he had given 'mind' a religious dimension. But this slip had seemed so natural that commentators have forgiven it and made nothing of it. In the end we know that Heidegger admired Luther, and we admire Heidegger for being part of this tradition. But what does it mean that Heidegger is a part of the Christian tradition, despite his protestations to the contrary, wherein the condemnation of idealism and Greek philosophy is only presumed also to condemn Christianity and Judaic language? Heidegger seemed never to have commented on religion because it was not part of his work to go into that area, and so commentators have thought that they should do likewise, and not mention religion, or assume that atheism is straightforward.[2]

In the way in which we could say that Heidegger *refashions* religion, we see him refashioning the concept *Geist*. In his late essay on Trakl, who uses the adjective *geistlich*, Heidegger is at pains to show that the use of the word by Trakl is new, and is not Christian. Heidegger goes so far, in other places, as to argue that only the Greeks and the Germans have the word or concept *Geist*, the concept of a mind infused with a mystical power, and ultimately that only the Germans have the concept *Geist* (something so obvious that it might mislead one into thinking that it is deep, when it is in fact trivial). Heidegger never asked about *Geist* as he did about other classical concepts like Freedom, or Truth, or the work of Art, for there is no treatise on this concept, only remarks and uses. Why is this, and how much difference does it make that Heidegger consistently returned to this word, which is, it can be shown, used in a religious sense despite contrary declarations?

It is by means of Spirit that Being becomes metaphysical, Heidegger says in his 'Andenken' paper (Heidegger 2000b, 101–74). Spirit is found to be essentially temporalization. The fall of Spirit into time is history. The Spirit is thus, as it first appears, and as accepted by Heidegger, the spirit of a people, and the nation in its historical unfolding in time. It is voluntarism and decision. So how is Spirit related to Being? It is the force which questioned on behalf of man into Being and works in tune with the revelation of Being or Nature, as Hölderlin had it. The Rectoral Address is founded on the ability and the necessity of questioning, and the whole project of national revolution in the 1930s as Heidegger saw it would be based on this historical and revealing Spirit.

Derrida is concerned to show that Spirit is, for Heidegger, a human thing: animals do not have it. Hands are required for it. That is, as the human is the difference between god and animal, this concept, especially as Heidegger uses it, is a theological concept dependent on the difference between man, who has gods, and animal, who does not. Spirit is part of Heidegger's scheme of Being as Germany, and hence philosophy, is a super-anthropology. Now in the reading of Trakl, published in 1952 in *Unterwegs zur Sprache* ('Die Sprache im Gedicht; Eine Erörterung von Georg Trakls Gedicht'), it is found that the more original meaning of Spirit is 'fire'. In Hölderlin it had been related to *Sehnsucht*, and to be able to go out of oneself is the essence of spirit for Hölderlin, since Spirit is not at home in its human ground. This spirit-fire has nostalgia for its own essence (Derrida 1989, 80), especially in the lectures on 'The Ister Hymn' (Heidegger 1996), and in his long essay on Hölderlin's 'Andenken' (Heidegger 2000b, 101–73). Heidegger will find the essence of *Geist* by reading Schelling, Trakl and Hölderlin, in whom it means 'desire', and historical revealing. The final description, in 1953, is of Spirit as fire, flame, burning, conflagration. Flame because it touches and is consumed by things, never leaves things as they were, but dies or lives amongst things, revealing and enlivening Being. It is thus that in the 'homely' place, the lands of Germany, there was a fire of creation and destruction, coming and going: time. In Heidegger's poetic and non-metaphorical thinking, the essence of all things is in fact *fire*, especially timely things, like the sunset and dawn, and the sun's course over the year, which, being fire, permits beings to be. The poet's view of this Spirit, in which Being is setting the path for its unfolding, is more essential than the Christian view of fire and light, in which the pathfinder is God and creation. This poetic view is more spiritual, more in touch with Being, he says.

Now Derrida shows that the Judaic *ruah*, translated into Greek and Latin as *pneuma* or *spiritus*, contains, actually, the notion of fire in it too. Heidegger had chosen to leave the religious usage aside, but he had simply ignored it, and had ignored the religious origins of his formulations. Nazism was born in the realm of Spirit and culture in this maze of unconscious filiations which, as in this essay, have only begun to be followed. This questioning of these dark forest ways is leading, Derrida says, not to linking this to that, or making histories. It is the activity of following the entirely Other, what is origin-heterogeneous, and, following its trace, it crosses the Other (origin). That is, not the national origin, but the Other one. By exhausting and merely repeating the formulations of Heidegger, Derrida seems to say, one opens on to something totally Other, something from the future, an Other which is not one amongst many, but the most concrete opposite, and a progress towards something which is not Christian, or Nazi, or Judaic. By means of rereading and reinterpretation we will come upon a hidden, saving meaning for the future. Derrida speaks for Heidegger, and says on his repetitious retracing [*retraite*]:

> It opens onto what remains origin-heterogeneous. What you represent as a simply ontological and transcendental replica is quite other. This is why, without opposing myself to that of which I am trying to think the most matutinal possibility, without even using words other than those of the tradition, I follow the path of a repetition which crosses the path of the entirely other. (Derrida 1989, 113)

This is in fact a Heideggerian/Hölderlinian technique itself. As Hölderlin revived the Greeks, he also brought to light their underside, their Other. As Caputo (1997b, 103) points out, the Judaic texts also put fire in a prominent position as regards Being and the nature of what provides life. But the fire of the Hebrew God is the fire which destroys, rather than the fire which sheds light. The ashes of what fire produces by destroying create not Platonic truth, but non-knowledge, no light, the delimitation of knowledge. This is not to say that Heidegger knew that fire was also darkness and non-knowing, but that in the discourse of fire in the West as Spirit is implied the darkness of night, and if Spirit is fire, then it is also blind, and formed from the impossible and secret. By reading Heidegger in this way we find that the Spirit which guides the West, and which led the period of the Nazification of university and state, cannot lead to a good end, as one would hope, for it is blind and heads for the darkness. The fire's light does not reveal, it turns its objects to ashes; so genuine thinking and Spirit recognizes ghost-entities, not 'real' things. The religious fire which Heidegger has invoked is actually blind, it cannot lead to the reawakening of a particular *Volk*, and must not lead to exclusion, and so on. But it should, Derrida says, change into the spiritual sight/blindness focused on the Other.[3]

The conclusion then: Heidegger is Christian when we look at him now, or when rereading him. Derrida's task however is to read the text, to repeat it in another time, and to open it up to the Other, to find the Other beyond these Heideggerian and Judaic-based religions.[4] It works by placing these traces, or reading them as traces laid upon, inscribed within, that Other and what we know, for their basis was never firm, and was always the unknown Other. In Heidegger's failure to go beyond, to cross over, we read the success of it in another time.[5] Nevertheless this is still Heidegger's project.[6]

16.3 The Assault on De Man and Heidegger

Victor Farías released his work on Heidegger in 1987 (Farías 1989) condemning the German thinker in a quite unscholarly way, a way which shows that Farías had not read much Heideggerian philosophy at all, and Derrida was already prepared to defend Heidegger, as he had been continuing his work on him on nationality and nationalism in a series of lectures. Following the reception of Farías' book he gave an interview for the *Nouvel observateur*, 'Heidegger: The Philosopher's Hell' (1995b, 181–90), in which he affirms the value of Heidegger studies, dismisses Farías' claims and his scholarship, and says that it has nothing which real scholars did not already know.

The de Man affair, which was unrelated, but possibly motivated by a similar desire to discredit deconstruction, was first triggered by a *New York Times* article of 1 December 1987 ('Yale Scholar's Articles Found in Pro-Nazi Paper'), straight after the Heidegger affair, and implicating deconstruction with one of its two main agents. Jameson (1991, 257) says that de Man was simply writing for the paper as part of his job, and his later liberalism is not inconsistent with it. He also says that de Man's journalism was, in its anti-Semitism, ironic, and that usually, as is accepted, it attacked French/Belgian culture in the name of a superior, not biologistic German culture. For the sake of this, de Man had joined the discussion with anti-Semites in France and Belgium to rouse them to improve French culture, using the anti-Semitic rhetoric so as to make his point to them (Davis and Schleifer 1985, 258). In one of the articles (McQuillan 2001,127–9) he speaks of the Jewish influence on culture, and of this having done little to undermine the French novel. De Man refers to the Jewish influence as the anti-Semites referred to it, as an external rival.

These two crises in deconstruction were responded to by Derrida definitively only several years later when books were being published discussing Derrida's affiliations and taking his attitude for granted. The occasion was Richard Wolin's book, *The Heidegger Controversy*, in which, in its first imprint, Wolin had included a translation of Derrida's interview 'The Philosopher's Hell'. Ultimately Derrida had the interview removed from Wolin's book. Wolin says that what he had intended to show by publishing Derrida's interview was that

> the deconstructive gesture of overturning and re-inscription ends up by threatening to efface many of the essential differences between Nazism and non-Nazism. As a result, in the case at issue, the specificity and extent of Heidegger's commitment to National Socialism is severely relativized. (Wolin 1993, xiii)

Wolin says that if Husserl, as Derrida said in the interview, can be found to be of the same tradition as the rectoral Heidegger, still this confuses more than it clarifies. For, he says, Husserl tied his invocation of Spirit to no particular specific political programme. What Wolin seems to be saying is that Nazism was a historical oddity and that it is above all important to singularize Nazism and show how un-Western it is. Derrida, on the other hand, insists that in Heidegger, and the general German conservative culture to which he belonged, we see political gestures which are very familiar in history, but which had hitherto not been confronted. Traditional ideas were being repeated by the Nazis in a new form, because the Nazis were essentially, not merely ironically, Western European, so that on our part it will take more than a certain set of incantations and popular formulas, which simply repeat again Western Europe's logocentric imperialism, to avoid Nazisms of the future, and to understand the past. It is confusing that there are not actually very good distinctions between the Nazi/Heidegger voluntarism and the Christian tolerant, Husserlian voluntarism, which permits coexistence with others by force of volition. The subtext to Wolin's preface and to the whole text seems to be the simple and childish affirmation: 'I will not tie my work by public declaration to Nazism regardless of whether such an alliance exists in fact. There are some binary oppositions that need to be strengthened rather than "deconstructed" and, hence, relativized' (Wolin 1993, xviii).

Derrida's reply was that Wolin is simplifying and this is why refinements are confusing for him. He said of *The Heidegger Controversy* that it is a simple and unreflective distortion of a complex matter. Besides, what Derrida has done in his work on Heidegger, nationalism and philosophy is in line with established belief on the causes of Nazism in general; that is, that it was due to internal problems with the European tradition of transformed Christianity, imperialism and the exploitation of nature and the foreign as resources. Derrida has transferred this to the domain of its most recent thought and philosophy where a similar heritage is found to be at the heart of the crisis. For now, however, the Farías book and the scandal over Heidegger remained confined to France and would not bother him until it reached the USA.

16.4 'Force of Law' [1989]

October 1989 saw Derrida involved in a conference dealing with law, at the Cardozo School of Law, in New York,[7] the theme or title of the conference being 'Deconstruction and the Possibility of Justice'.[8] This colloquium marked an important development in the deconstructive research in philosophy, or in the theory of law in the US. The new expressions of humanistic concern, of ethical tones sounding in the lecture he delivered there ('The Force of Law'), indicate a turn in Derrida's thinking, a new openness, a post-communist leftist voice, which perhaps he had always had, but that now, in an age where genuine socialist thinking seems weaker than ever and deconstruction need not fear deconstructing the Marx who is already buried, he could express more openly. The essay is not really openly ethical. It is the setting in which it is given, and Derrida's approval of the colloquium which is new, even though its title is ironic in that genuine justice is the impossible, rather than the possible. It is new also in openly discussing politics, and law, the ethics of politics. Prior to the end of communism in Russia, to deconstruct Marx or the Left may have seemed to be a criticism of it, and may have appeared to the public and to his associates to be the tearing apart of what ought to be nurtured. But at this time there was no need to hold back from deconstructing the pillars of the Left because they had fallen already, and simultaneously, perhaps due to his fame and age, Derrida began to aver openly that deconstruction is actually a positive process of renewing old structures, keeping them going by presenting them with obstacles to overcome (rather like the capitalist system which thrives on objections). Deconstruction, which before had seemed aggressive and uncaring, taking apart what was structurally useful and apparently sound, and neglecting the interests of those depending upon it, was now said by Derrida to have always been an act of rendering justice. It makes realistic the dreams at the heart of a confused and aggressive system. It is this which, by evoking responsibility or choice in those who face these structures, forces the subject to recognize the Other, and to choose in responsibility this Other, this dream, ethically, and with a religious awe. 'The Force of Law' is one of the first texts to announce this new openness and religious feeling in Derrida, marking his late phase of writing and activity. It was here that he began famously to say that justice is not the same as law, and that justice can guide the thinking through of laws, but that law is often unjust. In other words, any law is deconstructible, but justice cannot be deconstructed. Purest, most real justice, is impossible.

Of the 'Force of Law' (Caputo 1997a, 17) Derrida says: 'Justice is never fully answered, I tried to show that justice again implied non-gathering, dissociation, heterogeneity'; and, 'A judge, if he is to be just, must never content himself with merely applying the law.'

In order to read and prove this, he examined a thinker who, with Nietzsche and Heidegger, he says, is the precursor of deconstruction, since he and the others thought it appropriate to destroy the present state of things so as to make way for a renewed future and history of the West – Walter Benjamin. In his essay 'Zur Kritik der Gewalt', Benjamin had described the need and manner of overcoming the state, with a biblical, not Western, or Greek violence. Benjamin's 1921 essay on violence and justice is Marxist in intention, and attempts to attack the power of the state and the legalistic power of the police and the government. He brings to attention the biblical power of violence and absolute revenge, favouring this unforeseen, and pure, violence, a violence of God, a law of freedom rather than of state and government. Derrida shows that this German-Jewish intellectual would, like Nietzsche, whom Derrida showed to have been in a similar state of complicity and apologetics with Nazism, have condemned the Nazis as those products of state violence and democratic representation which he had been arguing against in his essay. However, by the self-deconstructing logic of the text, Benjamin has actually legitimized the Holocaust, for he is unable to claim for sure that Nazism was not itself part of the Divine Justice, the destructive, life-favouring, state-destroying violence, the violence which could have been the non-humanly-comprehensible act of vengeance which is anti-democratic and anti-parliamentary, which annihilates. Hence, it was Derrida's intention to raise this problem in Benjamin's text, which complains that state violence is bad, while divine violence is good. Even though Benjamin is of Jewish descent himself, his ideas really make sense of the Holocaust as part of God's annihilation of the wicked so as to preserve the good, the agents of which can thus be seen to be the Nazis, agents, that is, of divine violence. 'One is terrified at the idea of an interpretation that would make of the Holocaust an expiation and an indecipherable signature of the just and violent anger of God' (Derrida 2001a, 298). Benjamin's text is too hasty in its explanation of the origins and nature of the Other; this discourse and others, all others, are complicitous in murder.

What is divine justice? It is opposed to nation-state modern parliamentary police-enforced mythical violence. State violence founds a state in a mythical and half-remembered act, and in subsequent violence it tends to sustain the state of affairs which it has created. Benjamin hopes to bring about a Judaic type of violence, of simple extermination of the wicked, rather than punishment of those who break the law. He wants utter freedom from the state, and utter revenge upon the unjust. Benjamin is trying to justify his desire to use violence against the entire body politic in a strike or a revolution. What makes the violence which he admires and wishes to see different is that this violence is absolute, not reparative. It cannot found a state, but only leave the wicked free to act until their day comes. In its practical aspect this violence is not really controllable or predictable, for God's justice exceeds our understanding and control. It destroys states rather than founding, in the name of the social claim of a people, like a revolt. Like *khora*, this divine violence is without borders, unforeseen, and sublime, it cannot be contained, and in this way, it defies Benjamin's clear-cut definition. But the Holocaust is a limit experience of state and total violence, so it blends easily into the divine type.

16.5 The Gulf War

Meanwhile, in 1990, Derrida's interest in the Final Solution, his incipient avowal of his Jewish identity and his 'secret' name, as well as his work on Europe, were added to with an opening lecture which he gave at an international colloquium organized by Saul Friedlander at the University of California (Los Angeles) on 'The Final Solution and the Limits of Representation'. The

West was at this time falling more and more into a fascination with simulacra and the fictionalized media event, from which it was imperative that it be given some sort of catharsis so as to save 'the event'. The hyper-inflation of the fictional, historical, mediatized, pre-interpretation of 'the event' by the Nazis and the Germans in general in the early years of the twentieth century had led them to lose their sense of justice and reality. It is clearly possible that such an aesthetic version of 'today' as a moment of a great period of history, based on an image of the past, or an ideologically produced, constructed, perfect state of the West, could again shove aside all scruples, suppress the real, produce an equivalent of the Shoah, or a catastrophic war in which dreams make the aggressors believe themselves destined to win, and in which reality comes back, if at all, only as utter catastrophe. The great Nazi dream was a 'twilight of the gods', mixed with a drive to continue Bismarck's expansion of Prussia, in which certain men become divinized by the fading away of gods, and the German people spreads itself thinly over all other types of peoples. Tragedy in the Greek sense follows along with this divinized feeling, as a fitting end for the actions of these chosen ones. Ironically, the keynote to Sophoclean tragedy is the 'reversal' or catastrophe, in which for once the protagonist sees the genuine event, the true state of affairs, with a clear head. In *Philosophy in a Time of Terror*, and in various interviews, Derrida stresses that thought cannot be rushed, that it must attempt to slow down political decision-making, since such decision-making will, if hasty, never reach the singularity of what really happens, the 'event' beneath the simulations, and henceforth it cannot decide properly. This whole debate was inaugurated by Heidegger amidst the breath-less decline and ruin of Europe in the 1930s, with reference to Nietzsche, when Heidegger said that the will to power expresses itself through art, and that power is the metaphysic which loses contact definitively with Being, or the truth of the spirit of the land and people. The question of technology and of every other Heideggerian theme is concealed here too. In spoken interviews Derrida reduces this complex to the problem of what an 'event' is, for convenience. This is a version of the old problem of what truth is, or what anything is – the question of the meaning of Being. In the end, Derrida is advising a discussion of Being, or truth, as a deterrent to the will to power, the excesses of art/media, and general irresponsibility in politics. Above all he calls for a slower growth, the greatest meditative caution, not to take truth for 'Truth', and not to take reality for the 'Real'.

At this time in the political sphere, the Berlin Wall fell, and with it Soviet communism, and, shortly after, the Gulf War began, with which French intellectuals seem to have had far more problems, and had more to say, than those in Britain or America. The French debate, involving famously Baudrillard and Lyotard, is reasoned, objective, though cynical, and is discussed in the terms of post-modernity, or in Derrida's case, of deconstruction itself. John Pilger (1994), Noam Chomsky (1999) and the Anglo-Saxon commentators of note on the Left take a more factual view, and condemn the events out of hand, somewhat to their detriment as critics. They do so in the same breath as they condemn any other Western activity abroad. Their isolation, unlike the French generational-movement tradition of forming cliques, mobilizing and voicing public opinion, makes the Anglo-Saxon Left despair of being heard if their voice does not rise to a continuous description of abuses, while the French tone is one confident of finding consensus and it theorizes. Derrida admired the French response of caution in dealing with the Middle East. He declared the Gulf War, then beginning, to be deconstruction at work in the political and factual realm, since it witnessed the repressed foundation of the West's culture resurfacing. He saw the West's culture in part to be founded on representation and technology. The origins of the second Gulf War of 2004 would be, for him, caught up in non-events founded on simulations, events hidden beneath commentary and representation, as Baudrillard had said of the first War. Derrida said that it was not so much a war as an event of the West deconstructing itself, finding its foreign allies and its very self as they are represented to be more or less illusions, and containing a *khora* or an impossible element hopelessly containing and contained (Derrida 2001b, 136). He called its recurrent crises with former allies and terrorists a system of 'auto-immunitary' processes in which the body attacks itself (Derrida 2002a, 98).

17

Autobiographical Years, 1990–91

17.1 *Memoires of the Blind*

Memoires of the Blind: The Self-Portrait and Other Ruins (Derrida 1993a) is the companion text to an exhibition of paintings shown at the Louvre. Derrida was invited to choose his own selection of paintings and drawings from the Louvre collection, as the first of a series of living thinkers and famous writers who would receive this invitation, a series entitled *Parti pris* by the museum's curators.[1] The exhibition was given between 26 October 1990, and 21 January 1991. Derrida chose the theme of blindness, and concentrated on self-portraits, selecting mostly drawings and paintings from the old masters (Caputo 1997b, 309). The text, which accompanies the exhibition, reveals the theory of drawing or writing one's self, and the blindness which always prohibits a proper view of the self by itself. This blindness, a crippling illness of the knowledge which the subject has of itself, is also a blessing since it allows the self to be open to the Other instead of being wrapped in its own existence.[2] Blindness is constitutive of any attempt at knowledge at all, and is a blessing in precisely this way: it demands faith and a certain passion for the unknown, a certain openness to the future and to others. As such the blindness depicted in the chosen paintings of Hebrew biblical stories is the occasion for thanking and welcoming God, as the pictures show.

On the cover of the book is a self-portrait by Fantin-Latour, one of whose eyes is hidden in shadow, the other staring at the observer, both half-seeing and open. To be blind is desirable. It makes one full of prayers and tears, open to the unknown and freedom, and though we have no choice in this, it is helpful to recognize the structural blindness of the knowing subject so that the Other may come.[3]

The period in which Derrida chose his set of drawings and paintings for the Louvre was also the time at which he was composing his own autobiography or self-portrait, in which he is seen to be so obsessed by blindness with regard to himself, and knowledge of a God whose proper name he cannot work out, about whom he is blind. It was a time at which he thought that – suffering from Lyme's disease, a painful facial paralysis[4] that affected one side of his face, never permitting him to close one of his eyes – he would die soon, even before his mother, who was then in her final year. The illness forced him to delay a meeting on 5 July 1990, with the curators of the museum, until 11 July (Caputo 1997b, 316). The whole text of *Memoires*, and the choice of the pictures, is littered with references to himself in quite unuseful ways for the writer of a biography. The gallery selection of pictures of blindness is clearly affected by his own paralysis, while the choice of Hebrew images is affected by his new revelation of himself, hitherto a secret, as the Last Jew. The self-portrait theme of *Memoires* self-consciously aligns itself with his secret work in *Circumfession* and 'The Book of Elie', the latter being written in the late 1970s.

Derrida admits that part of his fascination with 'drawing as a blindness' is due to his not being able to draw, a feature of his education and youth which caused him some discomfort and jealousy, especially towards his brother, who was a talented artist. Drawing's transcendental resource, as Derrida is at some pains to show, rather ignoring the exhibition itself, is the blindness which prohibits one from both seeing the drawing one is doing and the object drawn at the same instant. From the beginning the drawing is a ruin, or an artefact, which is not a complete reproduction of the original.[5] Again, the possibility of drawing, as with the possibility of literature for de Man, is due to there being an inherent opening of nothingness between the memory which the artist draws from in order to see what he is doing whilst drawing, and that which the artist or writer is describing itself. The self-portrait in the same way is a ruin, a fantastic, traced speculation on what one really looks like, for there is no seeing that sees itself seeing. Derrida almost doubts that there can be such a thing as the self-portrait, 'if there were such a thing, if there remained anything of it'. All symmetry is interrupted between the portraitist and himself. This structural inability, productive of works of art which attempt each to create a perfect estimate of the original, and failing to do so, ruined from the start, is like the inability of language to explain itself too, the inability of language or consciousness to catch up with itself, the fatal flaw of all sciences of everything hitherto and today. But the blindness to facts is traded off for another sight, as the Bible has it, and as the Greeks, who made Homer a blind man, had it also. What I cannot see of myself, the Other may see, and what I miss of myself, I see in the Other. This blindness grants to each individual the possibility of a community greater than itself. In a strange alignment to Paul de Man, or what Derrida said of de Man in his *Memoires*, Derrida characterizes such ruined art, or literature, and self-portraiture, as allegorical, in an economy of blindness which creates inadequate allegorical likenesses. Being blind to empirical things, the artist or believer is free to impose meaning on them, he is free to write because he is always incapable of doing so with perfect accuracy. In the terms of the year of *Circumfession* and *Memoires of the Blind*, Derrida puts it that the eye is not for seeing (not being able to see properly the truth), but for crying and weeping. The very tears which blind me to myself by filling the eye with a film of water are those which open up sight on to the Other, who is approached not with the eye of sight and the light of knowledge, but with the heart of passion and the faith that the Other is real and valuable. Life is carried forward by faith, the secret sets life in motion. God was for Aristotle (1961, XII) the cause of time and motion, and here Derrida puts the Other as its cause in much the same way, except with the difference, which is Hebraic, that God is not a Mover, or a Maker of the world, but rather an Unknown, an opening. Derrida likes the attitude of faith, and is persuaded also that in a situation of blindness, and of not knowing the future, faith, no matter how delimited by knowledge, is the correct attitude, and no mere religious injunction. One does not know the pure Other, one has faith, love for it.

The spectre of Kierkegaard's knight of faith seems to appear here, although it does not become corporeal (Kierkegaard 1985). Derrida was to challenge the faith of this knight in *The Gift of Death* (1995a), but not specifically insofar as Kierkegaard's faith was too limited, but because it was Christian and Western and lent itself to religious conservatism, an exclusive superiority, as Patočka was to read the knight's adventure. In fact the hyperbolic situation into which Derrida sends his reader is a situation less extreme and worrying than those conjured up by Kierkegaard, in, for example, his shocking *The Sickness Unto Death*, in which the sense of the failure of signs to account for reality drives Kierkegaard back into 'despair'. Of course, that this was a thinking which resorted to the 'leap' and to faith, and is a philosophy of 'acts', has its decisive importance in Derrida's work (Kierkegaard 1989). By the by, the faith and the leap also appear in Heidegger's *Contributions*, a book announcing that the thinkers of the future must wait and be faithful, must feel the turmoil of their inability to think meaningfully about deepest nature, with tears and prayers maybe, listening for the echo of Being, and prepared for the leap into its coming (Heidegger 1999, 257–8; and 216 ff.).

17.2 *Jacques Derrida* [1991]

Jacques Derrida was written by both Derrida and Geoffrey Bennington, but at different times, and at cross-purposes, yet by prior arrangement. Bennington's intention was to provide a summary of what he saw as Derrida's philosophy, but to do so without making any quotation of works, and to confine biographical information to an appendix. He had agreed with Derrida on these terms since it left some space for Derrida then to make his own sub-commentary, or answer to the text which Bennington was to write, in his own words (hence the absence of quotes by Bennington). Without biography or quotation, then, Bennington wrote a commentary on Derrida's work up to 1990 which tends to clarify the action of his texts, concentrating on what he has done to words, what he thinks of texts, and what is ethical in his books. In simple terms he gave what Derrida called a 'computer programme' for how to write books like Derrida's. Derrida's contribution was *Circumfession*, which had not been foreseen by that computer programme. It is biographical, emotional, tortured in its style, and makes a few important announcements. For instance, since this was the first sustained critique of himself, Derrida had, in order to escape being predictable, to reveal what is more secret to his works than hitherto he had revealed. He described his childhood, his personal feelings about himself, his Jewish ethnicity, his mother, and above all, a sort of religion without religion which he had always followed.

Bennington was as if the first to write a book on Derrida's philosophy as a whole, with the intention of popularizing and explaining it to that extent, in a brief schematic form. It should not go unnoticed for many reasons that he is an Englishman with links to the USA, and that Christopher Norris had recently published his own *Jacques Derrida* in 1987. It is unfair to be too hard on Bennington's part of the book, which is indeed like a computer programme, as Derrida says, for it was actually pre-programmed by Bennington and Derrida to be so in the initial dual-authorial agreement. Many of the things which Bennington did not know or see only came to light when Derrida responded to his work.

Bennington did not do too bad a job of describing Derrida's texts, although if we read him as Rorty does, for the enjoyment of reading what he has to say on philosophy, and for how he reads, rather than actually what he does which is original and apparently traditional, then this 'Derrida' is hardly recognizable. The pleasure of the text seems to get lost in Bennington's *Jacques Derrida*. Bennington has done to Derrida what Heidegger did to Nietzsche in his 1930s lectures. Bennington does, however, have some original ideas about Derrida, which he expressed when he wrote the text 'Mosaic fragment' collected in *Derrida: A Reader*, after having finished his *Jacques Derrida* and having read the reply (Bennington 1992, 97–119). In the earlier text he had not emphasized Derrida's Jewishness or his private life, but he had speculated that Derrida belonged to a time before time, to Egypt perhaps, where writing had first developed. In the later text he once again resorts to this place which is not a place, a time not of time, a point which was before history, a religious place without religion, a non-locatable place which somehow is still a site, if only a speculative site by which we can carry out a line of reasoning. It is called 'Egypt' because it is neither Greek nor Jewish, but since, as he shows, it could be suspected that the Israelites and the Spartans came from Egypt originally, then prior to the Jew–Greek opposition there was a site which could conveniently be called 'Egypt'. Derrida as an Egyptian when writing is neither writing of the law, nor writing of Being. Bennington, in this rather literary text, aligns Derrida to the early Egyptian god Thoth, or in Greek, Hermes, the god of writing and of trickery and messages, also the god of *life death*, the god who crosses the line. Most of Bennington's text is extracted from Freud's work on Moses (*Moses and Monotheism*) which explains how Moses was an Egyptian, maybe a member of the cult of Thoth, an old god who had been overcome by a new dynasty and a change in the times. Both Moses and Lycurgus, the mythical Spartan lawgiver, may thus be seen as old Egyptians who gave to their provincial teachings the aspect of eternal laws, as if in fact they were charlatans, and, in the perspective of Egypt, this is exactly what they would have been.

1989 saw the third serious decline in health of Derrida's mother, Georgette, who was then nursed at her home by hospital staff. Her illness and her loss of memory, and of awareness generally, was the occasion of Derrida's self-confession in his section of Bennington's work which was inserted at the bottom of the book's pages. In *Circumfession*, in contrast to the *Confessions* of St Augustine, with which it is in constant dialogue, the death of the mother, the motive for writing, has not yet happened. But it may happen at any time, and really has already occurred insofar as death is already with life. What is the point of this work which writes on the death of the mother? What effect is produced, if any at all, and has any been intended, or is it a personal whim that he writes on it, an artist's prerogative to take any inspiration as it were, an occasion for textual production? The question is, who or why would one write at a time like this? What is the occasion? How does Derrida secretly see this event, or coming event, so that he has created a text around it?

Maternity signifies most of all the moment of birth, the singularity of coming into life, and hence just as a person is singular, so is a person's birth. It is then a personal matter. It is also banal, and speaking of the death of the mother, this text deals with it crudely and without genuine feeling. Yet the author knows his style. He also knows that what is crude will possibly be missed, and will not even raise surprise. To begin with his mother herself will never read it personally, although maybe she would, he hopes, take that opportunity, should she hear of the scandal. Then, she is almost dead in her soul, her memory lost, and she does not recognize her son throughout the year of the text's composition. In sum, the other person does not need to be dead in order to be almost completely absent, ill or not.

So what would be the classically stated purpose of the text in respect to his life, and his fate as the 'Last Jew' as he tries to make sense of his circumcision? He attempts to rewrite upon his 'sex' a code of openness and servitude to language, to the nameless impossible Other, not to God or mother (who no longer sees), or to Geoffrey Bennington, his biographer/apologist, but to the absolute and the impossible which also does not see him, but perhaps may do so. In this respect, his mother, the Other, had to be brain-dead, like Bataille's Christian/Hegelian God who if 'he knew everything would be a pig'. And if a person knows nothing, then, actually sovereign, and knowing nothing, he is not a person at all (Bataille 1988, 103). The conflict opened up in *Circumfession* is the conflict of the individual with the imposition of a universal code of divine and human law upon that individual, and the struggle to gain a super-Hegelian recognition from the Other.

His mother, in fact, filled with the near immanence of death, takes the place of God, divinely unknowing like him, and in consequence Derrida's personal peculiarities, the secret of self, is liberated from the law. She is also the Other who sees or may not see his true character. What is most secret about those who are mortal, who are knowing and non-knowing, temporalized and, in respect to religion and philosophy, who are named, circumcised and known, communal? Most secret to them is that they are possessed of freedom. What is least known, unnameable about the body, the event, the actual world? Chance, the chance of error and failure, or of success. What the text circles around is probably, in metaphorical terms, or metaphysical terms, freedom, and the chance of liberty, the fact that chance is one's own and nobody else's chance, just as death is always singular, and unshared, totally singular. But 'freedom' cannot be a name for it, for freedom is a possibility for anybody. What is most secret must be genuinely singular.

'God' is also 'Geoffrey Bennington', and again his mother, Georgette. Any of them could be 'G'. In spoiling his mother's memory, recircumcizing himself and avoiding Bennington's totalizing computer-programmed predictable 'Jacques Derrida', nothing else is being done than expressing, but not saying, not voicing, but performing, the great capacity of freedom. Such freedom and chance, if it, as we suppose, is the essence of life, cannot fail to succeed in this endeavour either, for if it could not evade G, it would be of no value, and would not be the most free secret. But really this aim is 'the impossible'.

So the text sets about performing a circumfession in which it allies itself to its name and the law, and also asserts freedom by inscribing the traced line between the self and the law. Its intent is to constitute itself as abiding 'text', and to let flow on to the Other, after it has spectralized, machinalized 'G', so as to make way for the true self and to appreciate the real death which comes, rather than the pre-programmed, obvious one. The means thereto is the crude word, *le mot cru*, the word of blood, *cruor*, which flows. Simultaneously the text is a static entity, a material inscription formalistically composed, of fifty-nine sentences, which flow, and do not halt, except at a predetermined point of a given quantity of lines of published text. The number fifty-nine is arbitrary, like the fact of the continuous sentence.

It if were written in blood, in that it genuinely was a flooding into the Other, it would be the death of him: the impossible would come definitely. This is what he dreams of perhaps, a text of blood, one section for each year of his life, from birth from the mother, to her death, his life passing. It would express all of his inner body on a page outwardly, like a syringe pen. Incidentally the 'autobiographical' writing of which we have nothing in Nietzsche's text, would be written on the body, passing with time, neither a work of writing, nor the immediate self-awareness of the living, human 'Nietzsche'. But it would mean nothing but the passing of a life, from life to non-life, if it were simply death. A shock, a puddle of blood, would be a crudely intimate trace of a life expressing itself to the Other. This is an aim, but an impossible one, for then he would no longer be alive to recognize the

Other who recognizes him (one never sees the ghost, though it sees us, as *Spectres* has it, and without the desired intimacy Derrida and G are just ghosts). The relation of not being seen and yet confessing, asking pardon, is love.

Above all Derrida wants this puddle of blood to say 'I', but by writing he has always missed it, and cannot afford the loss of blood. The distance of this thesis from that of Lacan, and structuralism in general, is surely incalculable. But it was possible to read this utterly impossible confessional element in the very first works of deconstruction, one feels. The tone of impersonal aggression in *Writing and Difference* seemed to be a covert self-expression, a covert defence of pure subjectivity against the 'sciences of man' or structuralism and Husserlian phenomenology. All of his writing has aimed at saying it, but will always miss it, due to the effect of the Other's proximity. Rather than use crude words, and red blood, he uses periphrasis, for he has always turned around what he wishes to say in each impersonal philosophical text (Bennington 1999, 13). It never takes place if it is said, this immediate self-presence of 'I' and of 'I' to the Other. We called it freedom, but freedom, being free, precisely avoids names. Finally we must make do with a writing which flows, into the Other, by periphrasis and circling, and crudity, wandering, reading, in absent traces. And this is his autobiography! Just like his usual work. *Circumfession* as a concept is another chance for a written event of recognition by a sovereign superhuman mind and existence, aware that it is only written in a half-light, but pointing towards a more genuine revelation. He renames himself by this periphrasis, keeps his true name, the name which is normal and legal, yet also shows something once secret, the forbidden, and unforeseen, and totally individual. If the text does not name his complete individuality, it can at least circle around it.

18

The Future of Democracy and the Very Worst Moment of Capitalism

18.1 'The Right to Philosophy from the Cosmopolitan Point of View'

This paper was given at the first International Conference on Humanistic Discourses hosted by UNESCO with sponsorship from the CIP. Derrida turned to Kant to express the hopes for the future and the practice of the past. Kant had held that Europe must lead the world, and as Derrida said in *The Other Heading* (1992a) in the previous year, this Kantian vision of a Eurocentric modernism depends upon a certain Rome and Greece. This European centralizing tendency of empire building was something which Derrida held on to to orientate himself, as an object to deconstruct and to uphold. He saw hope in this project insofar as, for him, philosophy is universal and not conditioned by any language or place as, although it is Eurocentric, it can overcome specific boundaries such as this. Even if a philosophy derives from a specific land, by means of the spirit and language of a certain people, its concepts are always translatable.

What is required for a deconstruction of Europe's disastrous course, and the improvement of its ignominious diminishment in the late twentieth century, is a philosophy able to think this Other origin or 'other heading', a new vision, maybe derived from religion, certainly contained in the unfolding of the past of its culture. Thus he was against the epitomizing Western philosophy of Kant in certain respects. He was also against current philosophy, for there are several histories of philosophy, and why should one dominate? At present the two dominant hegemonies are the Analytic and the Continental philosophies, which, to free the thought of the political future, have to be deconstructed, and the colonial attitudes must be put aside.

In regard to the right to philosophy which Kant advised, Derrida remained a Kantian (Derrida 2002b, 13). Philosophy must be off limits to no one, man or woman, and must be autonomous with regard to religion and science, which cannot affect it internally, but can do so by force from without. It is indissociable from democracy, a 'democracy to come'. The right to think and the demand to think which Derrida conceived philosophy to be essentially, the right to question, is coterminous with the existence of genuine democracy.

Derrida discusses the economic imperatives of decision in liberal-capitalist societies:

> For me, it is not a matter of indiscriminately contesting all of these imperatives. But the more these imperatives impose themselves – and sometimes for the best reasons in the world, and sometimes with a view to developments without which development of philosophy itself would no longer have any chance in the world – the more also the right to philosophy becomes increasingly urgent, irreducible, as does the call to philosophy in order precisely to think and discern, evaluate and criticize, philosophies. (Derrida 2002b, 15)

Basically, philosophy is today in danger of being completely forgotten. Nowadays philosophy is suffering because of limited resources, since capital invests itself only in what will return to it. Military imperatives, end-orientated sciences and 'educational standards' take priority over this activity of mere wondering and dreaming. In regard to supporting philosophy, Derrida can be very direct, for if a universal union of the human race is to be attained, as a democracy, philosophy is essential, and UNESCO could help, he says, to aid philosophy, and thus lead towards its always hoped for, dreamed of, destination. Such is the core message he gave at the UNESCO conference on humanistic discourses.

18.2 *The Other Heading*: Europe

The Other Heading (Derrida 1992a) was occasioned by a request by a journal for the opinions of prominent thinkers on the subject of Europe in 1991. Derrida's response was marked by two distinctive sorts of feeling about Europe: first the experience of the outsider in Europe, projecting a Europe in which the New International of citizens could find its place; and secondly with a view to Europe's promise, as witnessed in its triumphal rise in its history, especially its destiny as the power which organized and recognized itself on religious and tolerant principles. Derrida had always felt out of place in Europe, but his expression of himself seems to balance between the feeling of being on the margins which Nietzsche had, and on the other hand the more hidden call for an improvement and strengthening of Europe which is quite conservative. More and more the first sort of explanation for his feeling, that of being condemned, took precedence with the years, so that looking back after his death, it seems as if what Caputo and Malabou had said all along may have been true, that he was a *marrano*, or the Algerian Arab, with dark skin as a child, and a painful feeling of being ethnically Jewish, in the way that most Westernized Jews like Wittgenstein, Husserl or Freud were not. In this way, it would be dishonest of Derrida to valorize an exclusionary Europe, and his response was pre-programmed. On the other hand, his response is no less the expression of a philosophical tradition, and no mere expression of reaction against European history. To progress, Europe cannot remain static, for stasis is death.

Like most of Derrida's positions (including his relation to himself), his position on the future of Europe is Nietzschean. A good Europe, composed of good Europeans, needs its Others. Nietzsche's 'blond beast' was the creation of Nietzsche's reading of the past, and of the Other: Japanese knights, Vikings, Homeric aristocrats, Teutonic knights, and so on were examples of this 'beast' – that is to say, examples of cultures distant from Athens and Rome, those of the prehistory and margins of Europe (Nietzsche 1994, 25).[1] Nietzsche's absolute openness to foreign influence, openness to Asian philosophy, to French culture, and Italian Gothic culture, mirrors the absolute hospitality of Derrida's future Europe. There is nothing particularly socialist about this, and its democratic element is only owing to the penchant Derrida has for absolute hospitality, without limits, which means that he does not wish to foresee arbitrary creations of elites, although he does believe in an aristocracy of sorts (Bennington 1999, 63). Being open to the Other could obviously just as well be the ruin of any socialist levelling or liberation as it could be of value to any Marxism or socialism of Europeans themselves. The Other cannot be controlled. Nietzsche said that such openness would ruin the weak and select the strong. So Derrida's attitude is really neither Left nor Right at its extreme.

This coming of the Other is implicit in Heidegger's waiting for the coming of the Other origin. Deconstruction must not merely do its duty in this, but be responsible to the good and bad for Rome and Athens. Derrida's grand and practical scheme for making way for the Other as a necessity is also similar to Bataille's scheme for post-war Europe, with its acclaim for the lavish spending of the Marshall Plan (Bataille 1991, 169–90), where he also says that many rational expectations must be set aside in the name of a General Economy, which, as an economy, gives funds for the self to be able to give itself to the Other, and yet be defenceless in a welcoming state which is ostensibly an event, but is also internal to us. Of course, Derrida holds himself open to 'sovereignty' for ethical reasons and not economic ones.

His work on education and philosophy continued, seeing the publication of his *Du droit à la philosophie* in 1990. In 1989 he had submitted a report to Lionel Jospin (the education secretary) with Jacques Bouveresse, on the content of philosophy teaching, entitled the 'Commission on Philosophy and Epistemology', which he chaired. He and Bouveresse, co-president for the commission, were cordially invited to form a study group, and they put in months of work consulting the unions, and all of the professional organizations. The French intelligentsia gave him their usual treatment: denunciations and insults. The government did not take the advice (Derrida 1995b, 336).

Louis Althusser died in 1990. Derrida had been visiting him for some time as his only permitted visitor at the hospital where he was incarcerated for the murder of his wife.[2] At his funeral Derrida delivered a speech, for which he returned from Prague, where he was at that time. Also a text was read at Joe Riddel's funeral at UCLA, delivered in Derrida's absence. A lecture was delivered remembering Foucault this year too, at Saint-Anne Hospital, Paris, on 23 November, discussing Foucault's *Madness and Civilization*, and the 'Cogito' essay which Derrida had written nearly thirty years before, in which he had left it undecided whether the cogito could be formulated by a madman, implicating every act of reason in a madness which could not be repressed by philosophy. The paper was later collected in *Resistances of Psychoanalysis* (1998a). The possible death of his mother is a concurrent subtext to these meditations on death too.

As we have already seen, in 1990 another problem arose over Heidegger, as the Victor Farías scandal reached the UK and the US.[3] It marked the start of persistent and open dismissal of Derrida by a large and authoritative part of the Anglo-Saxon academy, of a kind which he had been used to only in France. Bennington's assessment of the divide between France and the rest of the world, in terms of the hospitality offered him in the preceding few years, had not anticipated this. If Bennington is right to say that, prior to 1990 and his own *Jacques Derrida*, overseas Derrida had received great acclaim and a warm welcome (Bennington 1999, 331), then it was only now that he first received opposition and resistance from overseas institutions and groups, as America and the UK began to lambast and reject deconstruction.

Several attacks were launched simultaneously, or coincidentally. What their motives were is not entirely clear: for one thing, certain American and British writers may have thought that they were defending 'The Canon' from Derrida, although such a motive would have been misguided. Then again, some were defending the integrity of Heidegger, or other strong and typically conservative philosophers. Heidegger is not, himself, a typical member of the Canon, and the attacks have the appearance of a certain fratricide. Richard Wolin published his *The Heidegger Controversy* that year, being a collection of documents centred on the notion of Heidegger's guilt during the war era. Wolin's book, which had clearly been conceived by him as an English-language counterpart to Farías' work, assumes such guilt and organizes texts around it so as to prove it. At the end of the volume Wolin presents a round-up of Heidegger's influence, especially on the Continent. He had included in the first edition an unauthorized translation of the 'Heidegger: The Philosopher's Hell' interview which was supposed to give an indication of how structuralist France had received the news that Heidegger was implicated in Nazism. On its reprint in 1993 (by a different publisher), Wolin, having been forced to remove the unauthorized translation, had the book reviewed by Thomas Shehan, who devoted a third of his review to an attack on Derrida, and the fact that Derrida had forced Wolin to withdraw the first edition. A controversy ensued, held in *The New York Review of Books*. Derrida called the collection of documents weak, simplistic and compulsively aggressive towards Heidegger. It was 'a bad book', and the Derrida interview was, as a translation, 'execrable' (Derrida 1995b, 453). The controversy lasted some months, Derrida commenting on the low level of the debate, the fact that debate was being reduced by the media in which they were arguing, and the irresponsibility of *The New York Review of Books*. The 1993 edition of Wolin's book said in its introduction that Derrida was contradictory and irresponsible.

Derrida said of the year 1992, which saw the aftermath of the Gulf War, the end of communism, the heightening of problems in the Balkans, and his own problems with the journals and academy, that it was the worst moment, the very worst moment of capitalism. He was writing on Marxism, work that would be published the following year as *Spectres of Marx*. At that time, in 1992, a letter to *The Times* was published on 9 May, written by twenty intellectuals in ten countries, which Derrida called 'an abuse of power' (1995b, 401). The letter denounced Derrida's work, was obviously inaccurate, and those making it cannot have read much of Derrida's work at all. The occasion of the letter, which surely expressed a violent and uncomprehending hatred, was the nomination of Derrida to an honorary degree at the University of Cambridge, against which, for the first time in thirty years, there were objections amongst the panel of judges (who consist of the members of the university). Three dons expressed their disapproval by means of the *non placet*. Though Derrida's case for the degree had to be voted on, and he subsequently had more support than he had objections (with 336 to 204 (!)), it showed to him, in an area for which he had been working most of his life, just how bad the neglect of reading and philosophy had become, since those objecting had not read him, nor were they, in the case of the signatories to the letter to *The Times*, connected to the University of Cambridge. They had resorted to non-academic means to argue against him, using newspapers in which no invalid argument would be questioned, and in which the reader usually believes what is given. After this, *Der Spiegel* in Germany further betrayed the nature of the media and publishing industry, by entitling a piece on him 'Gift für den Geist'. Roger Scruton, without provocation, and with obviously little knowledge of what he was dealing with, said of Derrida, and was quoted in *Der Spiegel* ('Gift für den Geist', no. 16, 1992), that his work was 'pure nihilism' and was 'poison'. Scruton made numerous other allusions to Derrida in the same way, without any provocation, as did, it might be said, a large number of other British philosophers and writers (Derrida 1995b, 405–6). It was at this time that Derrida was beginning to announce the ethical dimension of his work, which he had kept quiet for tactical reasons in the past. That so many were suffering the same lack of moral rigour showed a disease in the academic structure, something also worrying to him, as he had worked for philosophy and philosophical standards for so long. There was something very wrong, it seems, with the establishment of philosophy.

18.3 *Resistances of Psychoanalysis* [1993]

Resistances contains three lectures given in 1990 and 1991, on Freud, Foucault and Lacan (Derrida 1998a). Despite his very great debt to psychoanalysis, in fact despite his applying to the history of philosophy psychoanalytic methods, and presuppositions of reading, Derrida has very little in the way of avowal of debt or gratitude to make here. That is, in his reading of Lacan and Freud, here, as elsewhere, he deconstructs, or implicates them in philosophy or literature, but he does not point out what he or we should find valuable. It is as if, and this is as it should be perhaps, he is so close, so much of a psychoanalyst himself, that he feels that such an avowal goes without saying. It is, besides, more urgent that certain features of the institution of psychoanalysis be deconstructed as if they were foreign to his own way of working. Like Marxism, Freudianism today needs defence, not attack. Lacan had revived Freudianism spectacularly in the 1950s. It suffered obscurity, as it always will, from a psychologism which seeks to find the structure of the empirical self, and form biologistic explanations, as well finally as psychiatry which gets rid of the unconscious by speculating on what it is, as if it were not precisely 'the unknown'.

The paper on Lacan was read at a colloquium entitled 'Lacan avec les philosophes' at UNESCO, which was sponsored by the CIP and organized by René Major, in May 1990. The philosophers with whom Derrida brings Lacan into proximity are himself, Nancy and Lacoue-Labarthe, and his lecture is an account of Derrida's personal and publication history as regards Lacan. It therefore traverses in an autobiographical and reminiscent way the publication of *Of Grammatology* and *The Post Card*, and recalls the few times when he met Lacan, once in 1966 at Baltimore, and later at a family event.

Derrida's major concern with Lacan (the lecture is entitled 'For the love of Lacan') was with his 1966 publication *Écrits*, and specifically its first binding essay, which deals with Poe's 'The Purloined Letter' (Derrida insists that this essay is pivotal to the *Écrits*, and so his reading is pivotal to all of Lacan's work). He points out here eight motifs which have been outlined in his reading with the years which show how philosophy has affected and been affected by Lacan's work. In this it is like the work following it in *Resistances*, which recalls his personal and publication history as regards Michel Foucault in the same way. Naturally, the use of the word 'love' in the title was loaded with a slightly remorseful significance, and did not mean any personal love for Lacan, or if it did so, only with the retrospective glance, and with the love which is always belated.

19

Derrida's World: Confronting Marx

19.1 Final Major Works

In the following chapters we examine the last two major collections which Derrida produced in his lifetime, perhaps his most important, the one basically examining the predominant course of modern politics in the twentieth century on the Right, the other examining the Left. *Spectres of Marx* (Derrida 1994) was delivered and released in 1993, marking the release of long withheld and propitiously delivered thoughts on Marxism and its future. It was published with a number of interviews before and after, on the same subject, which reveal the biographical reasons for his decision to speak on Marxism at this late date ('Politics and Friendship', 1989 (Derrida 2002a, 147–98)), and a discussion of his new political adventure ('The Deconstruction of Actuality' (Derrida 2002a, 85–116)), which reveals the political element of deconstruction which had remained hidden up until then, and also develops it as something which was hitherto unthought.

The second work, *The Politics of Friendship*, published in 1994, deals for the most part with Friedrich Nietzsche and Carl Schmitt, as well as with the mainstream of revolutionary thought in the West which had remained conservative, by and large attached to nationalism, and the Aristotelian Greek beginning of philosophy. It follows an entire tradition of dispute and meditation on friendship from Cicero and Aristotle through Augustine to Montaigne. It is a work of remarkable range and depth, revealing consistently new ideas and considerations. It was loosely based on a seminar given during the early 1990s at the EHESS, but was composed more or less as a treatise, something quite rare in Derrida's work, but better for that. It is the culmination of work done for over a decade in teaching at the EHESS in seminars on Heidegger and Nietzsche, nationalism and philosophical nationalism, as well as on the self, the Other and the feminine. In this way *The Politics of Friendship* precedes *Spectres*, and is a more careful study, concerned with the development of a new sort of democracy, a discrete intervention of the Other into the notion of the national, fraternal concept and practice of democracy and state nationalism, which we should call the conservative tradition. Accompanying it is the interview which expressed, in Derrida's own words, his enduring attachment to Nietzsche's books ('Nietzsche and the Machine', *Nietzsche Studies*, spring 1994).

I have said that these were his last major works or publications, and this is said both because up until his recent death the preoccupations remained the same in his public work – which saw seminars on hospitality, on Kantian politics, and on Marx – and also because the publications after 1994 see only minor books which repeat the preoccupations with Europe, and the Other, in slightly different ways, as in *Archive Fever* and *The Gift of Death*. Lectures and books given in the last decade of his life dwell on cosmopolitanism and politics, as well as the core new development or overt message of his work at this time – messianism.

The final years saw Derrida, with his weakening powers, working more and more with other thinkers and writers, producing joint books, and, in general, shorter pieces. To say that his strength failed, however, and that the last decade saw nothing new of importance, is only to assert the grandeur of the products of 1993 and 1994. They are inconclusive texts, written in various styles, and in large part reworkings from disparate expressions of his ideas. Another work of note at this time is *Aporias* (1999), which was Derrida's final address to a conference at Cerisy organized around a discussion of his own work, and which deals largely with the aporia of (or the impossibility of understanding), death, particularly as Heidegger tried to describe it.

19.2 *Spectres of Marx* [1993]

Spectres of Marx is a loosely held together study of Marxism today and in the past, with multiple meditations on various aspects of Marx, which makes no great noise on what is effectively new to Derrida's thought, namely a messianic politics. By and large *Spectres* ejects the caution and pedantry of *The Politics of Friendship*, its careful and beautiful hesitancy. Parts of it were delivered to a conference audience, other parts have been inserted merely to create the illusion of a whole work, and other parts have been pasted on to the conference lecture from seminars or from notes made in other times.

An interview, 'The Deconstruction of Actuality', was given in August 1993 for *Passages*, to mark the publication of *Spectres* in French in that year (the book appeared in English in 1994, with the interview translated and published that year in *Radical Philosophy* in the autumn). Whether this book is in touch with reality, as it seems to be more than any of his other books, is something which the interview started off with, and something which Derrida questions as a possibility for any book. If the thinker has, as one must, to read the newspapers today, then already he begins with a manufactured account of reality, and, with other forms of communication and globalization, reality becomes yet more distant. Actuality is today so massive that one can never, even in a naïve sense, be in touch with it properly. But as for the reality of Europe, a Europe which he has spoken of at length in *Spectres* in the perspective of revolution and Marxism, Derrida accounts for it as one whose only reality – echoing Heidegger in no uncertain terms – whose only 'actuality' is economic and national, and whose only law is that of the market (2002a, 87). As regards the reality of facts and the world, like Baudrillard, he points out that the artificiality of modern communication and reality is not a pure delusion, or a complete virtuality. There is a reality beneath the simulacra, a singular event always taking place, though it is difficult to account for it always anew. The role of deconstruction, as the thinking of simulacra and singularity (the Other), is to shadow reality by making sense of the concepts and actions of real/prosthesis. What makes it more difficult to think modern, present time is that journalistic, communicative-world-time is far too fast, far too fast for thinking, and hence thinking gets edged out of the space of discourse. Though it could account for the real, it has great difficulty in intervening in the culture of simulation. It is a matter of getting to grips with what is really the noumenal, as against the phenomenal, the genuine experience and event, as against the simulation, and thinking needs its own speed. The most fundamental element of experience, Derrida has said in *Spectres*, which has aligned it to the coming of the Other, is not the present moment, but that to which communication hurries so much, always missing it, namely the future. Again, we could say that the present is what the media desires to make the most of, but it is the present which is thus always lost in itself. Derrida characterizes events, real happenings and the unfolding of historical things, by analogy with, or by pointing to, the complete reality and yet unknown quality of birth:

> Families prepare for a birth; it is scheduled, forenamed, caught up in a symbolic space that dulls the arrivance. Nevertheless, in spite of these anticipations and prenominations, the uncertainty will not let itself be reduced, the child that arrives remains unpredictable; it speaks of itself as from the *origin* of another world, or from an *other* origin of this world. (Derrida 2002a, 95)[1]

Birth means here the meaning and reality of a new person with an unforeseen life ahead, and their inexplicable (in any but the most banal terms) emergence from nothing into the world of experience. In plain terms, 'I cannot know anything in advance' (Derrida 2002a, 95), and that, as time-future flows towards us, it contaminates time-present through and through, forcing hasty responses, ill-considered injustices, a conceivable example of which is recent policy in Western lands on the migration of peoples.

Derrida is not the first to point out that 'human rights' are non-existent, that the UN is not based on any scientific or higher legal basis beyond the good intentions of certain people.[2] This is why, as Derrida says (2002a, 101), everybody is in the end allowed asylum, the right to enter a foreign land and to enjoy its benefits, and at the same time it can be proved that nobody has this right. 'A right of asylum can be null or infinite.' For his part, Derrida does not fear immigration, but he fears the kinds of fear that immigration raises in people. What is being discussed here, then, is not the fact of this or that political crisis, but the politics of fear, of exclusion, and the static conservative revolution backwards, due to fear of the Other, fear of the future, not love of fate (like *amor fati*).[3] And it is obvious that not only good comes from the future, but the worst. But Derrida is discussing here the spectrology of Europe and France against problems such as immigration in which spectres of the past are returning, such as those of anti-Semitism and the hatred of other races by Christian nations, factors induced by fear, which return like ghosts. What is important for Derrida is to avoid the coming of the bad from the future, the bad Other, and also the bad from the past, for it is possible and essential to choose, not by conservatism and nationalism, or by approaching stasis and death, but by understanding the unforeseen quality of the future, and the spectral feature of events, because if we are not careful, they haunt us, and return. In the same way one must avoid certain things from the past and cultivate others. How can you avoid the coming of the worst, if not, as is usual, by recourse to conservatism? We always inherit ourselves, a stance which was first formulated by Hölderlin, says Derrida (1994, 54–5).[4] We always, that is, have to choose what to accept from time, and what to reject. We have to have courage and responsibility to do this. 'The democracy to come' means always renew your promise to democracy and justice, your belief in the better future, so as to remain changeable to events (Derrida 2002a, 181).

The conclusion of the book, or the second half, examines Marx's texts, specifically the *German Ideology*, and the explanation of commodities which Derrida shows to be an explanation haunted by ghosts of the past and future, and thus a haunted and haunting text. The problem at issue concerns whether Marx believed the communist event would arise and become present, and whether we were justified in ever believing in the perfect socialist revolution. In an economy of haunting (a hauntology rather than an ontology), both expectations are doomed to be unfulfilled. However if Marx was unaware of this, his text becomes subtly but dangerously involved in lack of presence, a lack which also hides a power, a ghostliness which Marx sought to erase. The lack and the ghost now come forth: 'hauntology' is possible because the spirit, or mind, continually calls the past to its aid, without alternative, and cannot settle and become steady, *grounding*.

The reaction to ghosts is terror and totalitarianism in politics. The ghost haunts Europe and to exorcize it the charnel houses of Germany and Russia were constructed and created. Prior to this the revolutions in Europe were each haunted by the past, in France especially by the Roman Republic. Each revolution inherits the ghost of the past, aligns itself to it, this past, and then revaluates its acts, while forgetting the past. Each revolution or act is then forgetful of what it owes; form, the mere imitation of the past, overcomes content, or the sense of justice, which was what ought to have guided the revolution, says Marx:

> Then, this done, the phantasm is revoked, which is the abjuration; one forgets the ghost as if one were waking up from an hallucination. Cromwell had already spoken the language of the Hebrew prophets. The bourgeois revolution accomplished, the English people prefer Locke to Habakkuk. (Derrida 1994, 112)

The event was in fact always bound up with another time. Each tragic or liberating event is haunted; every event is so. The spirit of revolution is especially anachronistic. The spirit too is contaminated by the ghost. To counteract this it was therefore Marx's notion that the good revolution of the future would not be anachronistic and haunted, but pure and present to itself, and hence that it should work (Derrida 1994, 113). Marx likewise attempts, by criticizing past thought, or current thought, to cleanse the spirit of its ghosts. For each event seemed to him, each revolution, to be mirrored by, and stuck in, a past which made it more thought than act, more memory than event. In Marx's terms the revolution of 1848 was the victory of phrase over content, and thus it failed.

But Derrida pointed out that in Marx's texts the ghost is at work as a sub-jacent layer of all that he says. Derrida is moving towards a position on Marx in which Marx himself can be seen to have been subconsciously aware that his own theory is a ghostly system, and will never be real, but will always haunt the world, as its conscience. He undertakes a textual analysis to prove that Marx fights ghosts because he has a faulty interpretation of time, and because they haunt his own words.

In the final chapter of *Spectres*, Marx is seen to read a Christian and ghostly writer, St Max, or Max Stirner. In this thinker, the spirit, or thought, makes the world into a ghost, an insubstantial thing, with Jesus' ghostly body at its centre. Stirner's crime against life and politics is that the material fact of the world has been reduced to a mere insubstantial and unreal ghost. Marx's own life's work was of course directed in the other direction, towards reducing the dialectic of Hegel to a materialism; but Derrida shows that Marx and Max are very similar.

For Marx, work is the way out of this ghostly Christian situation. What had been deferred in the past, the different and missing part, was practical work. But Derrida points out that Marx is obsessed by 'St Max' because he is his double, his Other, a ghost of himself whom he would like to oppose (Derrida 1994, 139). Marx made up ten illusions which the Christian and ethical Max Stirner had fallen into. He proclaims the spirit in which the world should work, and advises that one live up to it, or rather the other way around, he spiritualizes labour, and hopes that it will inherit the earth once it has been spiritualized. The time delay in which this project will occur, a delay which is necessary and interminable, will ensure that Marx's system will always be ghostly, and always haunt labour and actual events – as a hope for a future, and yet always to come. Labour and commodities are haunted.

Commodities are mystical, they are fetishes. The commodity is childish and mystical, though the market requires it. It has a double face, for, although not real, the commodity, the product of labour, permits man to become social. To possess a commodity is thus to be fetishized, ghostly, and haunted by its split face. The Marxist community is spiritual and a community of ghosts. The non-possibility of closing this system off, of making the community or the person real, permits the space for decision. The disjointure between labour/act, and thought/ideal, comes as a seismic event, and the text contains an earthquake as it were, announcing the split which comes also from the future when it ought to have been resolved, but will not be resolved. But this effort to make all of it cohere is the process of history, and Derrida rounds off by announcing that this split or deferral is necessary to events.

Marxism is inspired by religion, specifically, Derrida says, by messianism. In the text, at a point in his career when Derrida was beginning to speak on religion, the subject of Marxism is for the first time broached at length and at the same time the theory of 'religion without religion' is definitively worked out, about which he had more to say, in 'Faith and Knowledge' (Derrida 2001a, 40–101). It suffices here to point out that this text was not only a discussion of Marxism, but an experiment in whether a working hypothesis of Marxism and religion could be formulated, a problem which Derrida, in this text of broken questions and answers, of various voices, solved to his own satisfaction to some extent, although he kept searching.

> That is why such a deconstruction has never been Marxist, no more than it has ever been non-Marxist, although it has remained faithful to a certain spirit of Marxism, to at least one of its spirits for, and this can never be repeated too often, there is *more than one of them* and they are heterogeneous. (Derrida 1994, 75)

Having revealed the hope for a just revolution by deconstructing it, Derrida says that this hope is the aspect of Marx's writings which he has always thought to be valuable. It is the spirit of Marx which he would like to inherit, or to see embodied.

195

20

The Politics of Friendship

20.1 *The Politics of Friendship* [1994]

The aim of the book *The Politics of Friendship*, it is said on the final page, 'is to think and to implement democracy, that which would keep the old name "democracy", while uprooting from it all the figures of friendship (philosophical or religious) which prescribe fraternity, the family and the androcentric ethnic group' (Derrida 1997a, 306). That is, it seeks to examine a presupposed, more pure friendship, which is not nation-based or family/blood/metaphysics-based, but which is concealed, or repressed, or longed for, in the classical formulations of politics and of democratic friendship in the tradition. To such a tradition, the blood-relationship is often the precondition for politics and for philosophy itself, even for the self-possession of the self.

As the book progresses it recounts readings of Nietzsche and Heidegger, in the perspective of nationality and revolution, undertaken in the last decade, which Derrida had made largely in the lecture hall, just as, following this book, he would confine himself to studies of politics in the fully developed terms of the new hospitality and the cosmopolitanism which were first announced here. He is dealing with the tradition of Plato, Aristotle, Cicero, Montaigne, the thinkers of the Revolution and France, then of Nietzsche, and Schmitt. Nietzsche and Heidegger opened the debate and revealed the stakes of the contest, and Derrida is here showing himself finally to be what he always was, one who read them anew, seeking to place justice and fairness within these cruel and, contradictorily, ultra-moral works. The problem is: 'At the centre of the principle (Derrida 1997a, ix) [of patriarchy], always, the

One does violence to itself, and guards itself against the other.' The problem originates and abides in conventional metaphysics, even, and most especially, in Heidegger, because the physical understanding of nature and of existence prescribes the nature of things to be governed by place, blood and soil, prescribing that political loyalty goes with the place of origin, the time and sort of the origin of the persons involved. It is the tradition of finding and basing meaning on the One. To follow the tradition, a single binding thread, Derrida chooses a phrase from Aristotle, which few philosophers have not commented on, namely: 'O my friends, there is no friend.' Following this tradition, which is apparently homogeneous, especially in the continual reversion to Aristotle, Derrida finds peculiar ambitions to change the tradition from within. Montaigne, for example, who infinitized the meaning of friendship by interpreting the phrase of Aristotle to mean that one loses the friend because he is so close; Nietzsche, who apparently inverts it into a madness; and Carl Schmitt, who most clearly embodies the tradition's strength, and also its contradictions, insofar as death is at the centre of the relationship to the friend, and death defines the enemy. As for Derrida's own slight alteration of the phrase 'O my friends, there is no friend', he questions whether there is not always the longing for a purer friendship concealed in its saying, an appeal to a better relationship to the unknown friend in the sigh 'O friends . . .', and whether it is not more than a simple statement of fact that 'there is no friend'. In the distant, phantom friend whom one does not know, who is not related by blood or oath, there is the promise of a greater, truer friendship, and a truer self. This friend is no more than a fellow-philosopher, but is the reassurance that, in essentials, one is not alone.

On the whole Derrida only makes open-ended suggestions, about what destabilizing effects the woman makes in this equation, and the effects of a certain Other, a friend who is the bearer of the gift of self, the friend of Blanchot who is never seen or present, but is always dead already, one who is only a friend insofar as he also shares the total isolation which the genuine friend must suffer. Though it is not mentioned by name, the New International which Derrida had tried to create or foresee in *Spectres* is here formulated down to the precise delineation of its members. Derrida is no longer one of Aristotle's heirs, we are not one of his heirs (Derrida 1997a, 7). Again implicit in the rejection of Aristotle and of the Greek-German axis is a rejection of a very core set of standards and values in decision-making. 'Greece and Rome' have been the spectres and dream of Europe's awakenings since the Renaissance and consistently through the English, French, American and German revivals and revolutions. How much change would such a loss of bearings effect? Naturally, the most extreme statement of this wish is to be found in Nietzsche, who, contradictory as ever, is found to assert only that a 'perhaps', a messianic coming of what may never come, and is dreaded, is at the heart, linking the thinkers of the future, or thinking itself, with friendship. Friendship is also philosophy, the coming of the Other is the coming of the question 'who am I?'. In place of a new democracy and a new relationship to our friends Derrida puts 'the Other', calling on both Nietzsche and Blanchot.

Heidegger too wished to escape the Greek origin, and his emphasis on Greek thought, particularly pre-Platonic thought, is misleading because it seems to locate a new and fresh approach to Being by imitating these Greeks. Rather, as *Contributions to Philosophy* makes clear (1999, §106), this return to Greece is a return to find our own Greek origin, only so as then to catch an 'echo' of the Other (European) Origin within that chamber which is called history.[1]

Derrida seems to summarize the thinking which comes after Nietzsche, and which is contained in his own work, as the thinking stemming from *Beyond Good and Evil*, (Nietzsche 1990a, §1–2), a thinking and a friendship whose word is 'perhaps' (Derrida 1997a, 29), and whose friends are not present, nor may ever be present. In *The Gay Science* (Nietzsche 1974, *passim*) these friends, like Blanchot's, are friends who exist as entirely absent, whose paths cross only like stars, and they exist only in the future, though the hope for them is always expressed in the present. Nietzsche's friends are friends of solitude (Derrida 1997a, 40), they are also friends only insofar as they are also friends of a certain truth, a certain type of liberated thinking, a 'mad' truth which does not require the Other as a present member of a discussion, dissociated from the opposition which creates the dialectic of Hegel. Friendship only protects them from the abyss, it is an illusion. They are allied only in silence (Derrida 1997a, 55).

> Silence amongst friends will not work without laughter, and laughter bares its teeth, as does death. And the more evil it is, the better. Doing and laughing, *machen/lachen*, doing evil and laughing at evil, making each other laugh about evil. Amongst friends. Not laughing evil away, but making ourselves laugh at evil. Amongst friends. (Derrida 1997a, 55–6)

Clearly this leads us to Blanchot's extreme and isolated friendship which is that of the Other, and not of a recognized person. It is a friendship of philosophers, who are friends because they share a relationship to Being, and to a promise of a great friendship.

Later in the work Derrida turns to the radical futural otherness of friendship which goes on only as a link between the total strangeness and inhumanity of those without presence or friendship, but who desire the coming of something superhuman. If friendship, the blood and oath relationship, is the foundation of modern democracy and politics, what would a politics or democracy be like which was based on a friendship based in absence, and foreignness, and what would this democracy be capable of? Nietzsche has done most of the work for this future democracy and friendship (which is non-nationality based), for example in his refusal of Aristotelian virtue, the refusal of the proximity of friends, the refusal of community, and the subsequent acceptance of the loss of truth and 'wisdom' as the grounds for decision and philosophy; Nietzsche awaited the arrival, yet to arrive, of a love not based on possession. What Carl Schmitt valued – enmity, a sense of self and the existence of the community and sovereignty – are lost.[2]

Schmitt's politics has been called decisionism, and locates the bases on which decisions can be made in politics. He therefore required hard-and-fast distinctions, the most secure bases, a fairly cruel glance at what the essential concepts of politics must be, namely the recognition of whom an enemy is in each particular instance. Derrida's analysis revolves around whether an enemy is always a foreign state with a mobilized army, or whether partisan warfare and guerrilla tactics, even terrorism, are not coeval with classical warfare and statecraft, in which case there can be no well-defined enemy. What is gained is the future, the longing for a friend as the longing for better things. This requires a new interpretation and application of the word 'friend', for as familial friends ground democracy, then with a more just, or a new right application of the word in which blood, kinship and oath do not bind, comes a new political behaviour, even a disappearance of the political strictly speaking, and the arrival of universal hospitality.

The final chapters encounter a more recent concept of the friend, in the thinking of the brother and the universalization of brotherhood developed during the French Revolution, which tends, in the perspective of the whole text, to account for the history of philosophy as a history heading towards the absolute reception of the wholly Other, or maybe the non-reception, but a waiting for the friend who is so. Michelet, who is quoted with some approval in this matter, envisaged a universal state named 'France', which was also the example and model of all other states, a contradiction which could not be resolved by him, or by the Revolution itself, and a contradiction typical of the ideals of many other European powers who desired to socialize the world (Derrida 2001a, 137–88). Such an ideal is a community, or fraternity, without fraternity of the usual sort, a France which is not France (bringing the nation as the privileged site of political questioning to the fore). This sort of thinking, which appears to be a crisis of political rationality, using concepts which delete themselves, which Blanchot, Bataille and Nancy enunciated some time later, further outlines the course of this progression, which must become aware of itself, culminating in a present-day situation in which we must recognize that, just as Marxism is a dream which never will be real, so this will never be real either, but is to be hoped for nonetheless amongst philosophers. Peopling this democracy may be, or will be, friends such as those of Blanchot, thinkers who need friends who never meet, friends such as those of Nietzsche whose friendship consists in simply reassuring each other that in their life and death they are not alone.[3] Is not this as concrete as Derrida has ever been on what really matters: on freedom, on justice in practice? The whole text is both a thorough statement of a position which Derrida has taken, and perhaps the most fair reading of Nietzschean politics which currently exists. Again Nietzsche is contradictory, but then he does not obviously contradict his 'superman' thesis of a thinking for/of the future in any of his published work – which is precisely where Derrida picks out a Nietzschean theory. The biographical pictures (Hayman 1980; Safranski 2003; Hollingdale 1999) of Nietzsche in his dealing with his friends Paul Rée and his schoolday friends who lasted into his maturity (I refer to Franz Overbeck and others, with whom he kept up a correspondence until almost his final year with a touching devotion and almost mad attachment (Gilman 1987)) back up the idea that Nietzsche's life and work are an expression of a longing for a friendship without proximity and without the mundane physical aspect of friendship and love (his disastrous attempt to win Lou Salomé notwithstanding). A book devoted entirely to Nietzsche's politics with the same delicacy which Derrida shows would require discussion of 'the will to power', the Antichrist philosophy, and so on, but would result in inconclusive results since in areas such as these, with which Nietzsche is popularly associated, texts which prove that Nietzsche, for example, hated Christianity, also prove, within the same works, that he admired and wished not to destroy it, but to harness its spiritual power, and regretted its passing.

Derrida's concrete politics has been described rightly as banal and everyday in its practice. Who Derrida votes for, for example, brings us to reality in a depressing way. Besides his political assertions in the two major political works, which are highly theoretical, Derrida made only a few, and these the most occasional sort of interventions in politics (mostly collected in *Negotiations*

(2002a)). He was as distant from contemporary politics as Nietzsche was from Bismarckian reality, although Derrida did, unlike Nietzsche, form groups, write letters and attend meetings, often giving speeches for a few select causes, which deal with issues of the liberty and respect owed to those who are persecuted. When Derrida made a political critique such as he did in the 'Deconstruction of Actuality', he did so in cultural terms, pointing to the difficulty of being responsible or honest, and finding truth, in the age of media and world-communications. He was occasionally scathing about Liberalism's pretensions, but offered only the 'superhuman' alternative.

20.2 'Nietzsche and the Machine'

The 'Nietzsche and the Machine' interview was given in 1993, for the spring edition of *Nietzsche Studies* 1994, published in *Negotiations* (Derrida 2002a, 215–56). It echoes the sentiments of *The Politics of Friendship*, bringing with it the reliance on Nietzsche, which seems to have grown with the years, as Derrida was forced by circumstances to make a less secretive assertion of his position on politics. As the reader of Nietzsche is forced to agree, after the years necessary for such a reading, Nietzsche has no system of thought, and has not even the basic minimum for such a system, that is, self-consistency, something which Derrida, as a great reader of Nietzsche, points out here. This, he says, is why he has not made a general survey of Nietzsche, although if Nietzsche were systematic such a study would have been made. On the other hand, if he were systematic he could not have been the mainstay of deconstruction and of a politics to come. Nietzsche is characterized, in this very open essay of alignment, as what we had always supposed him to have been. He has several voices, and is a poetic-philosopher, a theatre of poetic philosophical forms (2002a, 216).

It is hardly as if Nietzsche did not know that he was inconsistent. His contrariness is of a piece with his saying that he does not have to give reasons for the positions he takes; he wrote that he should not have to carry his reasons around with him. Nietzsche also enjoyed taking on various personae or roles, without first explaining that it was not precisely 'Friedrich Nietzsche' who was then writing. This is of a piece with his poetry, which is usually dramatic monologue (see Nietzsche (1984), *Dithyrambs*). Nietzsche looked on it as a virtue both 'to become that which you are' ('How One Becomes What One Is' is the subtitle to *Ecce Homo* (1979)), and to be able to look at things from every perspective, that is, from the perspective of different types of people, so that he knew how it was to think and be *déca-dent*, to think and be sick, or healthy, or wicked, or Goethian, or completely free of human sensibility. *Human, All Too Human* (Nietzsche 1986) is one example of this, in which he pursues a psychological investigation. In *Spurs* Derrida made a virtue of this sort of self-expression by somebody who may or may not be Nietzsche, by saying that the play of meanings is what counts, not the absolute meaning, and in *Otobiographies* he set aside any true 'Nietzsche' in terms of a man giving a true account of himself. Nietzsche was the antipodes of Derrida in one essential way: while Nietzsche was a thinker of the quickest step, the lightest rhythm, Derrida was almost unprecedent-edly *slow*. They both valued superficiality and shadows.

In this essay, which puts in more practical terms the agenda which has motivated Derrida throughout his years of teaching on Nietzsche, and of for-mulating a politics to come, Nietzsche's active usefulness to a becoming futural of European and American thought is explained. In it Derrida points to the three forebears of his own practice of thinking, which with the years has given voice to itself in terms of religion and politics. These are Heidegger, Nietzsche and, in religion, Walter Benjamin.

Note the totally different preoccupations of this self-explanatory Derrida, which in the early texts were always only presupposed. One knew, reading the famous texts of the 1960s, that Derrida had a Nietzschean point of view on politics, that is, a distant one, a futuristic one, and also, because it is sit-uated in a dialogue with Kant and Heidegger, a rather backward-looking, religious one, which was concerned with Europe's recent past as much as with its present and future. Derrida does not emerge in these book publica-tions and interviews as a commentator on the Nazi history of central Europe, for he always seemed to be involved in this, but for the first time he is speak-ing of a certain dream of liberty, at length, and in explicit terms. His voice is grander, it is higher up in the political realm, he is now a public man, and not merely an academic. He had, he says, always sought to rescue Nietzsche from Heidegger, and thereby to release him:

> Heidegger's gesture is, in fact, extremely equivocal, he cannot save Nietzsche from the biologism and racism in which the Nazis want to enclose him except by making him a metaphysician; the last of the meta-physicians; that is, by reducing him in turn. I have tried to formalize this scene in several texts, Heidegger saves Nietzsche by losing him, and loses him by saving him. I try to read Nietzsche – the thinker of the perhaps (Vielleicht), as he says in *Beyond Good and Evil*. (Derrida 2002a, 221)

For those who are worried by this new Nietzschean vision of democracy, which is neither pure democracy nor yet the sort of representative democracy which is derived from territorial belonging, such as is found in England, the question would be: why attempt to save Nietzsche at all? His thought, life, and his metaphysics of power, each undermines the accustomed order in a way which is far more destructive than mere progressive decline, the like of which Western democracy is at present suffering. Though in decline, Western liberty is not so poor that it requires something which puts an end to its misery. For sure, those who see Nietzsche as a mere German nationalist (which was Robert Graves' estimate of him), one who was envious of England's tradition and history, will not appreciate Nietzsche either as a radical democrat, nor as the one who alerted Europe to the nature of its own fate as a machine-based, moralistic, soulless desert. But what makes this work universally applicable and appreciable, by conservatives as well as by socialists, is that the decline of the West is neither welcomed, nor sped on by deconstruction of the brand which is Nietzsche's, Heidegger's or Derrida's. For all three, the destiny, and the Being of Europe, is the will to power, and technology, or, finally, these two combined and exhausted in Anglo-Saxon globalization. This globalization is the metaphysical, and hence, inescapable destiny of all that people, statesmen, artists or labourers do. No elegy on a passed England, or treatise on justice, can affect this destiny, since they are products of it. What can alone affect this present and future is a concealed 'saving' and founding moment or space, which does not take part in globalizing will to power, but is its antagonistic Other, so far Other that the two cannot come to agreement or accept each other in any form. The space and moment of this origin is not in this land, not, as T. S. Eliot had it, 'Now, and in England', and not on the banks of, or at the source of, the Rhine, as Hölderlin had it, but it could found a world worth something, out of the overwhelming power of loss of the reality and living, which goes on today because of technology and will-to-power metaphysics, and which Derrida felt more and more with his last years.

21

Derrida's Religion

21.1 Messianism

Caputo, in *The Prayers and Tears of Jacques Derrida* (1997b), gathered together all of Derrida's texts since 1980, the year in which he began to speak more and more of the Other. Caputo formed what he argued is the religion which Derrida had been creating. It is possible to think of a 'new religion' in pejorative terms, as Scruton (2005) does when reflecting on Derrida as a phenomenon with religious features. On the other hand, those who have disliked Derrida's 'priestly' style, his supposed theatrical religiosity, are also the first to lament the passing of religion, and the demise of high culture which followed on that, little imagining that efforts to revive religion are not fruitless, nor unphilosophical, and that they and Derrida are, in the end, motivated by similar desires. This religion which Derrida had been developing properly in texts and lectures since *Spectres* at least, is a religion which exceeds and yet borrows from the religions of the Book. It abstracts the messianic from them, or as Caputo, who has discussed this with Derrida, puts it, dogmatic religions of the law have either created messianism, or have been created by messianism. In any case, this non-present, extra-temporal coming of what will never arrive, a justice greater than any instance of the law, is the core of Derrida's religion without historical place, or text, or dogma. It is thus both universal, as the core of the major monotheisms, and also potentially the reconciliation of all the Abrahamic orthodoxies, as a religious position greater than them. Caputo devotes most of his attention to the development of the messianic idea by Derrida in the 1993 *Spectres of Marx* lectures. There Derrida asserts that what is of most value in Marx is his messianic impulse for justice, so that potentially, all prior social and political enquiry can be subsumed into messianism too.

21.2 'Faith and Knowledge'

In 1995, after the publication of *Spectres of Marx* and *The Politics of Friendship* Derrida took a trip to South America, and wrote another semi-autobiographical piece, 'A Silk Worm Of One's Own', in Argentina, Chile and Brazil. At the beginning of the year he also wrote the second half of 'Faith and Knowledge', signed at Laguna, 26 April 1995. This presentation insists on the often repeated notion that religion has returned. The conference to which it was presented was held on the island of Capri, and its theme was decided by Derrida himself, who saw religions as returning. They were certainly returning for him. But whether the *Christian* religion was returning is open to debate. The Christianity which returns is the one with a new form, he says. It is a technological world-attitude, whose process of transformation Hegel had taken part in, along with Voltaire, Mill and the other renegades of the history of thought, as well as Christians themselves. The return of a barbarous Muslim religion, simplistic and 'fundamental', was, as he saw, a response to the power of the West over this old civilization, in desperate decline, which was only today entering into the global community, and with a conservative nervous reaction. So indeed Judaism had returned to Israel, and its long period of exile in Europe had concluded with a renewed orthodoxy. On the other hand, away from incidental features of random terrorism as a result of the growth of 'capitalism', the return of religions which Derrida sees can also be viewed as it involves the entire destiny not only of the West but of civilizations *per se*.[1] The conference was published as *Religion* (Derrida 1998g), and co-edited with G. Vattimo. Religion is theological-political (Derrida 2001a, 46), and in relation to it, we, his audience, are democrats and Christians (Derrida 2001a, 47). Christianity, with which we are allied in great part as democrats, is then, in its battle with other religions, the point of departure for the examination of such a return of religions. None of us can be indifferent to religion, and Kant is invoked as the pre-eminent voice of Christianity; Heidegger settles accounts with the same religion interminably, and Nietzsche's 'dead God' is integral to this Christianity with which we are in league, Derrida says. Derrida sees the patrimony of the Christian religion everywhere. The Christian community of openness and honesty, of confession and worship in public and in common, has given impetus to science; science of the modern kind depends upon it, as religion depends today on science in order to propagate itself. Its modern form is the set of values and ideals which all Western democracies religiously assume as their motivating and controlling laws: peacefulness, treaty-observance and human rights. '[G]lobalatinization (this strange alliance of Christianity, as the experience of the death of God, and tele-technoscientific capitalism) is at the same time hegemonic and finite, ultra-powerful and in the process of exhausting itself' (Derrida 2001a, 51–2). The foundation of this Christianity and its law is a mystical foundation, which is to say that our religion is deconstructible at the moment when it produces a concrete set of proposals to effect its sway through us from the ground of its mystical authority. As the religion of Christ is Latin in its moral aspect, it has survived most powerfully in the Anglo-American politics of right and international-ism, since these are languages of Latinity. But the religion is also a Greek and Abrahamic one. The Latin element of the religion, or of religion itself, is the law-promoting aspect of religion, while Abrahamic faith constitutes a second branch. This bifurcation of its genealogy with the twin branches of law and faith has at root an unknown origin, an unknown which any and every religion lives upon, but which it only interprets. Derrida ends the first part of 'Faith and Knowledge' by reminding those conscious of their power derived from religion, that at root, because religion is bottomless and mys-tical, it must also be the cause of some patient and unending tolerance, for the Other is its basis, and the Other cannot fill us with such certainty as our religious behaviour often inspires in us. Christianity's law is also fundamen-tally tolerance, and even Voltaire was a Christian insofar as he based all of his life on tolerance. Our uncertainty as to the ultimate ground of religion, a ground deeper than the written and spoken name of God, deeper than the recent history of the death of God, more real because this Other cannot die, and because it is surely at the root of it all – our uncertainty must teach us tolerance, Derrida says.

In general, modern Christians, or northern Europeans, have only inherited the law, the Latin power of right, the Protestant inheritance, Derrida says. Let us go back to the nature of Christianity, and its largely unconscious self-preservation in the West in its transformed guise of the tele-technological society. Firstly, Christianity infuses and impels all modern communication in the way of telephones, the internet, television, satellite communication and the general overcoming of distance and time. Secondly, religion also ensures that science flourishes and does not lose itself in untruth and unpragmatic research, since it dictates that statements of fact and truth be adequate and impersonal, as techno-science does, in its complete objectivity. Third, international organizations, the UN and so on, require religion, for they have no other justification than the demands made by the religious law, specifically the law of Christ and of the interpretation of it by the Latin Church Fathers, and later reformers through the modern era in the various countries of Europe. The omnipresence of communication technology today relies on the same demand amongst people for openness in communication, honesty and confession. While science has as its basis the communal benefit of finding out the truth of things in correct statements of fact, the Latin-Christian organization is devoted above all to communal truth-telling, a communal bond of speaking for which God and the law is essential, and to which an open and clear mediatized vision via TVs, satellites, CCTV, and so on, is essential. The outcome of the binding of communications, science and law-enforced communal honesty is Global-Latinization (Globalatinization) which Derrida seems to consider as pervasive a thematic as the thematic of capitalism, if once we understand this link between Roman law-based Christian history and modern globalization. This outcome consists of telecommunications, techno-science and absolute rights, an outcome for which a religious promise is the energy. Derrida also calls it a phallic process, a phallic-religious process.[2] The Phallic is both the pure, the fruitful and desired, which is acquired through the logos, but is also mechanical and machinal. By the way, the techno-scientific and Phallogocentric excludes various groups, the Islamic peoples, women, animals, the economically backward, and so on, so as to maintain a certain vision of the law. Such were Derrida's thoughts in 1995 in a lecture which shows the signs of being that of an old philosopher, one who has now reached the age at which the modern world seems to frighten, or maybe he has reached, at sixty-five, the age of wisdom, who knows? Similar religiosity or grand schemes for changing the attitudes of the world, as well as the course of history, seem to impose themselves on the work of most philosophers with age. Russell, for example, was more and more shocked by his civilization, and made bolder and more generalized statements.[3] On the other hand, generationally younger thinkers such as Baudrillard were saying similar things.

21.3 Late Publications

With Derrida's interest in religion developing, Levinas, the friend of Blanchot, and theorist of the Other, passed away in 1995, and Derrida delivered a funeral oration on 25 December that year. *Archive Fever* (Derrida 1996) was released in this year in French, dealing with the thesis that Freud was a Jewish thinker. Also in 1995 *Donner la mort* (Derrida 1995a) was published, a counterpart to *Donner le temps* from the 1970s, describing the intervention of death or the Other into European culture as Christian Europe perceives it. Again, as in *Donner le temps (Given Time)*, Being, or in this case, death, had been used to strengthen national and cultural unity against the onset of decay in morals. Derrida's destruction of this tradition focuses on the notion of a gift without return, which death, or the Other, or Being, must make if it is what we suppose it to be: ineffable. Though short, and on the subject of Patočka, a well-known Christian religious writer, *The Gift of Death* is crucial in Derrida's journey towards a messianic religion without religion, a classical religion which binds all of the others into one universal church incapable of dogma. For the gift of the Other, the intervention of which is totally Other, of death or of God, suspends the natural law of things, the law of this or that dogma, the law of a particular political unity, and comes uncalculated. That is to say, one cannot put laws on how to return the Gift or worship the Giver. To obey the call of the Other can be to obey no specific instance of a historical law, and no ethics. For philosophy, from Plato to Heidegger and in Kierkegaard's day, has made use of the Other, sanitized it, and made it into something that 'if it does not kill me makes me stronger'. Patočka's intention is to cultivate a re-Christianization of Europe to make it responsible and ethical, related to a history of Christian responsibility, to European places and times and a definite orthodoxy, in which death is a border against which Europe builds its authentic existence. Derrida takes issue with this for what it excludes; for while it takes account of death, and overcomes death's obvious limit to life, it does not overcome other limits, such as national boundaries.

1996 and 1997 saw the final years of Derrida's massive output for journals, although with the final years Derrida was to be involved in published dialogues which express his hopes, fears and reflections. Here are interviews showing the same interest in a multitude of aspects of culture.

Aporias (1993b), on Heidegger's *Being and Time*, was released in 1996 for the first time in French, having been translated and published in English in 1993, and being Derrida's concluding address to a Cerisy conference on Derrida himself. *Echographies de la télévision*, with B. Steiger, appeared in 1996, and *Monolingualism* (Derrida 1998e) translated and published in English in 1998, by Patrick Mensah with Stanford, which deals with personal and general reflections on the disturbing effects of language on the personality and liberty of its users, particularly of Derrida himself. The effects are put into practice, unavoidably, in the text. He gave interviews on film, and continued to give papers on theology, law, education and psychoanalysis, though half of the published work for 1996 is translated work, predominantly into German.

In the new year of 1997 Derrida gave seminars on hospitality, lectures which were carefully memorializing Levinas, published for the first time in the English collection *Acts of Religion* (2001a). These indicate Derrida's lecture style at EHESS, and the manner in which he composed his lectures, for although they are largely unedited lecture notes, these chapters are finished pieces. They actually seem not to deconstruct anything in particular, but to unfold in a Levinasian way the idea of the Other, not deconstructing a text, but, as is more frequent in these final years in lectures and seminars, deconstructing a concept, or a conceptual network, mostly ethical concepts being used in contemporary politics, such as 'forgiveness', 'hospitality', 'cosmopolitanism' or 'justice'.

Derrida was also to write a preface to a Michel Servière text (Derrida 2001b, 135), and publish a text on Sarah Kofman for *les Cahiers de Griff*, following her recent death. Aside from these occasional pieces, and *Marx en jeu*, showing his continued freedom to deal with this thinker, there were fewer French publications. It seems that at this point Derrida was slowing down and in retreat, concentrating instead on expressing ethical ideas, instructing others in how to be more liberal, yet harder in their thought. But this was in line with his turning away from the theme of the singularity of the self, of his own self, which culminated in *Circumfession*. It was his interest in his own peculiar fate, or the fate of each individual, which had sustained his popular approach in the late 1970s and through the 1980s. As we have seen, the political work on Marx, on the politics of friendship and the like, show a turn towards an ethical writing, more concerned not with the self, but with the Other, in the manner consciously of Levinas. This turn is, of course, not in another direction, for the singularity of the self is very much of a piece with the singularity of the Other; they are the same, but approached from a different perspective. Derrida with age seems to have become more restrained, involved in classical statements of how one should behave, how laws should be passed and framed by the French parliament, more concerned, but less revolutionary.

With the lectures on hospitality, there is also a book in French released of the same name, and another on cosmopolitanism named *Cosmopolites de tous les pays, encore un effort!* after the Marquis de Sade's ultra-materialistic and post-French revolutionary work *Philosophy in the Bedroom* which contains a *reductio ad absurdum* of Robespierre's revolutionary principles entitled 'One More Effort If You Wish To Be Republicans'. 'On Cosmopolitanism', as Derrida's work is known, was published in 1997, and given to an audience protesting against 1996 policy on immigration in France. The political idea, which is a positive doctrine, rather than a secret intention hidden beneath a deconstruction, is to align the politics of states, which usually deal with one another as enemies and threatening others, to the Levinasian doctrine of the Other as the image of God, in each actual other person. This is an ethical stance, and Derrida, writing on peace, and forgiveness amongst nations (cosmopolitanism), is moving the ethical Other into the place of the political Other, and, unusually, in a straightforward declamatory way. This is the age of the uprisings in the Middle East, of religious revival there, of migrations from the Third World, and the East, of growing media and popular unrest about foreign people, a time of the revival of religions, as Derrida had noted at the time of the Capri conference.

In 1998 a new edition of *Psyche*, with augmentations, was released, and *Demeure*, on Maurice Blanchot. Interviews, contributions, joint publications giving help to sympathetic and younger writers, and memorial works to dead friends set the tone for his final years. So, in 1997, several works were released in dialogue or in cooperation with other writers: *A Taste for the Secret* with Maurizio Ferraris; *Marx en jeu*, which was with Marc Guillaume; and *Choral Works*, with Peter Eisenmann, the American architect. There were also to be interviews with Elizabeth Roudinesco (Derrida 2004c) and Giovanna Borradori (2003) in the first years of the new millennium, as well as *Counterpath* with Catherine Malabou (2004a), wherein Derrida did not merely take part in a joint effort as a participant, but was using joint works as a means of expressing his ideas and approaches to problems then current.

22

Thoughtful Welcoming of the Other, Death[1]

22.1 'On Cosmopolitanism'

In his late English-language collection of two occasional pieces, *On Cosmopolitanism and Forgiveness* (Derrida 2001c), true ethics and ethical decision is cast in its purity as mad and sovereign, because it transcends the merely human (the rational). Derrida calls the argumentative orientating point for ethics the 'hyperbolic' by which he means the most pure instance of ethical action. It alone, this hyperbolic instance, must orientate us if we are to change actual existing laws, for, as the extreme limit of commonly used concepts, it is the purest meaning of them. This reflects Derrida's belief and practice that the law is given, and can be just or unjust, but justice, which is always hyperbolic, is separate and beyond the law, undeconstructible, having no structure, and belonging to nobody. It must however guide the law as it is applied.

'On Cosmopolitanism', or the first paper in *On Cosmopolitanism and Forgiveness*, was given on request to the International Parliament of Writers, December 1996, as an address on asylum seekers, while 'On Forgiveness' was commissioned by a journal.

In these late 1990s speeches and papers, Hannah Arendt is representative of the humanistic element, or the human discourse of politics and law; especially she is the post-war commentator on international law, and the humanist approach. Kant also is the representative of the merely human: good and exemplary, but limited, a thinking which must be subjected to the logic of the hyperbole. Kant acts as a limit on what, Derrida says, must be infinite, namely an international government, and the harmony and ultimate disappearance of all nation-states. Interestingly, Derrida sees a step towards this ultimate situation of pure democracy, which he is sure will never be complete, and would be dangerous if it were, by means of the political and military unification of Europe.

1996 marked a time of crisis for immigration in France, even though, as Derrida was to say often, immigration figures had not risen annually for twenty years (Derrida 2002a, 137). The Debret Laws were passed which permitted the police to extradite *sans papiers* even after they had lived in France for decades. There was also the matter of it becoming a crime to harbour a foreigner for more than eight days, which was being called 'a crime of hospitality'. It offended Derrida that France thought much of its spirit of cosmopolitanism and hospitality even while passing laws like this. In a familiar pattern in these years, he retraced the history of French politics on this matter, from 1938 to 1945 (when it became a criminal act to help a foreigner whose papers are not in order, passed on 2 November 1945), and back into the history of medieval France, Greece, Israel and other lands. There were mass demonstrations in Paris after the Debret Laws were passed (Derrida 2001c, ix). Not that Derrida was completely opposed to renewal of the laws on immigration and citizenship. But such renewal must see the double bind, as Derrida put it, that hospitality has to be offered as a right of refuge, but then has to be conditional on other circumstances, and the Debret Laws had erred on the side of caution. Laws must be passed with a continual eye to circumstances, and to undeconstructible justice, in a negotiation between the conditional circumstances and unconditional, hyperbolic instance.

22.2 'Derelictions of the Right to Justice (But What are the *Sans-Papiers* Lacking?)'

'Derelictions', which was originally improvised and later transcribed (published in *Marx en jeu*), was delivered on 21 December 1996, at the Théâtre des Amandiers in Paris at a mass demonstration against government policy on asylum and immigration in France. It often seems to revert to published work that Derrida was working on, which he calls up by memory, and is slightly impassioned in its style. Derrida hates it that states can be inhospitable, that it can be a crime to be hospitable. There is genuine hatred and passion in his use of terms and language applied to those who are swaying policy. 'Desperate incompetence', demagoguery, xenophobia, the administration is 'sad, depressed, depressing, desperate, despairing' (Derrida 2002a,

141). As Derrida sees the matter, the 'sans-papiers' lack human dignity, the right to be considered as people. Their treatment is due to government efforts to win an election by countering Right-wing parties that were then growing in strength by seizing on their policies. The immigrants in question, Derrida points out, are being, and have always been, used as resources by governing bodies, shown by the fact that the rich 'neo-liberal' countries have allowed immigration while there was economic necessity for it, only to deny it when elections must be won. The basic understanding of the 'sans papiers' as people, due rights, is thus from the first denied them. He calls this a renewed racism (Derrida 2002b, 140). The person who is *sans-papiers* is also naked thereby, and without recourse (Derrida 2002b, 135). That year and the next he gave seminars at EHESS, and in America, on hospitality, as we saw, so that it may indeed seem that events in politics, rather than in academic studies, had shaped his teaching and publication history at this time.

Another UNESCO lecture of these times was given by him in November 1999, showing him to be a complete patron of UNESCO. This was 'Globalization, Peace and Cosmopolitanism' (Derrida 2002a). Derrida sees globalization as a benefit and the opportunity for challenging new hegemonies, but he says that it requires vigilance and continued critique in deconstructive manner because the apparent homogenization only hides new inequalities.

In the paper Derrida apologizes for only giving a personal profession of faith. His point is that the opening of borders depends less on technology, which is in fact recreating itself into blocks of knowledge and power, than on ethical decisions and military political justice, as he has said in his paper 'Faith and Knowledge'. 'Globalization, Peace and Cosmopolitanism' reflects the latter in a few other ways, so that it appears that Derrida was trying to repeat and propagate a single message. The problem of language, specifically English, was such a recurrent issue, calling for a hyper-systematic position beyond the double bind, for the universal language which is not universal is both beneficial and also exclusive. To decide for or against in any situation is impossible, and requires simply a sense of justice, for a general rule or principle cannot help. Anglo-American language is Christian, he says, and is Christianizing the world in a pre-programmed way, bringing with it Roman history. His plan would be to uproot this history and yet to trace it, to recognize it as actual history, and to reinvent it on the basis of the Other, or justice, always anew. That is, as a trace-language, which recognizes that it is traced upon the image of a better future. The 'crime against humanity' is such an Anglo-American concept, and it offers such a possibility if we see it as a trace.

Following his introduction, four points of faith are given which Derrida would like to devote himself to, so as to make the maximum effect: first work and the end of work, the right to work which globalization sets into chaos, and which it seems to have ended by means of computerization and information labouring (following Lyotard to some extent in this, he disputes that it is as clear-cut as being a simple third revolution in labour);[2] second the drama of forgiveness and repentance for modern crimes which governments commit, the cult of recognizing the faults and crimes of modern states which Derrida finds problematic and which is bringing about a false cosmopolitanism;[3] third, the question of peace which demands intervention into state sovereignty, which in practice means that the strong take a hand in deciding for the weak, and which, again, interferes with true globalization and finally the question of the death penalty which is a punishment applied only on the disadvantaged. These are some of his professions of faith at that time, he said.

22.3 'On Forgiveness'

Originally 'On Forgiveness' was written for *Le monde des débats*, December 1999. A question had been put to Derrida on the phenomena of states reconciling themselves to each other; his answer refers back to 'Faith and Knowledge' [1995]. Modern present-day acts of forgiveness and repentance, asking for forgiveness, admitting guilt, are based on ending disputes and finding reconciliation. They are staged and political. Today's heads of state ask forgiveness, admit guilt, take on responsibility, and do so as if it i a key part of their role, a dramatic state ritual or ceremony, and they do i almost gladly, even with the appropriate feelings. It is since the concep 'crime against humanity' was formed that states guilty of such crimes, often in war, are made accountable with the peace. Since then, a metaphysical concept of man as god, or man as sacred, and human life as untouchable which is religious, even specifically Christian in its language, has taken over the language of international diplomacy and law. Derrida kept an eye on this. He was annoyed by this fake, banal ritual of semi-forgiveness for guilt over crimes in the past by nation-states, and the avowal of them on occasion for state-based economic advantages, since the guilt and the forgiveness are not genuine and will not lead to real respect. It is forgiveness with an aim in mind, limited forgiveness. This globalization of Latin/Roman religious feeling is like a universal religion, fed by the media which does no even need a church or ministers, since it uses Christian templates to guide its rhetoric, and expects Christian responses (Derrida 2001c, 31). The idea of the reality of globalization and the latinization of the globe is of a piece with what had become a world-view for Derrida, a world of unfulfilled cosmopolitanism, of mediatic globalization, of the rebirth of religions, and the occluding of the real state of things by the media, which promotes Christian values. To this half-light of false, halfway professions, nervous reactions, ghostly mixings of honest virtue and pretence in the name of economic advantage, Derrida brings the harsh, biblical standard of virtue which will not compromise. It is the promised and genuine, impossible, true, forgiveness and repentance, rather than the sort of thing which heads of state practise as part of their job, and as a routine.

In Derrida's late triadic scheme – of the pure instance of the concept, the circumstances limiting the use of the pure concept, and the final impossible choice between the two – the Christian religion-media plays the role of what is now taking place contrary to, but not too distant from, this triad of good conduct. However, this is not to say that the Christian world is bad through and through; it is only that this is not religious or Christian enough. Europe, which formed this mediatic world space, needs to develop its Christian heritage more thoroughly in fact; not, definitely not, to reject this religious inheritance wholesale (Borradori 2003, 118; Derrida 2004b). Also note that *The Other Heading* severely criticizes the Greco-Roman Europe and the recent trajectory piloted by the phallic, mastering, Platonic-logos.

22.4 'As if it were Possible'

The title of this journal contribution refers to the request that Derrida summarize his work to 1998 for the *Revue international de philosophie* for an edition devoted to following his work by a group of academics who had studied his ideas for many years. A number of contributors had submitted articles on his work, and he decided to reply aphoristically. The papers which were included in the edition were, one each, by Christopher Johnson,[4] Christopher Norris and Arkady Plotnitsky, each speaking from the scientific and Anglo-Saxon side of things; and from John Sallis, Daniel Giovannengeli and Michel Meyer from the more continental side. He said that he was giving seminars on forgiveness, excuse and perjury at the time (Derrida 2002a, 349), and was interested in how the possible derives from the impossible, or how the possible is impossible, a logical statement which disrupts the logic of the propositional form. In solving it he has turned to the gift, the secret, testimony, hospitality and forgiveness, and so on, and had imagined a place, or site, prior to the distinction possible/impossible (Derrida 2002a, 350).

For the benefit of his readers, and answering their demand to summarize, he points to his continual preoccupation with the question of *the question* which first concerned him in print as far back as 'Violence and Metaphysics', where he had said that this question of questioning, like a Bataillean unending quest for non-knowledge, alone can institute a philosophical community. Bataille does so in the context of making an estimate of Heidegger's work and lecturing (Bataille 1988, 28), specifically of the 1930s where Heidegger had called on a 'community of thinkers', and earlier, a national enterprise to initiate a national revival (Wolin 1993, 29–39). Bataille could not let his question of the question be compromised by common standards of intelligibility, or by the constraints of ethical judgement and accountability. Of course it is precisely to Heidegger and Husserl that Derrida is turning when he says that the question of the question must ground the philosophical community, and from them that it gains its legitimacy, insofar as Derrida points to a tradition. To discuss this further, we should need to sort out which sort of 'community' he means. Though he spoke in 1964 of a community of researchers, like Heidegger, by the 1990s he was speaking of that Nietzschean community without proximity.

Also he shows how his question of the impossible gift is not new either, but begins to show itself in *Given Time*, and before that in 'Ousia and Gramme' where it is said that 'Time is the name for this impossible possibility' (Derrida 2002a, 358). It is because of the paradox that the impossible is the origin of the possible, that the gift is primarily a gift of time, hence 'Given Time'. He says that *The Post Card* continued the questioning of this gift of time, and it led finally to *The Politics of Friendship*.

The gift of the impossible is the precondition for the possible to occur, for how can anything happen at all, how not be machinal and pre-programmed, spectral, if everything is pre-possible and simply possible? Only what is genuinely unforeseen and chance-like is a genuine occurrence. What really comes with time in the future has, if it occurs at all, and contrary to Aristotle's scheme of potential/actual, come from what was previously unforeseen, and has been gifted to existence, by the impossible.[5] Before it occurred it was impossible. If it was simply possible all along then it never really occurs properly, it merely comes to pass. What really *occurs* is always unknown, never foreseen, never possible, Derrida says. One cannot but reflect that, finally, Derrida is creating the reasoned arguments for 'the coming', the Other, the hyperbolic, spectrality, the double-bind, différance, as if he were preparing to shut up shop.

This portion of his self-assessment and his work in recent years was intended for his colleagues Sallis, Meyer and Giovannengeli. When he turns to what Norris, Johnson and Plotnitsky have written he turns to science, and tries to estimate what these 'analytic-tradition' writers have done for him. Norris, he says, has fought for deconstruction, fighting against misunderstandings and a host of prejudices, and he has fought persistently and originally (Derrida 2002a, 366). Norris tended to put Derrida amongst the US/UK thinkers and to show them that Derrida is serious, and a good thinker, in the lineage of Wittgenstein.[6] Derrida says this makes him smile really, to see himself defined as a transcendental philosopher by Norris (Derrida 2002a, 367). Of course Derrida is interested in the conditions for the happening of the real, and Norris is right in a way, but mostly this is to do with the coming of the Other as the real, not the analytic representation of things, which he considers to be machinal. Plotnitsky and Johnson on the other hand align Derrida with Niels Bohr and quantum theory, something again which he says he does not object to, although he had not said it himself. It is a strategy of alignment which could be useful.[7] But Johnson says that Derrida's position is outside of science, something which seems to mirror Heidegger's view on science (science does not think), and Derrida objects. There is a boundary between thought and science, which his own work epitomizes to an extent, but he still does not believe that this boundary is unbreachable. Deconstruction is not *against* science as Heidegger opposed 'thought' to science.

23

2000 Onwards

23.1 A Contemporary Philosopher

Acts of Religion was published in 2001a in English translation, having been collected first in English for an American public. The collection of essays on religion from the previous fifteen years is a sign of how Derrida was being interpreted in the years directly preceding his death. A book of this sort would not previously have been possible, for lack of work by Derrida on this subject. But it also showed what his critics and readers were searching for in his work, because such a religious side had been there, underneath, from the start, even in the 1962 introduction to the 'Origin of Geometry'.

As a sign of Derrida's loss of power but his continuing inventiveness and desire to work, we see an extended discussion of his friend Jean-Luc Nancy, and the following year something similar published with the CIP on Jean François Lyotard, *Lyotard and Us* (Derrida 2001b, 211–42). He also released a book on the filmic media with Safaa Fathy.

23.2 *Philosophy in a Time of Terror*: 9/11

Philosophy in a Time of Terror records discussions organized by Giovanna Borradori occasioned by the events of 11 September 2001 in New York. They were held there three weeks later, organized by Borradori so as to gather the responses of Jürgen Habermas and Derrida, 'the two foremost voices of contemporary philosophy' as she puts it. To begin with Derrida took issue with her naïve use of the word 'event', in the phrase 'major event', when applied to 9/11. He handles the 'event' in conceptual terms, dealing with the name or date '9/11' as itself a problem, and also deals with the metonymies 'Bin Laden' and 'Bush', and what it is that decides whether anything has occurred: then with the concepts 'war' and 'terrorism' in his own way, a way which had always, since ENS, been standard for him, that is, the way in which key concepts which the media and philosophical critics were using without much reflection are problematized.[1] His point is that this event as an isolated phenomenon has been abstracted from the wider origins of itself. Throughout it is not clear whether Derrida disagrees with the first rumblings of the Bush response, the threats against Afghanistan, and then against Iraq, or whether he disagrees with Bin Laden. He does not again seem to consider it to be a major event at all, outlining it rather as an episode in the world's auto-immunitarian crisis, a process wherein the West is producing the means to injure and destroy itself, the actors playing out this drama having little to do with the events which symptomize it.[2] He thus sees it as part of a larger 'event'.

His view of the concept 'event' tackles the Anglo-American empiricist usage of the concept, splitting it up into impression and sensation, and then into interpretation, and the way that today's events have always been given such empiricist evaluation, so that they are events which are also first of all 'created'. His whole approach is cautious and slow and, using all of his learning, in psychoanalysis, sociology and philosophical enquiry, it tends to advise caution in our response. First one must know whether anything has happened, or whether something more normal and perennial has occurred, so that the response should be more mournful than vengeful.

When questioned on what he saw as the future of the world given this sort of crisis, while the rest of the world was tending to form itself against the West, or the 'North' as he now terms it, Derrida considers that the chance of a more just future lies in Europe, which, unlike any other part of the globe, any other culture, has successfully transformed a civil society and legislation, by effective action and revolution, from its roots in religion by changing the dogma of Christianity into a working democracy, so that there are really no active vestiges of pure religion or irrational faith left there, since they have been transformed organically and from within, and yet the moral imperative and sense of faith and search still remains. This struggle could bring with it in future the chance of further development towards what will be genuinely redemptive, namely, the foundation of an international law-and-order scheme, roughly similar to the UN, but without the problems which beset the UN, in particular its reliance on the strongest members for backing and implementation of its plans. For such a strengthened UN or new international body to be born, the conditions seem, from what he says, to be as follows: this transformation will come from Europe, but must do so from a Europe which no longer needs or desires to follow America, and, since America is a military bloc, such independence must involve military independence from the US.

At present, New York and America represent the centre of the world, and without this centre there would be no world as we know it because we know it by means of the capital and information systems running out from New York. And furthermore, the world, the countries in Europe and the rest, just do need a heart. Problematically, only a militarily powerful Europe, and one united politically, could put an end to this subservience, one which could be considered to be a nearly classical totalitarianism. Once achieved, the transformation of the world into a cosmopolitical space could be undertaken from within Europe's traditions. This could lead towards the equalization of power amongst states and their possible dissolution, a situation in which, with Europe's help, the 'American dream', or the deconstructive history called 'America', could become universal. In 2004, Derrida's final interview, given for *Le Monde* (Derrida 2004b), restates this position as if it had become a hardened agenda. It is of course very problematic in that, while he says that militarily – and he emphasizes the military aspect – Europe must find its strength – a strength to involve itself in world order – on the other hand he says he does not desire Europe to become another superpower, a bloc involved in a war of nerves against the USA, or the East. Rather, it, with its spiritual riches, should be able to back up its moral positions on international matters with a sort of immediate reaction force, for example in Israel, and other troubled places.

Once, Derrida had called the USA 'deconstruction' (Derrida 1986b, *passim*) because it seemed to offer an alternative to Europe and Europe's ills. In this day Europe does not have a self-identity and cannot therefore constitute an opposition or an Other to the USA. It is hard not to remember Oswald Spengler's *Decline of the West* (1934) when thinking of the USA, a superpower composed and guided by military energies, and by decisions made on the basis of military priorities. Spengler had noted that late civilizations always have a period of civil wars, dominated by money, followed by a period of military tyranny dominated by the love of bloodshed. Late civilizations are cultureless and barbarous, dominated by the love not of existence, but of spectacle and vice. For him a culture is primarily based on the love of freedom and the impact of an ideal or guiding structure which forms the way in which the people belonging to it behave and express themselves. It is both frightening and depressing that, like Machiavelli, Derrida has had the clarity to adopt views which look forward to wars which would be good because the outcome may result in freedom and a guiding idea, of, in his case, justice. The challenge to Europe to fight its way free of America is a challenge to the spirit of Europeans, and yet is depressing, since it looks forward to a form of warfare with no guarantee of coming out to the other side with anything left.

It seems that here, more than ever, Derrida is quite Heideggerian. His appreciation of empirical and represented events, as subject to *Ereignis*, or unpossessed by Being, is particularly Heidegger-based. His view of global politics, based in Europe is, of course, also Heideggerian in a straightforward way in that he sees Europe as a place of the centre, neither theocratic like the Muslim world, nor determinedly economic and rootless like the USA. Finally, the rather silent gesture of a future quarrel with the US over who governs the world is even quite belligerent, and, we could say, Right-wing, if such terms could be of relevance to such a mobile and sensitive thinker on politics. Derrida's faith in the past of Europe, his neo-religiosity, and his considered recommendation that a European Armed Forces are ultimately necessary, echoes Heidegger perfectly. He admired the French government's cautionary response, and its persuasion that immediate action by the USA in reply to the attacks against an enemy which it could not locate would be inappropriate. It was this response which could not be heard due to France being so small (Borradori 2003, 119):

> Right now the French and German governments are trying, timidly, to slow down or temper the hastiness or overzealousness of the US, at least with respect to certain forms this 'war on terrorism' might take. But little heed is given to the voices coming from Europe. (Borradori 2003, 119)

In the discussion he also hints at what he sees as the role and future of philosophy and philosophers. He sees them as overseers and governors of this new international community, especially with regard to matters of justice and law – 'those responsible for the language and institutions of international law' (Borradori 2003, 106).

> A 'philosopher' (actually I would prefer to say 'philosopher-deconstructor') would be someone who analyzes and then draws the practical and effective consequences of the relationship between our philosophical heritage and the structure of the still dominant juridico-political system that

is so clearly undergoing mutation. A 'philosopher' would be someone who seeks a new criteriology to distinguish between 'comprehending' and 'justifying'. (Borradori 2003, 106)[3]

Several of the new books were published in English, keeping time with the French editions of *Cosmopolitanism and Forgiveness* (specially collected for an Anglo-American audience), *A Taste for the Secret*, and *Voiles* (1998c), as well as another Anglo-American collection – *The Work of Mourning* (Derrida 2001b), translated and collected for an English-speaking public from past publications (which would have been familiar enough to the French-speaking educated public, but from which we are cut off in many ways), gathering many of his speeches and papers on the dead of his generation. He published a work with Hélène Cixous, whom he admired and counted as a friend.

2001 saw Derrida, now seventy-one, as active in teaching and lecturing as he had been at the height of his powers, fulfilling obligations to teach at EHESS and U. C. Irvine along with work at the Cardozo School of Law, New York. He lectured at Liège, Brussels, Murcia, Saint-Paul, Florida, as well as at Beijing, Nanjing and Shanghai, from all of which Chinese universities he received honorary doctorates that year. His work at EHESS is recounted in passing at various places in *For What Tomorrow . . .* (Derrida 2004c) and involves questions of the death penalty, of anti-Semitism and animal 'rights'. Video footage taken by Amy Ziering Kofman for her film *Derrida* from this time shows him to be in good health, and fully in possession of his faculties, though his work had become more accessible and simpler in recent years.

In 2002 a collection of filmed interviews was released, and an interview in which Derrida recognizes 'the three ages of Jacques Derrida', although he had refused to have his work put into separate periods. Mostly the releases of that year are English translations, notably the first volume of *The Right to Philosophy*, entitled *Who's Afraid of Philosophy?* (the second volume was translated and published two years later as *Eyes of the University*), and the collections *Negotiations*, *Without Alibi* and *Echographies*. He was aware of his approaching death and had turned his thought to his posterity and reflection on what he had achieved, finally contrasting his own view of death with that of Plato's Socrates.

In 2004 Derrida still had work at the *École des hautes études en sciences sociales*, from which he had by this time retired officially. In the first part of this year he was organizing student and staff protests against the anti-intellectual behaviour of the French government. He gave an interview for *Le Monde*,

September 2004, in which he spoke of how philosophy is the science of getting to know life and having to live life. Derrida said that unlike the philosopher Socrates, he was not ready to die and did not look forward to it, but refused it, wishing to experience more.[4] He also feared that in today's barbarous climate, despite having 'many very good readers', his name and work could all but cease to exist shortly after his death, but that this is just how it goes in this age, and oblivion is all the more possible because the media and fashion dominate the universities and the presses.

23.3 Life Death

On 8 October 2004, Derrida died in as definitive a way as he could, yet was it a real death, or just the pre-programmed, routine, machine-event which is predictable and, therefore, not real? Without a real death the subject lives on. The cause of death was the cancer about which he had been aware for the past two years and which had been broadcast in the French newspapers. *The Times* immediately announced the fact in the UK, along with *The Guardian*, both dwelling on his influence in the USA after his breakthrough in the 1960s, and his initial reception by literary scholars rather than philosophers. *The Guardian* concluded that he had lent a voice to the voiceless and had fought for the interests of the excluded in society. *Le Monde* had followed Derrida's illness and his career with growing interest in the preceding years, and, on his death, issued a ten-page supplement on 'the greatest and most talked-about living French philosopher'. Jacques Chirac gave his own testimonial in the same edition, saying, along with others, that with Derrida France had given to the rest of the world a great thinker, probably not unconscious of the fact that, unlike his contemporaries, Derrida had not favoured French audiences or places, but had given his life to the world in general.

Derrida finally ceased to be alive, but continued to haunt as it were, living still in the writing which was already dead, and which had already put an end to Derrida as a biological thing well before 8 October. His disappearance was unforeseen and, maybe, due to his having always lived for the future and the coming of the Other, it came despite the illusion that he may live for as long as it is possible for one to live. Nine years before, Richard Rorty, in his contribution to *Derrida: A Reader*, had concluded that, despite the hopes of his negative critics, Derrida was 'still going strong'. The sense of this gesture was more loaded with significance than would seem. It was intended to point out that Derrida was relatively old, but yet seemed to be as young and as strong as ever. But this is precisely what shocked his contemporaries when Derrida did 'cross the line'. Derrida was going strong, as strong as ever, changeful as ever, although becoming more ordinary in the later 1990s as he concentrated on contemporary facts in his analysis of 'the event', and the hyperbolic in ethics, applying these analyses to concrete events and governmental policy in France.

It seems now that the strength of Derrida in those last years was illusory, as indeed it of course was. No one is untouchable, but Derrida seemed to be so throughout his life and in his writing. But he never recognized death as an end, though he knew that it was, and never desired to 'live for the day', even though there is nothing existent beyond what is present. It was pointed out by Bernasconi that Derrida made his position impervious to attack or internal criticism by any means at all, by changing position, or by simply making a doubling reading, which, as a reading, a mere reading, could not be faulted. What this means is that Derrida seemed to be impervious to criticism, and in terms of the life and vigour of works, this gave the impression of a sort of inhuman, immortal strength perhaps. In Derrida's texts, that is, in his mind and his life, only the Other got the upper hand. Only the Other and the promised coming was that to which he would submit and hand over authority. Apart from the undeconstructible itself, which Derrida seemed to command, while avowing that he submitted to it, he had to the last, and always, the power to avoid being overcome in argument. So death seemed inappropriate as an event in regard to him, since he was always already at its mercy and thus out of its way. Besides, having been foreseen, death was not truly an event anyway, just a machinal pre-programmed occurrence with nothing mysterious or marvellous about it. In the end he preferred to think of life, and a life unaffected intrinsically by this non-event, a life of living-on beyond death, which the passion and faith in true life could overcome.

For those who read the books and knew nothing about the coming end, this event had an uncanny and surprising shape, as he had said it always would. The event had a bizarre and supremely modern shape as well as something archaic and holy about it. Derrida did not think much of death, but those alive after it recognized it as he could not.[5]

He had continued to publish, to be interviewed, and to travel, to work with younger writers, and to deal with the avant-garde. More surprising still, a film was released in 2003 entitled *Derrida*, by an American director who had chosen Derrida, it appears, because he had the appearance of being a genuine philosopher after the old Western model of the genuine genius and thinker. Amy Ziering Kofman was one of his students at Yale in 1984. She approached him after a lecture in the mid-1990s and proposed a documentary. She received grants, and also the approval of Derrida himself. Work took place at random over several years. Kofman is not a film maker and was having difficulty editing her material, and so she invited an established director, Kirby Dick, to help. The aim was to let the life and thought come together but not explain each other. (Derrida disputes what Heidegger said about the details of a philosopher's life being 'he was born, he thought, he died' (Kofman and Dick 2003)). As well as being a documentary, the film is odd for having several quotations from Derrida's work, which make it more exciting. As the director says, it is interesting and valuable to have a genuine philosopher on film for the future. Asked if he would like to hear Heidegger or Hegel speak on tape as he was then doing for the film, he said after a short pause that he would like to hear them speak not on their philosophy, which was public, but on something not in their books, namely on their sex lives, for this is most private. They are always impersonal, he said.

The last year of his life reconciles these odd attributes of thinker and of modern celebrity, or leaves them unreconciled maybe, maybe just assorting together: of the distracted and empty-hearted life of the one who travels all over the world and has no place of rest, whom friends reproached, the busy and restless intellectual, who, moreover, allowed himself to be filmed and reproduced for the movie industry; and on the other hand, one of the few thinkers who continues in a vital way the tradition of Nietzsche and Heidegger, one whose most similar contemporary must be accounted perhaps Immanuel Kant. Perhaps what we see here is a person who could disregard himself and his private life for the benefit of the Other, or others, who would travel for them, speak for them, be filmed, and written on, and who always sought justice for the past and the future, irrespective of his present. One who knew also that, if he could not express himself, tell his own story properly, so that the story had something which signed him alone, could not write on his own body, and could not see himself, then he knew that both his writing, and an other person, would be able to do so.

Conclusion

Because this work has studied a philosopher, or, as some have it, a literary writer and theorist, it will be appropriate to make some sort of remark on the philosophy itself in conclusion. I do not hold that Derrida was not a philosopher because I do not hold that analytic philosophy is the only way of thinking, and it is only analytic philosophy which would attempt to consign Derrida to literary studies. Along with Richard Rorty, I hold that Derrida is a philosopher, or even, a 'literary philosopher', and look forward to the growth of a post-analytic philosophy. Derrida was popular amongst literature departments in America and the United Kingdom because analytic philosophy has such a hold on the philosophy teaching in those countries, and has forced many philosophers to leave, or not to join, philosophy departments, but this is no reason to deny that Derrida's work is 'philosophical' in the historical sense. In fact, the contrary is the case.

Jacques Derrida's philosophy, despite its never having been set out systematically, does have a radical coherence, even if 'deconstruction' tried to avoid creating or revealing a system. Thinking that broaches the problems which Derrida broaches positively abhors a system, but is still coherent.

In plain terms, that is, without reference to the occasions in which it was set out, or the terminology used, one should begin by allowing that Derrida's work is an ontology dealing with existent things as if they were 'spectral'. As an ontology, it took its bearings from Heidegger, and ultimately from the original philosophical project set out in Plato's works. For convenience and brevity, I would put it like this: when the chained man left the Platonic cave, as described in *The Republic*, he saw that the world which he had been looking at prior to his escape was one which was a shadow-play, cast on to his prison walls; in his liberation he saw that there is another possible life, where the true objects exist, rather than their shadows, and a true light shines, rather than a mere cave-fire. Plato's liberated philosopher saw, when he was released, a world of the truest light, and the most real existent things, which was revealed by, and constituted by, the paths of logical thought. This was metaphysics. Derrida also refers to liberation from a cave to epitomize his own philosophy (Derrida 1998d, 178),[1] but I should rather put it like this: in the cave, as before, the enchained man sees mere shadows reflected upon a prison wall; they are real objects, but outlined by a mere prison fire; once he is liberated, he does not find a true sunlight, nor a true world of existents, as Plato had it, but instead, he sees that the truest light is the light of dif-férance, and the truest objects are mere shadows, but nonetheless true shadows. The world revealed is not sensible or intelligible, though it is, again, constituted and revealed by logical thought. He may as well have not been liberated, then, if he is still resident only amongst ghosts, machines without life, and has no source of light, or goodness (in Plato's Greek, *to agathon*). But the liberation has allowed him to see clearly, and he also sees that, in the absence of a true good, he may still hope for such a good, and more important, the philosopher will be determined to love this absent or distant good. Fully to translate the Platonic world into the Derridean world it is appropriate to say that, instead of existent things, the liberated philoso-pher finds ghostly and machine-like things which do not exist in the present, nor do they have 'life', but he desires one day to locate them in a pure form. Instead of *to agathon*, he finds only the fires of différance, which, neverthe-less, give the hope that an infinitely good Goodness may, perhaps, reign over existent things in the end. The justification for the hope which the philoso-pher feels is in the promise which these real shades hold out, the promise in the way that they exist as shadows, and in which they are understood. It is because they are only promised that they are 'neither sensible, nor intelligi-ble' (Derrida 1998d, 178). Finally, the justification for his hope is that 'life', and every other gift, must have a Giver, and it may only require a better understanding of this source for him to be able to gain the most true life.

The purpose of deconstruction was to show that the fire of différance is the light beyond the Platonic cave, and in reading the history of philosophy, it has been shown, or found, that hitherto, philosophy has not discovered a way of improving this fate, this destiny of thinking, that it is governed by différance.

Objections to Derrida's philosophy have, perhaps, taken exception to this philosophy as it has just been outlined. On the whole, however, it was never this philosophy to which Frank (1992), Abrams (1977), Scruton (2005) or others were objecting. The statement that 'life is illusory' is not something with which historical philosophy has disagreed, and that 'there is no Platonic light beyond it' is not something which can be scoffed at either. Who can deny that life, and whatever rules over it, defeats the hopes of those who try to come to terms with it, or to love it? Or who deny that the riddle of things cannot be answered, but that still we have hopes, and desires? Scientific approaches to existence turn the circle of what exists into a machine, so that grasping the world, we simultaneously lose it, keeping hold only of a machine, a dead process. Despite what we feel and know, we only ever approach other people as if from a great distance, and, attempting to know others with philosophy, we find only ghosts, tangential features, or a thing with properties which are universal, and which crush the individuality of the person beneath platitudes and generalizations.

What offends deconstruction so much about the 'commonsense' or analytic philosophies, is that they give in to these processes of loss and 'fading' too easily. Not that common sense is of no use, or is not partly right, but that a dead world, and a ghost-other, are not the things themselves. Never mind that the ghost and the machine are all that we can reasonably expect; deconstruction's passion to fulfil the promise of language and the world is irrational. A reign of Being as Germany and its people, or a Platonic universe of Ideals revealed by the logos, or the dialectic progression of philosophy and the state towards Absolute Knowledge, cannot be set within the light of différance and survive. Heidegger, Plato and Hegel, however, do offer us the hope of a reconciliation with Being, or a pure and ideal world, and a genuine science, and it is this distant promise which, by deconstructing the philosophies which appropriated them, Derrida hoped to redeem.

Derrida's philosophical beginnings are rooted in Nietzsche and French existentialism; his philosophical training begins with Husserl; but the initial vision of a 'grammatology' and a 'deconstruction' was witnessed in the conflict between Being and Technology, or Being and Nihilism, outlined in Heidegger's work of the 1950s, which is basically poetic and religious in overall perspective. In Heidegger's view, as he discussed it with Jünger in *The Question of Being* (1959), the essential attribute of a religious feeling is a strenuous happiness, the burden of the happiness and the sense of destiny which only a god can bring by giving release from the heaviness of Being, and which is utterly foreign to a world obsessed by human achievements, infinite ambition, and lack of oneness with simplicity and steadiness.

To remedy what he saw as a crisis, Heidegger turned to Hölderlin's religious poetry, which is very consciously meant to fly in the face of the modern, rational metaphysics. The word of the poet is the word formed in the silence of an innocent heart which can bear the nearness of god. The god can only come near when his name and his attributes are stated in our language. A heart, or a mind, which fears loss, or is obsessed by power and machination, is simply not ready for this, and, while not above worship and community with gods, is yet afraid of the destruction which Heaven brings to human ambition and human cares. Today, the word of the poet is just a trace, and there is no poetry, except for the poetry which looks to the future, and the coming of something. Without that coming the world is unreal and joyless, except in the most fleeting and pre-programmed of ways.

The word 'Being' need not be mentioned, even though this is a Heideggerian perspective, since Being was only the privileged way of expressing where and how one lives, a word which brought to mind the possibility of understanding what rules over our existence, and how to refashion it. Hölderlin's god was not an entity in any case, but a power of renewal, an inner secret, non-existent core of Nature, just like the force which would lend reality to Derrida's spectral, machinal world of existents. The grammatology of Derrida developed from this situation analysis when Heidegger began to discuss this coming god, and the meaning of Being in *our time*. He said that today, on the metaphysical plane, Western man belongs to nihilism, and must cross the line to Being, or at least be able to read the line. At present, then, we are still on the line, and, because of this, signs such as 'Being' mean nothing. Words do not sign anything, except for what is in the future perhaps, what is beyond the line, and thus, words are just traces and marks, signifying the 'line'. Derrida once went so far as to grant that even his own words are just a rhythm in the end, and that their content is just a play of meanings, not a real meaning. But this is due to the time in which we live, our position on the near side of the line separating us from a genuine life.

But while Heidegger awaited the god in our time, it is not clear, but seems to be the case, that Derrida did not wish to see such an arrival, but thought in terms of a generalized 'arrivance', in which the coming miracle, the impossible moment at which the soul would return, and genuine peace and justice prevail amongst peoples and nations, was infinitely deferred. He thereby transformed a temporary philosophical response into a permanent description of existence. Each great thing from the past, be it 'the soul', 'happiness', science, or 'life', are all just traces, their content lost, and this content may only return in a messianic time, when perhaps language would be redeemed by the great meaning and joy which besets a people when they are stuck by the arrival of a god, or thrown beyond the domination of the '*il y a*'.

The same is the case with all of the things which were deconstructed by Derrida. 'Speech-acts', Hegelian Christianity, Freudian psychoanalysis, 'national awakening' and democracy, each is founded on the hope that somehow their words will one day, or do already, have a meaning in real terms. Derrida, not wishing to give these logocentric hopes the advantage of saying that they are *partly* true, held that such a coming meaning would never come in actual fact. Rather, meaning is just a tradition, and is extracted from words simply by repetition of them, so that even an affirmation of happiness, in the 'yes' of a welcome or an agreement, has to be repeated in order for it to make sense.

To come back to the Platonic alignment which was made earlier, in which it was said that entities are spectral, and that différance rules over them, we should say that language itself is spectral too, and this is put into words in the thematic of 'the trace'. Words do not signify, they merely separate Being from Nothing, and each thing from any other thing. Again, in the Platonic scheme, Derrida held that a great true justice might one day hold sway, a god could come and bring a deep innocence and industriousness to people, a great happiness to the philosopher amongst his shadow world – but the chances are that this is close to impossible.

Because such a burst of reality is impossible, it is slightly improper to write of Derrida's life and his work as if they were 'real' things which could be aligned with the words of a book. Such a book will always simply present a dead and spectral object by means of dead and worn-out, pre-programmed sentences and styles. When Geoffrey Bennington did so in 1990, Derrida responded by trying to give a more true, pure version of himself at the bottom of Bennington's pages. Not that this was of any avail. It would have been impossible for Bennington ever to have got to the heart of 'Jacques Derrida' or his work, no matter how much accuracy, information and wisdom he applied to the task. When Derrida aided the work, and replied, his effort too was doomed, but it was still his hope that something would come across, something real. That is the hope of Heideggerian and Derridean philosophy. That indeed was the content of his reply, that he was full of hopes, passionate, in love with reality, with the truth, even though they fled him. The impossible is the only thing which is real in this age of nihilism, when, perhaps, only a god can save us, and the impossible is the one thing worthy of love, so that deconstruction is, in the end, the desire for an impossibly high standard of goodness, justice, purity and existence.

Notes

Introduction

1   The conference was held at Baltimore in 1966 and invited several French structuralists to speak of their work on the human sciences, entitled the 'International Colloquium on Critical Languages and the Sciences of Man'. De Man attended the conference and popularized Derrida's work by writing on him at length in his 1972 *Blindness and Insight* (de Man 1983).

2   Ted Honderich mentions a survey of British academic attitudes to philosophers in the late twentieth century in which 'the most over-rated philosopher of all time' was Derrida (Honderich 2001, 384).

3   To Geoffrey Bennington's book *Jacques Derrida* I must give, at the outset, the acknowledgement which I owe it. Bennington's account of Derrida's life in 'Curriculum vitae' (Derrida 1999, 325–36) gave a basic outline for the preliminary sketches of this biography. Bennington was fortunate enough to have undertaken his own account with the active assistance of Derrida himself.

4   Particularly *Counterpath*, with Catherine Malabou (2004a), and *For What Tomorrow* . . ., with Elizabeth Roudinesco (2004c), as well as the earlier *Monolingualism of the Other; or the Prosthesis of the Origin* (1998e). Finally, the collections of interviews, *Points* . . . (1995b), and *Negotiations* (2002a).

5   Derrida, in a film by Ken McMullen (*Ghost Dance* (1982)) in which he appeared, went so far as to say 'I am a ghost'.

1 Algeria

1   For the sake of convenience I have provided the titles of Derrida's books almost always in the form of their English translations, even where I refer specifically to French releases.

2   Derrida held back photographs of himself from the press until the 1980s, fearful that they might detract from his work's reception for itself. By the time he did permit photographic likenesses of himself to be distributed by the press his appearance had taken on a pure white, silver tone, due to the greying of his hair and the fading of his natural skin colouring.

3   It was his first question insofar as he decided to begin a questioning of literature in terms of 'The Ideality of the Literary Object', a projected title which betrays a confused adherence to Husserl, and yet a notion that Husserl's phenomenology would not be able to incorporate 'the literary object'. The title in question was that of his postponed *Thèse d'État* in 1957. 'Punctuations' recalls this projected thesis (in *Du droit à la philosophie* (1990)).

2 Paris and ENS

1   The course is generally three years. Derrida took four.

2   The text which fascinated Heidegger at a similar point in his life. Heidegger recalled famously that he was so fascinated by the book that he even used to pore over how the pages were laid out, and had it permanently on loan from the university library for several years.

3   A claim which Derrida made, and reaffirmed in the early 1980s after nearly two decades of reflection on this.

4   See also 'Language', in *Poetry, Language, Thought* (Heidegger 1975, 187–210), which is identical to the theory of a 'grammatology' in all but its style of exposition.

5   There are two ENS: one on rue d'Ulm, and the other, for women, at Saint Cloud.

6   François Dosse locates the political and cultural crisis of having to enter the wider European community, initiated by de Gaulle, at around 1974/5, some twenty years later (Dosse 1998b, 269–75). The crisis amongst intellectuals centred on the revelations from Stalinist Russia. Liberalism and democracy became worth defending in 1974 definitively, becoming the sure alternative to the revolutionary politics which had been in steady decline with successive revelations of cruelty, imperialism and gross injustice in Soviet Russia throughout the post-war years.

7   A typical deconstructive questioning of concepts in even normal statements in Nicholas Royle's *Jacques Derrida*, where he introduces his book with more than ten problems with the provisionally meaningful, and unproblematic sentence: ' "Derrida" is the name of a man, a Jewish Algerian-French philosopher, born in 1930' (Royle 2003, 1–13).

8   Again Lacan (2001, 78–9) sought to give back to the subject its creative subjectivity in a cultural revolution along socialist lines ('Rome Report', 1953,

Lacan 2001, 33–125). Lacan, the great adaptor of others' ideas, here sums up the feeling of the 1950s. Lacan's 'Rome Report' was delivered while Derrida was a second-year student at ENS.

9   See Derrida (2001a, *passim*).

3 After ENS

1   Fredric Jameson even went so far as to say that deconstruction is essentially the imitation and recreation of works from history, which attempts to improve on them and replace them, with, one must add, the advantage of a vision of justice (see his remarks on de Man in Jameson (1991, 220)), that is, insofar as de Man rewrote the texts, recreating them with a new vision of them, like a 'piece of homemade furniture'.

2   This structuralist shortcoming, in structures themselves and in Husserl, was later to be valorized, by Foucault, with reference to the history of science and knowledge, as 'discontinuous progression' (in *The Archaeology of Knowledge*).

3   I have been assisted in clarifying Husserl's progress and the development of his ideas over a lifetime of research and study, by David Bell's publication *Husserl* (Bell 1990).

4   See 'Kant, the German, the Jew' in *Acts of Religion* (2001a, 135–88).

5   Jean Cavailles was an epistemologist logician who had died in 1944, a hero of the Resistance, under Nazi fire (Dosse 1998a, 84).

4 The First Book

1   Freedom, or the equality of choices for any and everybody, is no doubt a good 'idea', but 'freedom' is a concept whose validity and meaning has only ever meant something to the self-aware mind, or logocentric thinking based in the 'same'. Freedom has no referent beyond the concept of it in the conscious, and is thus pernicious in the end – while responsibility to the Other has something of the same imperative nature, the same universal feature and justice, yet is not 'conceptual' but responsible – for the 'Other'. The further reaches of freedom are no doubt those positions which D. A. F. de Sade's heroes take up in his *120 Days of Sodom*.

2   I would draw attention to the fact that deconstruction was not primarily, as Derrida first framed it, a typical linguistic philosophy. It dealt with language and signs, but it did so in a manner contrary to post-Russellian and post-Saussurian linguistics. That is, it was interested in language so as to debunk linguistic, speech-centred philosophy (it 'debunked' linguistic philosophy, as Rorty has it (Rorty 1982, 96)). The trace is not a language or even meaning, but the pre-conditional differential basis for language.

3   The repressed nature of writing, its having a place in the, as it were, 'uncon-
     scious' of Western culture, indicates how it has been possible to say that
     Derrida has carried out a psychoanalytic reading of that culture.

4   Heidegger's essay 'Language' ('Die Sprache'), which appears in English
     translation in *Poetry, Language, Thought* (Heidegger 1975), is quite obviously
     the first instance of a grammatology prior to Derrida's own. Indeed, one may
     go so far as to say that the only element which Derrida has added or changed
     has been the alteration of the terms 'speech' and 'spoken' in Heidegger's
     description of language's essence, for the terms 'writing' and 'written', so
     that for the first time this Heideggerian theory can be a theory of the *gramme*.
     The fact that language is always already speaking, that it acts as a differenc-
     ing power because it is a line of separation and of unity, or, finally, that lan-
     guage brings together a unity of non-present things into a relationship of
     play, is all explicitly outlined in Heidegger's essay, and was clearly taken up
     by Derrida almost to the letter.

5   Caputo is referring to the work *Finnegans Wake* (Joyce 1992) almost every
     word of which is a pun or a neologism utilizing various languages, and con-
     sisting of sentences with no one meaning, if they have any meaning at all.
     The austere precision of *Dubliners*, *The Portrait of the Artist*, or even *Ulysses* is
     not the Joyceanism to which he is referring.

5 Against Structuralism

1   See Heidegger, *Basic Writings* (Heidegger 1978, 'A Letter on Humanism'), a
     text written for Jean Beaufret who also taught at ENS, in response to French
     existentialism.

2   Not mentioned here is Roland Barthes, who was the most famous struc-
     turalist literary critic, and with whom Derrida was to collaborate in *Tel Quel*.

3   There are exceptions in the work of each. Freud's later work made the
     unknown [*Unbewusst*] into a portion, a restricted area of the psyche, along-
     side the Ego, the superego, and the various drives and so on, so that the
     'unknown' became slightly 'known' in character. Similarly, in his note-
     books, collected as *The Will to Power*, Nietzsche laid out a metaphysics of
     power and will which disqualifies his 'end of God/Plato' theory somewhat.
     Finally Heidegger seemed to put forward a 'result' in the work and speeches
     of the Rectoral period (1933) although Heidegger's real work never had a
     result or system.

4   Dosse (1998a, xxiv) seems to include Derrida in his list of epistemic struc-
     turalists. It may be as well to consider early Derrida to be a renegade struc-
     turalist in this way, as a structuralist who imagined a structure which has no
     core, which is nevertheless a structure. By 1966 Derrida was finishing off his
     Of Grammatology and had rounded off his understanding of it. He was

publishing work on Lévi-Strauss and Rousseau. Such is the basis of his triumphant announcement at Baltimore.

6 Structures in French Thought

1   Dosse lists Derrida amongst them (Dosse 1998a, xxiv). He also was the first to reach America. ·

2   Lévi-Strauss was still alive when Dosse completed his work in 1991, and still working on anthropology.

3   Again, in 'Language' (Heidegger 1975, 187–210).

4   These formative ideas which Derrida had developed came to him just before 1966 when Lacan's first major publication, *Écrits*, came out.

5   Major organized the *Lacan avec les philosophes* conference at which Derrida spoke in the 1990s (see Derrida 1998a). It was organized at a time when there was controversy between different interpretations of Lacan's work – especially amongst his followers who, like Derrida, were beginning to see him not as a scientist but as a thinker and philosopher. Lacan himself considered Freud to be a philosopher of a sort, a descendant of Hegel (Dosse 1998a, 95). In his contribution to the colloquium, Derrida allies himself to Lacan, after decades of resistance, because it was strategically necessary to do so, he said later (Derrida 2004c, 186). He saluted Lacan.

6   Derrida himself knew that his own prose was not very 'French', and pointed out that even Lacan, amongst the structuralists who were all quite conventional stylists in prose, was far more French than himself (Derrida 2004c, 14).

7   This is the gist of the 'Purloined Letter' lecture ('Le Facteur de la verité', or 'The Purveyor of Truth') first published in 1975, and subsequently collected in *The Post Card* [1980]. This lecture is actually an event of Derrida's early reading of Lacan's work.

8   That is, the *Autre* with a capital 'a', as opposed to the *autre* with a small 'a', as it is understood as an object which resists signification (*objet petit a*). Derrida made use of this perhaps with his 'a' in différance, suggests Dosse (1998a, 244).

9   Dosse helpfully refers this to Heidegger's statement that 'Thinging is the nearing of the world' (Heidegger 1975, 163–86), meaning that when the world appears as near to us or is in our purview, it does so as a mere 'thing'.

7 1967

1   With this gesture Derrida is making use of the spoken voice's similarity to writing which he elsewhere characterizes as dead, or the sign of the death of the writer, a point made particularly at Baltimore in 1966 in response to Barthes' paper.

2   The Aristotelian-Kantian view of time.
3   See G. C. Spivak's introduction to the English language translation of *Of Grammatology* (Derrida 1997b, lxxix).
4   Derrida maintained the distinction between 'philosophy' and 'thinking' throughout his life, expressing it in 'Violence and Metaphysics' and in *Of Grammatology* itself. This permits us to put an end to philosophy and yet to continue to do philosophy in an indirect way, while still concentrating on the mystery of the one, the unity of this existence, which has been philosophy's perennial object.
5   'To counter this simple alternative, to counter the simple choice of one of the terms of one of the series against the other, we maintain that it is necessary to seek new concepts and new models, an *economy* escaping this system of metaphysical oppositions.'
6   Hence the invitation from André Green, to deliver 'Freud and the Scene of Writing' (2003, 246–91) at the *Institut de psychoanalyse* in 1966.

8 Avant-garde Philosophy

1   Althusser had held a very public debate with Sartre over Marxism in 1960 in the Sorbonne in which Sartre was defeated, while Lévi-Strauss had been invited to contribute to *Les Temps Modernes*, Sartre's journal, but had quickly gained support by repudiating Sartre's methods and his existentialism.
2   'A Podium Without a Podium' (Lyotard 1993).
3   The paper's proximity to *Of Grammatology* is due to its having been presented in January 1968.
4   Derrida never attacked a text as a target, as it is common to do in Anglo-Saxon philosophy, where criticism is undertaken so as to improve one's own point of view, or the current beliefs as to what past efforts have been. Such efforts are in general set against the backdrop of contemporary findings. Derrida said, and his practice does not contradict his statement, that he never discussed a work unless it interested him, and he was sympathetic to it (Derrida 2004c, 6). Around 1974 French structuralism began to speak of doing theory and philosophy for the pleasure of reading, but Derrida had been doing it for this reason well before Barthes, and Derrida (in *Glas* particularly) stated this explicitly.
5   See the conversion, and the discussion of what Plato's cave allegory meant to Heidegger, in Heidegger (1998b, 155–82). The discussion of the doctrine of truth [1942] emphasizes the distinction, unquestioned by any Greek thinker, that truth was 'revelation' or unconcealment. See a full discussion of the Greek destiny, as opposed to the modern version, in Heidegger (1994, 105–7). In regard to this see also Nietzsche's own discussion of what he saw as Platonism, or what had become Platonism due to the incorporation of the

Republic into Christianity, as 'Platonism for the People', in *The Twilight of the Idols* ([1889] 1990b), at the point where the origins of the 'other world' are discussed. Nietzsche tended to reverse Plato, in a manoeuvre which neither Derrida nor Heidegger, both of whom admired this passage in *Twilight*, could follow in their own swerve away from Plato. Derrida chose a middle path, between truth and mere appearance, the word which is neither sensible, nor intelligible.

9 America: Derrida as Literary Theory

1   Heidegger calls the field of thinkers over history a mountain range, in this way doing away with any sense of linearity in the unfolding of philosophy over time, and giving to these thinkers the solidity and 'grounding' power of the German land itself (Heidegger 1999, §93).

2   (Nietzsche 1968, §95): 'In Goethe a kind of almost joyous and trusting fatalism that does not revolt, that does not flag, that seeks to form a totality out of himself . . .' See also the passage in *Zarathustra* in which the sage meets a gigantic ear beneath which he discerns, with difficulty, a miniature set of limbs, and a head, the ear being Wagner's, a man who responded only partially to reality, not with an openness to the future, but to a future which he had decided to create and force (with his *Musik der Zukunft*).

3   Derrida involved himself in the city, with his notion of 'Cities of Asylum' (discussed in 2001c), and also in his architectural collaborations (to name but a few related matters).

4   I would refer here also to the Heidegger who found his opening of truth in the middle of forests (Safranski 1998), and in his Black Forest home at Todenauberg (Petzet 1993). That era of grand solitude, and love of nationalistic fatherland, of heroic, sovereign solitude has come to an end in Derrida's type of post-structuralist thought in which there is no ultimate *Ding an sich* to reveal by meditation, and no referent ever to reveal with a sign, and finally, no life ever to possess, no death to suffer.

5   Bernasconi pursued this matter in his contribution to *Derrida and Difference* (Wood and Bernasconi 1985, 17–44).

6   Derrida's late messianism is a case in point.

10 *Glas*

1   See Heidegger (1999) on the Other Origin, and the Echo, two 'joinings' [*Fuge*] of the projected way of thought to which he was making a 'contribution'.

2   Habermas based his critique on the *Of Grammatology* and *Writing and Difference* (Habermas 1987) as did M.H. Abrams (Lodge and Wood 2000, 242–52, also

in *Critical Inquiry*, 3, [1977]). Most adverse criticism does this, seeing in these early works only what is obvious, and not the riches which were concealed and which were revealed with time, namely Derrida's ability to revive a tradition and to make way for a future by destroying the structuralist tradition. Unfortunately, few were then aware of Derrida's very ancient Dionysianism, his search for the hidden unity amidst the broken and ghostly.

3 Insofar as this vocalic element is at its heart, Derrida is also showing the repressed side of the voice as well as the repressed side of writing. D. F. Krell, who makes this point in the Wood/Bernasconi collection *Derrida and Difference* (1985, 11–16), is correct in this statement, especially since Derrida does not take sides with the repressed Other, but overcomes their opposition, favouring neither.

4 Howells (1989) is of great use in understanding the cultural background of *Glas*, insofar as *Glas* is a response to Sartre's *Saint Genet*.

11 GREPH

1 The cultural Foundation against Apartheid, of which Derrida was part of the guiding council (Bennington 1999, 335); and also the Writer's Committee for Nelson Mandela (texts about which were collected in *Psyche* (1987c)).

2 This campaign for philosophy has an admirable consistency with his activity. It is of value to society to increase or maintain philosophy since it conduces to a true democracy.

3 Dosse catalogues this in *The Empire of Meaning* (Dosse 1999).

4 Government initiatives to put an end to the lack of acceptance of 'otherness' in philosophy would not be out of character in an age which has seen it become illegal to be overtly discriminative in the matter of otherness in racial matters, where the natural affection of disliking non-natives, and excluding them, in order to strengthen the original population, has had to be educated out of institutions and public life by means of force, in the long-term interests of those natives.

12 Yale

1 See T. S. Eliot on Milton (1947). Eliot says that he does not appreciate the lists of names of places which Milton creates. This objection is characteristic of Eliot's preferences and says little about *Paradise Lost*.

2 De Man considers T. S. Eliot to be the great exemplar of pre-Theory modernist New Criticism in his personality and ideology (Lodge and Wood 2000, 335).

3 A sentiment similar to the suggestion that Europe, and no other place on earth, could transform religion into governmental policy, since it alone has a tradition of transformation.

4 Hillis Miller in a round table following the delivery of the lecture in the US refers to the treatment which Richard Rorty's book *Philosophy and the Mirror of Nature* received in philosophy departments from staff, despite and because of student and public interest in his new brand of post-analytic deconstruction which he pretends is native to the US.

5 While following one of Hegel's contemporaries, one famous for despising Hegel's work, namely the philosopher Arthur Schopenhauer (Heidegger calls him an 'epigone' (Heidegger 1984, 112–13), insinuating that he is not a 'genuine' philosopher).

13 *The Post Card*

1 The original seminar by Lacan, Derrida's review, and the discussions these two texts gave rise to, are collected in *The Purloined Poe* (Harvey 1988).

2 A primary source of this doctrine for Heidegger was Hölderlin's poetry, and was outlined by Heidegger in his paper on 'As When On a Holiday . . .' (Heidegger 2000b, 67–99). This sending was questioned by de Man in his *Blindness and Insight* (de Man 1983), in an essay devoted to Heidegger. The problem centred on whether Being, or Germany metaphysically understood, can both be immediate, and, at the same time, mediate between things, as the Law. But the major exposition of the doctrine, which both de Man and Derrida took issue with, was propounded by Heidegger around the year 1950, when, while not describing exactly how it was possible, he said that it is the poets who hear Being, and found the destiny of the world. Heidegger, of course, tried to provide the enemy to pure technological metaphysics with his fourfold unity of gods, heaven, earth and mortals, a fourfold which he believed was the only alternative destiny for Western Being.

14 Nietzsche and Heidegger

1 In commentary like this on Heidegger's post-*Being and Time* work Derrida is remarkably clear on the newly published and secret work, so that very little can be said as regards Derrida's inaccuracy on Heidegger's public and private doctrine. I refer the reader to the *Contributions to Philosophy* text composed as notebooks by Heidegger (Heidegger 1999), adequately called the most important of his works after *Being and Time* – an assessment based on its compiling the post-*Being and Time* work in a systematic and exhaustive format. There are, of course, very good reasons for believing that there is no Heideggerian system, and that 'thought' means exactly this: that there shall be no system, only thinking of the essential. The same thesis seems to have been held by Derrida.

2   I have relied on Hugh Silverman's own contribution to Silverman (1989) in
    this discussion of a Heideggerian text by the older Heidegger.

3   The event was to become Derrida's preoccupation. The text *Zur Seinsfrage*
    was to be a crossing and meeting point for Derrida in many ways.

4   See Cumming (1981) on the great similarity of Derrida's view of art to that
    of Heidegger, but in which Derrida puts the 'frame' [*Gestell*] within the
    picture itself, in the form of lattices. One of the most originary levels at which
    these Derrida and Heidegger concur, and which they both study, is that of
    'representation'. The representation which Derrida congratulated Heidegger
    for understanding so well is both the counterfeit, artistic form of the world,
    and also the world itself, as an interpreted 'event'. This mixing of world with
    art is what Derrida is questioning, since Heidegger had maintained their dis-
    tinction, while Derrida did not, at least he did not so easily accept it.

5   The saving power contained in Technology, or the Being of the present day,
    is very helpfully and lucidly contained in *Heidegger's Confrontation with
    Modernity* (Zimmerman 1990).

6   See Heidegger (1975, 143–62), 'Building, Dwelling, Thinking'.

7   Hollingdale (1999, 341) suggests even that Nietzsche feigned his madness,
    aware of how much credit a thinker could receive from having gone hero-
    ically into the beyond of sanity. Hölderlin's example, he says, had taught him
    much, while the Greeks considered their philosophers to be insane – and
    thus divine. This credit, which he had to give to himself, and which would
    return only with his death, was precipitated and recouped with his death-
    in-life, so that he did perhaps enjoy a decade of genuine reward.

8   In *On Nietzsche* ([1944], 1992) Bataille said that Nietzsche's type of ecstatic
    plethoric states of mind described in *Zarathustra*, and in which the philoso-
    pher attains to a grasp of all things, thematized as early on as *The Birth of
    Tragedy* [1872] in which the satyr who sees this vision considers it best to be
    dead (a reference to the captive Solon's words prior to being burnt by the
    Persian king), is likened to the moment regained in Proust's *In Search of Lost
    Time*, in the stepping on the uneven kerb, or the drinking of tea in the
    Guermantes' mansion (Proust 1972). As Berezdvin describes the Eternal
    Return it seems so. On the other hand, aside from these Bataillean partiali-
    ties, Nietzsche admired Dostoevski's *The Idiot* (Dostoevski 1955) because it
    seemed to him to be an expert psychological study of a 'Christ'-figure. That
    is, not of superhumanity, but of *décadence*. Maybe Proust is Nietzschean,
    maybe Proustianism is *décadent*.

15 The 1980s

1   Robert Bernasconi further elucidates the story by referring to the revisions
    which took place in the original publication of 'Violence and Metaphysics',

followed by the inclusion of these early revisions into the main body of the text in the 1967 publication of *Writing and Difference*.

2   Described as the Mother figure of structuralism by Dosse (1998a, 71) where Lacan would provide the figure of Father.

3   The first printed photographs of Derrida for the media had been issued on the occasion of his taking part in the Estates General of Philosophy in 1979. He is seen with a flowing cravat, swept-back greying hair, and a philosophical seriousness, seated at a desk (see the photographs in *Jacques Derrida* (Bennington 1999)).

4   Collected in Derrida 1990 (619–58).

5   Habermas in *The Philosophical Discourse of Modernity* (1987) represented Derrida as a French neo-conservative. Derrida and Habermas moved beyond this, attending conferences and speaking together, as in their late agreement to consider 9/11 in a single work with Borradori (Derrida 2003).

16   1987–90, Deconstruction and National Socialism

1   Translated as 'spirit' usually, and in the English translation of 1989, but *Geist* is elsewhere synonymous with 'mind'.

2   The essays constitutive of *The Companion to Heidegger's Contributions to Philosophy* for example make almost nothing of religion's relationship to the dominant Western religion of Protestant Christianity (Scott, Schoenbaum, *et al.*, 2001) except insofar as Heidegger himself says that medieval philosophy has decided the history of philosophy in such and such a way. To read Heidegger in such a servile way is not genuinely to understand his work, for it is easy simply to appropriate his language, but it is not easy to apply it in an original or appropriate way. Heidegger's own stated view on religion is that it is a 'faith'-thinking and thus not genuine questioning. On religion itself, Heidegger had received his education because of Catholic sponsorship, and he was intended for the priesthood, a duty which he finally had to set aside due to ill health at crucial moments of his career. He married into a Protestant, Prussian family and set about avoiding religion and theology altogether.

3   This new textual blindness of *Geist* is the new, Other text, that Derrida finds by rereading, concealed in the Heideggerian trace/metaphor of fire.

4   This is Derrida's conclusion, a description of a method of rereading and overlapping texts (here Heidegger and Hebraism), so as to create a new trace, a third text, but one with a future, rather than a (ghostly) present such as we have now.

5   This is the time of the text, the time of the line (see Silverman 1989, 168).

6   See the other origin of Being's interpretation in the Other beginning [*Andere Anfang*], *Contributions to Philosophy* (Heidegger 1999, §89), a nonmetaphysical thought which is similar to Derrida's.

7   Derrida received an honorary doctorate from the New School for Social Research, New York, this year.

8   Subsequently published (Cornell 1992).

17 Autobiographical Years, 1990–91

1   Note that Derrida inaugurated this series too, just as he tended now to be the first to speak or act whenever he was invited to an event. No doubt this was no accident. In his dealings with Lacan and Foucault he could not abide taking second place.

2   See the fire which consumes rather than discloses in *Of Spirit*.

3   Caputo's discussion of *Memoires of the Blind* constitutes a good study in his book *The Prayers and Tears of Jacques Derrida* (Caputo 1997b, 308–29). His analysis of Derrida as a thinker of the messiah and the coming of the other person, the utterly Other, only came into its own, perhaps, when he began to study *Circumfession* and the other texts of confession. *Circumfession* is the obvious inspiration for his study of Derrida in the light of religion, but his study of *Memoires of the Blind* is invaluable.

4   See the selection of *Memoires* in Derrida (1998d, 169–83).

5   The impossibility of seeing the mirror-image and the page at the same time, thus constituting a 'margin', is a theme seen previously in *Glas'* two columns and in other texts like *Circumfession*. Derrida was convinced that such a margin was also a trace, and thus a third text whose meaning was yet to be found.

18 The Future of Democracy and the Very Worst Moment of Capitalism

1   Also discussed in the context of 'we good Europeans' in Nietzsche's most political work – *Beyond Good and Evil* (1990a, *passim*).

2   See *The Future Lasts Forever* (Althusser 1992).

3   It had reached France in 1987, while it had reached Germany in the 1930s, and had never been forgotten. Hugo Ott, a historian, had involved himself in the life and history of the philosopher some years before in Germany (Ott 1988). This only served to make the storm aroused by Farías' work all the more ridiculous.

19 Derrida's World: Confronting Marx

1   There is an alarming consistency in Derrida's notion of the sign versus the unnamed thing, the coming, the birth. It also figures in Derrida's early 'manifesto': 'Structure, Sign and Play'.

2   MacIntyre also throws this weakness of good sentiments at the reader – in the name of Christianity, which is the true foundation of these rights (1985, 251).

3   A Nietzschean formulation for his type of 'Dionysian pessimism' delivered
     at the time of his *Gay Science*, after his analysis of pessimism had begun in
     the *Untimely Meditations*. It does not, like Stoicism, merely accept facts and
     the delight and horror of life because they are illusory, but decides to enjoy
     and love them – from a place beyond value judgements of delight or horror.
     Ronald Hayman notes that, according to Nietzsche, Orphic wisdom had told
     the Greeks that their genius was founded on the acceptance of destructive-
     ness and conflict (Hayman 1980, 159). The sentiment is quite similar, but
     the style of Nietzsche's bizarre Latin hieroglyph could not be further away
     from Derrida's own considered, infinitely laborious metonymy.

4   It was said there that this aspect of Hölderlin is the most core attribute of his
     poetry, and that his hymns on gods 'Wie wenn am Feiertage', 'Der Rhein',
     and so on (Hölderlin 1986), and the coming of a new race, a new god, is
     nothing but the reading of Greek culture in the perspective of what can be
     saved from it of good for a post-French Revolutionary Europe. Heidegger too
     seems to see Hölderlin in this perspective, as the poet of the revitalization
     and inheritance from the Greeks, when he treats of Hölderlin when reading
     his translations of Sophocles, and 'The Ister' in lectures devoted to them
     (Heidegger 1996); also in the *Introduction to Metaphysics* lectures (Heidegger
     2000a).

20 *The Politics of Friendship*

1   See *Basic Questions of Philosophy* (Heidegger 1994, 105–7) on Greek thought,
     which despite being very deep and beautiful, is in fact an overturning, or a
     deconstruction of, Greek thought.

2   See Schmitt 1996, *passim*.

3   Who lived for the future and 'lived off his own credit' but never received
     that credit back in kind while actually 'alive'.

21 Derrida's Religion

1   Arnold Toynbee (Toynbee 1957) outlined in the later books of his *History* a
     growing prevision that the only part which a late, or third-generation, civi-
     lization can contribute, from within the internal and external proletariat, is
     the birth of a new religion – as is proved by what remained of Rome, or of
     various other over-extended universal states from biblical times, in the
     Americas and in the Indian subcontinent, for what they had to leave behind
     them was a new religion. Toynbee finds it hard to give a structural picture
     of our civilization or universal state because it is unprecedented by and large,
     but he speculates that a religion must come which will give strength to a
     future culture, a seed sown in our ruined and elderly world which will be

the origin of a new genuine culture. Such work on religion, and religion itself, has value not only because religion promises an afterlife, and is therefore potentially a great benefit to the believer, but because religion does in fact make way for a future of civilization in the empirical sense. Finally it may bring about, as Derrida hoped, a democracy to come.

2   In a reference to Lacan, Derrida also means this phallus is the truth, the logical and the rational.

3   In the work of poets this greater abstraction comes with age too – as we see Yeats turn to his grand scheme of life, desire and death involving the coming of a new age (Yeats 1962), and Heidegger, who had been careful about how practical his plans were in the rectorate, and avoided otiose prophecy in his early work, but who in the end said that 'Only a god can save us' in an interview for *Der Spiegel*. The reliance on a god was a candid admission of his own failure, but was it not also integral to his philosophy, both to fail, and to need a god, a god to show the truth, and to push aside the world of desire and calculation.

22 Thoughtful Welcoming of the Other, Death

1   Stephen Spender (1951) refused to commit himself to describing the most recent ten years of his life in *World Within World* since to do so would be to break his rule of having a complete picture of his life – something hard to do with events which had not been digested fully in the course of time. Nevertheless, we have to come to the end.

2   Lyotard (1984). *The Postmodern Condition* was originally a report for the Canadian government on the state of knowledge and science in the present day. Lyotard created a work in which he suggested ways in which to equalize the potentially harmful effects of a powerful minority taking control of the new industries of information and technology, thereby disenfranchizing the majority.

3   Which he was to deal with in 'On Forgiveness'.

4   Author of the short popular work on Derrida, under that title (1999). It concentrates almost exclusively on Lévi-Strauss in *Of Grammatology*.

5   Heidegger (1995) devoted a seminar series to this problem of possible/actual and its machinal aspect, its pre-programmed side, in his work on Aristotle. He is there unsatisfied both by the logical underpinnings, and by the classical exposition wherein Being must become ideal, before it is actualized in things.

6   See the early article in *Partisan Review* (Greene 1976).

7   The German physicist Heisenberg had a friendship with Heidegger, and, while laying out the future of physics, made some gestures towards letting the philosophers sort out the question of Being and of, perhaps, 'the gift'. See Heisenberg (1963).

23 2000 Onwards

1   See *Spectres of Marx* on the event.
2   In this he seems to have been trying to diminish the importance of the event and at the same time advising 'Bush'-followers that it was something they should expect and then put up with calmly.
3   This is said with regard to a projected war. It is one thing to understand the conditions under which and because of which war could be waged, but it is another thing to justify going to war.
4   See *Living On* and *Life death* above.
5   An economy of sight worked out by Caputo (1997b, 323).

Conclusion

1   Roughly, he had left Plato's cave not to get to Ideas, but because the trace is 'neither sensible nor intelligible', something that the cave hid, and which Plato could not see either. In other words, the final ground of things is neither sensible nor intelligible, and the effects of this run throughout all which is built of the trace.

Works Cited

Abrams, M.H. (1977), 'The deconstructive angel', *Critical Inquiry* 3, 425–38.

Althusser, Louis (1992), *The Future Lasts Forever*, trans. Richard Veasey. New York: The New Press.

Aristotle (1961) [c. 330] *Aristotle's Metaphysics*, ed. John Warrington. London: Dent.

Aschheim, Steven E. (1994), *The Nietzsche Legacy in Germany (1890–1990)*. London: University of California Press.

Barlow, J. and Nadeau, J.-B. (2004), *Sixty Million Frenchmen Can't Be Wrong*. London: Robson Books.

Bataille, Georges (1987), *Eroticism*, trans. Mary Dalwood. London: Marion Boyars.

—— (1988) [1943], *Inner Experience*, trans. Leslie-Anne Boldt. New York: SUNY Books.

—— (1991), *The Accursed Share* (two vols), trans. Robert Hurley. New York: Zone Books.

—— (1992), *On Nietzsche*, trans. Bruce Boone. London: Athlone Press.

Bell, David (1990), *Husserl*. London: Routledge.

Bennington, G. (1992), 'Mosaic fragment, if Derrida were an Egyptian', in *Derrida: A Critical Reader*, ed. David Wood. Massachusetts: Blackwell, pp. 97–199.

—— (and Derrida) (1999), *Jacques Derrida*. Chicago: University of Chicago Press.

Berezdvin, R. (1989), 'Drawing, (an), affecting Nietzsche, with Derrida', in *Derrida and Deconstruction: Continental Philosophy II*, Silverman, H. (ed.). New York and London: Routledge, pp. 92–107.

Bernasconi, R. (1992), 'No more stories, good or bad: de Man's criticisms of Derrida on Rousseau', in *Derrida: A Critical Reader*, ed. David Wood. Massachusetts: Blackwell, pp. 137–66.

Bernet, R. (1989), 'Derrida's *Introduction to* Husserl's "Origin of Geometry"', in *Derrida and Deconstruction: Continental Philosophy II*, Silverman, H. (ed.). New York and London: Routledge, pp. 139–53.

Bloom, H. (1995), *The Western Canon*. London: Papermac.

Bloom, H., de Man, P., Derrida, J., Hartman G. and Miller J. H. (1979), *Deconstruction and Criticism*. New York: Seabury Press.

Borradori, Giovanna (2003), *Philosophy in a Time of Terror*. Chicago: The University of Chicago Press.

Brogan, W. (1989), 'Plato's *Pharmakon*, between two repetitions', in *Derrida and Deconstruction: Continental Philosophy II*, Silverman, H. (ed.). New York and London: Routledge, pp. 7–23.

Caputo, John D. (1997a), *Deconstruction in a Nutshell*. New York: Fordham University Press.

—— (1997b), *The Prayers and Tears of Jacques Derrida*. Bloomington and Indianapolis: Indiana University Press.

Chaffin, D. (1989), 'Hegel, Derrida and the sign', in *Derrida and Deconstruction: Continental Philosophy II*, Silverman, H. (ed.). New York and London: Routledge, pp. 77–91.

Chomsky, Noam (1999), *The New Military Humanism: Lessons from Kosovo*. London: Pluto.

Cornell, Drusilla (1992), *Deconstruction and the Possibility of Justice*. New York: Routledge.

Cumming, R. D. (1981), 'The odd couple, Heidegger and Derrida', *Review of Metaphysics*, 34, 484–521.

Davis, R. C. and Schleifer, R. (eds) (1985), *Rhetoric and Form; Deconstruction at Yale*. Norman: University of Oklahoma Press.

De Man, Paul (1983), *Blindness and Insight: Essays in the rhetoric of contemporary criticism*. London: Methuen.

Derrida, Jacques (1973), *Speech and Phenomena, and Other Essays on Husserl's Theory of Signs*, trans. David B. Allison. Evanston, IL: Northwestern University Press.

—— (1974), *Glas*. Éditions Galilée.

—— (1978), *Edmund Husserl's 'Origin of Geometry': An Introduction*, trans. J. P. Leavey Jr. New York: Harvester Press.

—— (1979), *Spurs: Nietzsche's Styles/Epérons: Les styles de Nietzsche*, trans. B. Harlow. Chicago: Chicago University Press.

Derrida, Jacques (1981a), *Dissemination*, trans. Barbara Johnson. Chicago: University of Chicago Press.

—— (1981b), *Positions*, trans. Alan Bass. London: Athlone.

—— (1982), *Margins of Philosophy*, translation and annotation by Alan Bass. Brighton: Harvester Press.

—— (1985), *The Ear of the Other: Otobiographies, transference, translation; texts and discussions with Jacques Derrida*, trans. Peggy Kamuf. Lincoln: University of Nebraska.

—— (1986a), *Glas*, trans. J. P. Leavey, Jr. and Richard Rand. Lincoln and London: University of Nebraska Press.

—— (1986b), *Memoires: For Paul de Man*, trans. C. Lindsay, J. Culler and E. Cadava. New York: Columbia University Press.

—— (1987a), *The Post Card: From Socrates to Freud and Beyond*, translation, annotation and introduction by Alan Bass. Chicago and London: University of Chicago Press.

—— (1987b), *The Truth in Painting*, trans. G. Bennington and Ian McLeod. Chicago: Chicago University Press.

—— (1987c), *Psyché: Inventions de l'autre*. Paris: Galilée.

—— (1988), *Limited Inc.*, trans. Samuel Weber and Jeffrey Mehlman. Evanston, IL: Northwestern University Press.

—— (1989), *Of Spirit: Heidegger and the Question*, trans. G. Bennington and R. Bowlby. Chicago: Chicago University Press.

—— (1990), *Du droit à la philosophie*. Paris: Galilée.

—— (1991), *A Derrida Reader: Between the Blinds*, ed. Peggy Kamuf. Hertfordshire: Harvester Wheatsheaf.

—— (1992a), *The Other Heading: Reflections on Today's Europe*, trans. Pascale-Anne Brault and Michael B. Naas. Bloomington: Indiana University Press.

—— (1992b), *Given Time*, trans. Peggy Kamuf. Chicago: University of Chicago Press.

—— (1992c), *Acts of Literature*, Derek Attridge (ed.). New York: Routledge.

—— (1993a), *Memoires of the Blind: The Self-Portrait and Other Ruins*, trans. Pascale-Anne Brault and Michael Naas. Chicago: University of Chicago Press.

—— (1993b), *Aporias*, trans. Thomas Dutoit. Stanford: Stanford University Press.

—— (1994), *Spectres of Marx: The State of the Debt, the Work of Mourning, and the New International*, trans. P. Kamuf. London: Routledge.

—— (1995a), *The Gift of Death*, trans. D. Wills. Chicago: University of Chicago Press.

Derrida, Jacques (1995b), *Points: Interviews 1974–1994*, ed. E. Weber, trans. P. Kamuf. Stanford: Stanford University Press.

—— (1996), *Archive Fever*, trans. Eric Prenowitz. London: University of Chicago Press.

Derrida, Jacques (1997a), *The Politics of Friendship*, trans. G. Collins. London: Verso Books.

—— (1997b), *Of Grammatology*, trans. G. C. Spivak. Baltimore: Johns Hopkins University Press.

—— (1998a), *Resistances of Psychoanalysis*, trans. Pascale-Anne Brault. Stanford: Stanford University Press.

—— (1998b), *Le Rapport bleu*. Paris: PUF.

—— (1998c) *Voiles* (with Hélène Cixous). Paris: Galilée.

—— (1998d), *The Derrida Reader: Writing Perfomances*, ed. Julian Wolfreys. Edinburgh: Edinburgh University Press.

—— (1998e), *Monolingualism of the Other; or the Prosthesis of Origin*, trans. Patrick Mensah. California: Stanford University Press.

—— (1998f), *The Secret Art of Antonin Artaud*, trans. Mary Ann Caws. Cambridge: MA: The MIT Press.

—— (1998g), Vattimo, G. (ed.) *Religion*. Cambridge: Polity Press.

—— (2001a), *Acts of Religion*, ed. Gil Anidjar. London: Routledge.

—— (2001b), *The Work of Mourning*. Chicago: University of Chicago Press.

—— (2001c), *On Cosmopolitanism and Forgiveness*, trans. M. Dooley and M. Hughes. London: Routledge.

—— (2002a), *Negotiations: Interventions and Interviews, 1971–2001*, ed. Elizabeth N. Rottenberg. Stanford: Stanford University Press.

—— (2002b), *Ethics, Institutions, and the Right to Philosophy*, trans. Peter Pericles Triphonias. Maryland: Rowman and Littlefield.

—— (2003), *Writing and Difference*, trans. Alan Bass. London: Routledge.

—— (and Catherine Malabou) (2004a), *Counterpath: Travelling with Jacques Derrida*, trans. David Wills. Stanford: Stanford University Press.

—— (2004b), 'Je suis en guerre contre moi-même', *Le Monde*, 19 August 2004.

—— (and Elizabeth Roudinesco) (2004c), *For What Tomorrow . . . : A Dialogue*. Stanford: Stanford University Press.

Dosse, François (1998a), *History of Structuralism: The Rising Sign*, trans. Deborah Glassman. Minneapolis: University of Minnesota Press.

—— (1998b), *History of Structuralism: The Setting Sign*, trans. Deborah Glassman. Minneapolis: University of Minnesota Press.

—— (1999), *The Empire of Meaning*, trans. Hassan Melehy. London and Minneapolis: University of Minnesota Press.

WORKS CITED

Dostoevski, Fyodor (1955), *The Idiot*, trans. D. Magarshack. London: Penguin.

Eliot, T. S. (1947), *Milton*. London: Oxford University Press.

—— (1974), *What is a Classic? An Address delivered before the Virgil Society*. New York: Haskell House.

Farías, Victor (1989), *Heidegger and Nazism*, trans. Paul Burrell. Philadelphia: Temple University Press.

Ferry, L. and Renaut, A. (1990), *The French Philosophy of the Sixties: An Essay on Antihumanism*, trans. Mary S. Cattani. Amherst: University of Massachusetts Press.

Foucault, Michel (1989), *Madness and Civilization*, trans. R. Howard. London: Routledge.

Frank, Manfred (1992), 'Is self-consciousness a case of *presence à soi*? towards a meta-critique of the recent French critique of metaphysics', in *Derrida: A Critical Reader*, ed. David Wood. Massachusetts: Blackwell, pp. 218–34.

Freud, Sigmund (1991), *The Interpretation of Dreams*, trans. James Strachey, ed. A. Richards. London: Penguin.

Fried, G. (2000), *Heidegger's Polemos*. New Haven: Yale University Press.

Gasché, Rodolph (1986), *The Tain in the Mirror*. Cambridge MA: Harvard University Press.

Genet, Jean (1993), *Le Miracle de la rose*. Paris: Éditions Gallimard.

Gide, André (2002) [1935], *Fruits of the Earth*. London: Vintage.

Gilman, Sander L. (1987), *Conversations with Nietzsche: A Life in the Words of His Contemporaries*, trans. David J. Parent. Oxford: Oxford University Press.

Greene, Marjorie (1976), 'Life, death and language: some thoughts on Wittgenstein and Derrida', *Partisan Review* 43, 265–79.

Habermas, Jürgen (1987), *The Philosophical Discourse of Modernity: Twelve Lectures*, trans. Frederick Lawrence. Cambridge MA: MIT Press.

Hanley, D. L. and Kerr, A. P. (eds) (1994), *May '68, Coming of Age*. Oxford: Oxford University Press.

Harvey, Irene (ed.) (1988), *The Purloined Poe: Lacan, Derrida, and Psychoanalytic Reading*. Baltimore: Johns Hopkins University Press.

Hayman, R. (1980), *Nietzsche, A Critical Life*. London: Pheonix Giants.

Hegel, G. W. F. (1977) [1807], *The Phenomenology of Spirit*, trans. A. V. Miller. Oxford: Oxford University Press.

Heidegger, Martin (1950), 'Wozu Dichter?', in *Holzwegn*. Frankfurt-am-Main: Klostermann.

Heidegger, Martin (1959), *The Question of Being*, trans. W. Kluback and J. T. Wilde. London: Vision.

—— (1975), *Poetry, Language, Thought*, trans. Albert Hofstadter. New York: Harper and Row.

—— (1978), *Martin Heidegger: Basic Writings*, ed. David Farrel Krell. London: Routledge and Kegan Paul.

—— (1984), *The Metaphysical Foundations of Logic*, trans. Michael Heim. Bloomington: Indiana University Press.

—— (1994), *Basic Questions of Philosophy: Selected Problems of Logic*, trans. R. Rojcewicz and A. Schuwer. Bloomington: Indiana University Press.

—— (1995), *Aristotle's Metaphysics, Theta 1–3: On the Essence and Actuality of Force*, trans. W. Brogan and P. Warnock. Bloomington: Indiana University Press.

—— (1996), *Hölderlin's Hymn 'The Ister'*, trans. William McNeill and Julia Davis. Bloomington: Indiana University Press.

—— (1998a) [1927], *Being and Time*, trans. J. Macquarrie and E. Robinson. Oxford: Blackwell.

—— (1998b), Pathmarks, ed. W. McNeill. New York: Cambridge University Press.

—— (1999), *Contributions to Philosophy: From Enowning*, trans. Parvis Emad and Kenneth Maly. Bloomington and Indianapolis: Indiana University Press.

—— (2000a), *Introduction to Metaphysics*, trans. Gregory Fried and Richard Polt. New Haven and London: Yale Nota Bene.

—— (2000b), *Elucidations of Hölderlin's Poetry*, trans. Keith Hoeller. New York: Humanity.

Heisenberg, Werner (1963), *Physics and Philosophy: the Revolution in Modern Science*. London: Allen and Unwin.

Hölderlin, F. (1986), *Selected Verse of Hölderlin*, ed. and trans. Michael Hamburger. London: Anvil Press Poetry.

Hollingdale, R. J. (1999), *Nietzsche: The Man and his Philosophy*. Cambridge UK: Cambridge University Press.

Honderich, T. (2001), *Philosopher: A Kind of Life*. London: Routledge.

Howells, C. M. (1989), 'Derrida and Sartre, Hegel's death knell', in *Derrida and Deconstruction: Continental Philosophy II*, Silverman, H. (ed.). New York and London: Routledge, pp. 169–81.

Husserl, Edmund (1931) [1915], *Ideas. A General Introduction to Pure Phenomenology*, trans. W. R. Boyce Gibson. London: Allen and Unwin.

—— (1970) [1901], *Logical Investigations*, trans. J. N. Findlay. London: Routledge and Kegan Paul.

Husserl, Edmund (1973) [1926], *Cartesian Meditations*, trans. D. Cairns. The Hague: Nijhoff.

—— (1991), *The Phenomenology of the Consciousness of Internal Time*, trans. John Barnett Brough. London: Kluwer.

Jameson, Fredric (1991), *Postmodernism, or the Cultural Logic of Late Capitalism*. London: Verso.

Joyce, James (1992), *Finnegans Wake*. London: Minerva.

Kant, Immanuel (1883) [1790], *Critique of Practical Reason and other works on the theory of ethics*, trans. T. K. Abbott. London: Longmans, Green and Co.

Kierkegaard, S. (1985) [1843] *Fear and Trembling*, trans. Alastair Hannay. Harmondsworth: Penguin Books.

—— (1989) [1849], *The Sickness Unto Death*, trans. Alastair Hannay. Harmondsworth: Penguin Books.

Kofman, Amy Ziering and Dick, Kirby (2003), *Derrida*. New York: Zeitgeist Video.

Lacan, Jacques (1994), *Four Fundamental Concepts of Psychoanalysis*, trans. Alan Sheridan. London: Penguin.

—— (2001), *Écrits: A Selection*, trans. Alan Sheridan. London: Routledge.

Lacoue-Labarthe, Phillipe, and Nancy, Jean-Luc (1981), *Les fins de l'homme: à partir de travail de Jacques Derrida*. Paris: Éditions Galilée.

Lacoue-Labarthe, Phillipe (1990), *Heidegger, Art and Politics: The Fiction of the Political*, trans. Chris Turner. Oxford: Blackwell.

Leavey, J. P. Jr and Ulmer, G. (1986), *Glassary*. Lincoln and London: University of Nebraska Press.

Levinas, Emmanuel (1969), *Totality and Infinity: An Essay on Exteriority*, trans. A. Lingis. Pittsburgh: Duquesne University Press.

—— (1998), *Entre Nous*, trans. M. B. Smith and B. Harshav. London: Athlone Press.

Lodge, D. and Wood, N. (eds), (2000), *Modern Criticism and Theory: A Reader* (2nd edn). London: Longman.

Lyotard, J. F. (1984), *The Postmodern Condition: A Report on Knowledge*. Manchester: Manchester University Press.

—— (1991), *The Inhuman: Reflections on Time*, trans. G. Bennington and R. Bowlby. Cambridge: Polity Press.

—— (1993), *Political Writings*, ed. Bill Readings. London: UCL Press.

MacIntyre, Alistair (1985), *After Virtue*. London: Duckworth.

McQuillan, Martin (2001), *Paul de Man*. New York: Routledge.

Mann, T. (1949), *Dr Faustus: The life of the German composer Adrian Leverkühn as told by a friend*, trans. H. T. Lowe-Porter. London: Secker and Warburg.

Monk, Ray (1990), *Ludwig Wittgenstein:the Duty of Genius*. London: Cape.

Nietzsche, F. W. (1968), *The Will to Power*, trans. Walter Kaufmann. New York: Vintage.

—— (1974) [1887], *The Gay Science*, trans. Walter Kaufmann. New York: Vintage.

—— (1979) [1889], *Ecce Homo*, trans. R. J. Hollingdale. London: Penguin Books.

—— (1980), 'On Truth and Lie in the Extra-Moral Sense', in *The Portable Nietzsche*, ed. Walter Kaufmann. New York: Random.

—— (1984), *Dithyrambs of Dionysus*, trans. R. J. Hollingdale. London: Anvil Press Poetry.

Nietzsche, F. W. (1986) [1880], *Human, All Too Human: A Book for Free Spirits*, trans. R. J. Hollingdale. Cambridge UK: Cambridge University Press.

—— (1990a) [1886], *Beyond Good and Evil: Prelude to a Philosophy of the Future*, trans. R. J. Hollingdale. London: Penguin Books.

—— (1990b), [1889], *The Twilight of the Idols/The Antichrist*, trans. R. J. Hollingdale. London: Penguin Books.

—— (1994) [1887], *On the Genealogy of Morality: A Polemic*, ed. Keith Ansell-Pearson. Cambridge UK: Cambridge University Press.

Norris, Christopher (1986), 'Deconstruction against itself: Derrida and Nietzsche', *Diacritics* 16 (4), 61–9.

—— (1987), *Derrida*. London: Fontana Modern Masters.

Ott, Hugo (1988), *Martin Heidegger: A Political Life*, trans. A. Blunden. London: Fontana Press.

Petzet, H. W. (1993), *Encounters and Dialogues with Martin Heidegger*, trans. Parvis Emad and Kenneth Maly. Chicago and London: University of Chicago Press.

Pilger, J. (1994), *Distant Voices*. London: Vintage.

Plato (1966), *Plato's Cosmology, The Timaeus*, ed. F. M. Cornford. London: Routledge and Kegan Paul.

—— (1977), 'The Republic', in *The Portable Plato*, ed. Scott Buchannan. New York: Penguin.

Plessix Gray, F. (1999), *At Home with the Marquis de Sade*. London: Chatto and Windus.

Proust, Marcel (1972), *Le temps retrouvé: À la recherche du temps perdue (vol. 8)*. Paris: Gallimard.

Rorty, R. (1980), *Philosophy and the Mirror of Nature*. Princeton: Princeton University Press.

Rorty, R. (1982), *Consequences of Pragmatism*. Minneapolis: University of Minnesota Press.

Rosenberg, Alfred (1970), *Selected Writings of Alfred Rosenberg*, ed. Robert Pois. London: Cape.

Royle, Nicholas (2003), *Jacques Derrida*. London: Routledge.

Sade, D. A. F. de (1992), *Les 120 journées de Sodome: precedé de La machine en tête*. Paris: POL.

Safranski, Rüdiger (1998), *Martin Heidegger: Between Good and Evil*, trans. E. Osers. Cambridge MA: Harvard University Press.

—— (2003), *Nietzsche: A Philosophical Biography*, trans. Shelley Frisch. London: Granta.

Saussure, Ferdinand de (1960), *Course in General Linguistics*, trans. W. Baskin. London: Owen.

Schmitt, Carl (1996), *The Concept of the Political*, trans. George Schwab. Chicago and London: University of Chicago Press.

Schopenhauer, Arthur (1969) [1844], *The World as Will and Representation (vol. I)*, trans. E. F. J. Payne. New York: Dover Publications.

Scott, C. E., Schoenbaum, S. M., Vallega-Neu, D. and Vallega, A. (2001), *The Companion to Heidegger's Contributions to Philosophy*. Indiana: Indiana University Press.

Scruton, Roger (2001), *England: An Elegy*. London: Pimlico.

—— (2005), *Modern Culture* (2nd edition). London: Continuum.

Shelley, P. B. (1945), *The Complete Poetical Works of Percy Bysshe Shelley*, ed. G. Cumberlege. London: Oxford University Press.

Silverman, H. (1989), 'Derrida, Heidegger and the time of the line', in *Derrida and Deconstruction: Continental Philosophy II*, Silverman, H. (ed.). New York and London: Routledge, pp. 154–68.

Spender, Stephen (1951), *World Within World: The Autobiography of Stephen Spender*. London: Hamilton.

Spengler, O. (1934), *The Decline of the West*, trans. C. F. Atkinson. London: George Allen and Unwin.

Sturrock, John (1998), *The Word from Paris*. London: Verso.

Syberberg, H. J. (1977), *Hitler, A Film from Germany*. London: Academy Video.

Toynbee, A. J. (1957), *A Study of History (Abridgement of vols VII–X by D. C. Somerville)*. London: Oxford University Press.

Wiener, John (1989), 'The responsibilities of friendship: Jacques Derrida on Paul de Man's collaboration', *Critical Inquiry* 15 (4), pp. 797–803.

Wolin, Richard (1993), *The Heidegger Controversy*. Cambridge MA: The MIT Press.

Wood, D. and Bernasconi, R. (1985), *Derrida and Difference*. Warwick: Parousia Press.

Wyschogrod, E. (1989), 'Derrida, Levinas and violence', in *Derrida and Deconstruction: Continental Philosophy II*, Silverman, H. (ed.). New York and London: Routledge, pp. 182–200.

Yeats, W. B. (1962), *A Vision* (2nd edition). London: Macmillan.

Zimmerman, Michael E. (1990), *Heidegger's Confrontation with Modernity: Technology, Politics and Art*. Bloomington and Indianapolis: Indiana University Press.

Index

À partir du travail de Jacques Derrida 145
A Taste for the Secret (Derrida/Ferraris) 210, 222
absolute difference 107
Absolute Knowledge 85, 87–8, 90, 114, 228
Acts of Literature (Derrida) 150
Acts of Religion (Derrida) 209, 218
Adami, Valerio 121, 139
'Aesthetic Ideology' (de Man) 155
Algeria 10, 13–16, 18–19, 23–5, 32–3, 40–1, 81, 83, 98, 184
Algiers 11–13, 17, 19, 40, 83
Althusser, Louis 24, 31–2, 34–5, 42, 45, 47, 55–6, 58, 60, 62, 65, 70, 74, 145, 150, 185
analytical philosophy 182
'Andanken' (Heidegger) 165
anthropology 67
anti-Semitism 16, 161, 167–8, 192, 222
Aporias (Derrida) 190, 208
archi-writing 77, 78, 84, 89, 134, 141, 146
Archive Fever (Derrida) 208
Arendt, Hannah 211
Aristotle 76, 85, 127, 176, 189, 196, 197, 199
'Art Against Apartheid' (exhibition) 152
Artaud, Antonin 90
Aschheim, Steven E. 140
'At This Very Moment Here I Am' (Derrida) 146
atheism 164
Aucouturier, Marguerite 31, 39–41, 42, 47
Augustine, St 189
Austin, J. L. 129
auto-immunitary 219
autobiography 141–2

Bachelard, Gaston 55
Barthes, Roland 57, 59–60, 66, 74, 87, 89, 150, 234n.2, 241n

Bataille, Georges 54, 69, 94, 179, 185, 216, 240n.8
Baudrillard, Jean 173, 191, 207
'Before the Law' (Derrida) 151
Being 6–7, 27–9, 45, 51, 53, 56–8, 60, 67, 77–8, 84, 92, 102, 106–7, 110–11, 134–8, 139, 145, 162–6, 172, 176, 198, 203, 208, 221, 228–30, 237n, 241n.6
Being by Being 131, 239n.2
Being and Time (Heidegger) 29, 30, 85, 164, 208, 239n
Being-in-General 146
Benjamin, Walter 170, 202
Bennington, Geoffrey 3, 12, 17, 95, 105, 144, 152, 162, 177–80, 185, 230
Benoïste, Jean 58
Berezdvin, R. 143
Bergson, Henri 19
Berlin, University of 83, 110
Bernasconi, Robert 29, 43, 101–4, 224, 237n.5, 240–1n.1
Bernet, R. 49
Between the Blinds (Kamuf) 138
'Between Brackets' (Derrida) 121
Beyond Good and Evil (Nietzsche) 130
Beyond the Pleasure Principle (Freud) 130
Bin Laden, Osama 219
biography 141
birth 192
Birth of Tragedy (Nietzsche) 57
Blanchot, Maurice 59, 83, 97, 145, 147, 149, 197–8, 200, 210
blindness 174–6
Blindness and Insight (de Man) 136
Bloom, Harold 123, 131
Bodleian Library 128
Bohr, Niels 217
'Book of Elie, The' (Derrida) 128, 141, 175

Borradori, Giovanna 210, 218
Bourdieu, Pierre 23
Bouveresse, Jacques 185
Brogan, Walter 89
Bush, George 219

California University 99
'Cambridge Affair' 3
Camus, Albert 22
Canguilheim, G. 55
capitalism 108, 119, 183, 186, 205, 206–7
Caputo, John D. 4, 29, 34, 39, 54, 93–4,
    156–7, 161–2, 166, 184, 204, 242n.3
Cardozo School of Law 169, 242n.7
Carmel, Titus 139
Cartesian Meditations (Husserl) 44
Celan, Paul 83, 90, 150
Cerisy-la-Salle 42, 45, 56, 67, 87, 106, 108,
    147, 208
Chaffin, Deborah 85
Chessman, Carol 150
Chevènement, Jean-Pierre 156
Chirac, Jacques 158, 223
Chomsky, Noam 60, 66, 173
Choral Works (Derrida/Eisenmann) 210
Christianity 13, 21, 23, 31, 148, 164–9, 176,
    192, 194, 200, 205–6, 207, 213–19, 242n
Cicero 189, 196
circumcision 12, 179–80
Circumfession (Derrida) 12, 36, 48, 92, 152,
    162, 175–6, 177, 180, 209
Cixous, Hélène 222
Clinton, Bill 17
'Cogito and the History of Madness' (Derrida)
    37, 185
Cohen, Hermann 46
Collège international de philosophie 109
Commission on Philosophy and Epistemology
    119, 185
'Committee of Writers for Nelson Mandela'
    152
communism 27, 31, 32, 55, 70, 89
community 199–200, 216
consciousness 28, 45, 57, 75, 77, 124, 130,
    146
construction 60
Contributions to Philosophy (Heidegger) 164,
    176–7, 198, 241n
Cosmopolitanism and Forgiveness (Derrida) 222
Counterpath (Derrida/Malabou) 93, 94, 95, 210
Course of General Linguistics (Saussure) 66
Critique of Practical Reason (Kant) 4
'Cultural Foundation Against Apartheid' 152
culture 61, 62
Cumming, R. D. 139

Daedalus, Stephen 154
Dasein 58, 137
de Man, Paul 2, 19, 43, 59, 87, 92, 98–104,

    122, 124–5, 133, 142, 150, 152, 154–5,
    167–8, 175–6
death penalty 222
death/life 84, 93–6, 113, 125, 137–8, 141–3,
    179–80, 192, 197, 208, 227–8
Decade de Cerisy 145
decisionism 199
deconstruction 2–8, 18, 25–6, 34–5, 37, 43,
    51, 53–4, 59–62, 68, 74, 77–8, 88, 92,
    98–102, 104, 106–7, 113, 124, 129, 131,
    137, 139, 145, 150, 152, 157, 162–3,
    167–70, 173, 182, 184, 186–7, 189, 191,
    195, 206, 211, 213, 217, 220, 226–9, 233n
'Deconstruction of Actuality, The' (Derrida)
    189, 191, 201
Deconstruction and Criticism (Derrida) 137
'Deconstruction and the Possibility of Justice'
    (Derrida) 169
Deleuze, Gilles 108–9
Delorme, Michel 116
Demeure (Derrida) 210
democracy 118–19, 127, 148, 183, 193, 196,
    199–200, 203, 205, 238n
Derrida: A Reader (Bennington) 178, 223
Derrida, Abraham 11
Derrida, Aimé 11, 92
Derrida and Difference (Krell) 111
Derrida, Elie 11
Derrida, Eugène Eliahou 11
Derrida, Georgette Sultana Esther 178–81
Derrida, Jacques
    overview 1–8
    early life 9–21
    studies/early adulthood 22–38, 39–41
    teaching/early publication 42–8, 49–54
    structuralism and against 55–64, 65–73
    further publication 74–9
    May '68 and beyond 80–91
    travelling/teaching 92–109
    Glas and Berlin 110–15
    philosophy research group 116–18
    America 121–7
    turning inwards 128–32
    later years 133–43, 144–59, 160–73
    autobiographical years 174–81
    hopes for the future 182–8
    and Marx 189–95
    final years 189–95, 196–203, 204–10,
        211–25
Derrida, Janine 11
Derrida, Jean 39, 74
Derrida, Marguerite *see* Aucouturier,
    Marguerite
Derrida, Norbert 14
Derrida, Paul 11–12
Derrida, Pierre 39, 48
Derrida, Renè 14
Descartes, René 85, 86, 111
dialectic, the 34, 85, 113

différance 54, 64, 69–70, 77–8, 83–5, 96, 111, 129, 135, 137, 142, 145, 146, 227–8
Dissemination (Derrida) 87–90
Disturbance (Hill) 150, 162
Donner la mort (Derrida) 208
Dosse, François 65, 68, 232n.6, 234n, 235n.2
'Double Session, The' (Derrida) 87, 89
double-bind 94, 95
drugs 151
Du droit à la philosophie (Derrida) 133, 185
Dupin, Auguste 88

'Eating the Other' (Derrida) 161
Ecce Homo (Nietzsche) 57, 141–2, 201
Echographies de la télévision (Derrida/Steiger) 208
Eco, Umberto 100
École des hautes études on sciences sociales (EHESS) 96, 144, 156, 157, 159, 160–1, 189–90, 209, 222
École Normale Supérieure (ENS) 7, 22–5, 30–4, 36, 47, 55, 58, 69, 74, 83, 96, 116, 134, 141, 144, 157
economy 185, 191
Ecrits (Lacan) 69, 188, 235n.4
Ehrmann, Jacques 137
Eisenmann, Peter 139, 210
El-Biar 16, 19, 23, 24
Elementary Structures of Kinship, The (Lévi-Strauss) 61, 66
Eliot, T. S. 122–4, 154, 155, 203, 238n
Elucidations of Hölderlin's Poetry (Heidegger) 28, 30
enframing 139
epistemology 46, 47
Ereignis 136, 137, 221, 240n.2
Eroticism (Bataille) 94
Estates General for Philosophy 117–18
ethics 104, 211
Europe 101–2, 119, 126, 135, 182, 183–5, 191, 193, 206, 208, 212, 215, 219–21, 238n
event, the 131, 137, 172, 193, 218–19, 224, 240n.3
existence 10, 67, 149
existentialism 8, 20, 23, 26, 65, 228
experience 21, 192
expressions 75
'Eyes of Language, The' (Derrida) 158
Eyes of the University (Derrida) 222

faith 195, 206, 214
'Faith and Knowledge' (Derrida) 205–6, 214
Fantin-Latour, Henri 174
Farías, Victor 167, 169, 185
Fathy, Safaa 218
Faye, Jean-Pierre 105
Ferraris, Maurizio 210

'Final Solution and the Limits of Representation' (Derrida) 171–2
Fink, Eugen 39, 47, 49
For What Tomorrow... (Derrida) 222
'Force of Law' (Caputo) 170
'Force and Signification' (Derrida) 47–8, 56, 67, 78
Foucault, Michel 30, 32, 34–8, 45, 53–4, 62, 65–7, 69, 74, 109, 117, 150–2, 185, 188, 233n
Four Fundamental Concepts of Psychoanalysis (Lacan) 72
freedom 51, 52, 164, 180, 181, 233n
Freiburg, University of 46
'Freud and the Scene of Writing' (Derrida) 63
Freud, Sigmund 31–2, 34–5, 53, 60–4, 69–71, 114, 130–1, 178, 208, 234n
Freudianism 188
Fried, Gregory 104
Friedlander, Saul 171
friendship 189, 196, 197, 198–200
Fruits of the Earth (Gide) 20–1
future 68, 76, 192

Gasché, Rodolph 3, 113
Gaulle, General Charles de 32, 41, 80, 81, 82
Gay Science, The (Nietzsche) 198
'Genesis and Structure' (Derrida) 26, 42
Genet, Jean 15, 90, 112–13, 114, 150
geometry 49–50
German Ideology (Marx) 193
Germany 6, 19, 46, 80, 106, 118–19, 135–7, 154–5, 165, 197, 221, 228
'Geschlecht 1/2' 134
ghost 4–5, 13, 54, 76, 84, 193–5, 227–8
Ghost Dance (film) 150
Gide, André 17, 20
gift 107, 113, 136
Giovannengli, Daniel 215, 217
Girard, René 59
Given Time (Derrida) 147, 216
Glas (Derrida) 4, 36, 83, 90, 110–15, 121, 138
'Globalatinization' 206–7
globalization 107, 203, 213, 214–15
God 21, 44–5, 51–2, 60–1, 78, 97, 110, 112, 146–7, 153, 162–3, 166, 171, 174–5, 179–80, 206–8, 210, 228–9
Goethe, Johann Wolfgang von 98, 237n
grammatology 26, 53, 67, 111, 228, 233n
Graves, Robert 203
Greece 135–6, 197–8
Groupe de recherche sur l'enseignement philosophique (GREPH) 116–17, 120, 121, 145, 157
Guattari, Felix 107
Guillaume, Marc 210

Habermas, Jürgen 157, 218, 237–8n.2, 241n
Haby Proposal, The 117

Hartman, Geoffrey 123
Harvard University 39
hauntology 193
Hegel, G. W. F. 19, 34, 51–2, 57, 65, 83, 85, 90–1, 97, 112–13, 114, 127, 198, 205, 239n.5
Heidegger Controversy, The (Wolin) 168, 169, 186
Heidegger, Martin 4, 6–8, 20–1, 26–9, 30, 33–4, 46–7, 51, 53, 55–6, 58, 60–3, 68, 71, 75–8, 83–6, 90, 92–3, 105–7, 128, 130–1, 134–40, 162–8, 184–6, 190, 196, 198, 202, 205, 216–17, 221, 226, 228–9, 232n.2, 234n, 236n, 237n, 240n.5, 244n.5
Hill, Gary 150, 162
history 52, 63, 66, 67, 107, 110, 111
History of Structuralism (Dosse) 68
Hölderlin, F. W. 153, 165, 193, 203, 228–9
'Hölderlin's Heaven and Earth' (Heidegger) 53, 56, 90, 93, 97, 136, 165–6
Hollingdale, R. J. 240n.5
Holocaust, the 146, 170–1
Homer 154–5, 176
Human, All Too Human (Nietzsche) 202
Hus, Jan 151
Husserl, Edmund 22, 24–8, 30, 33, 36–7, 39, 40, 42–7, 49–51, 52, 54, 58, 60, 74–7, 85, 103, 124, 158, 168, 181, 216, 228, 233n
Hyppolite, Jean 34, 42, 45, 55, 58

Ibsen, Henrik 153
Idea, the 44, 51
idealism 77, 92
'Ideality of the Literary Object, The' (Derrida) 40, 145
Ideas I (Husserl) 44, 45
il y a 146, 229
immigration 17, 192, 212–13
impossible, the 34, 180, 215–17
'In Memoriam of the Soul: for Paul de Man' (Derrida) 152
intentionality 27, 45
International College of Philosophy (CIP) 117, 152, 156–7, 163
'International Colloquium on Critical Languages and the Science of Man' 59
International Conference on Humanistic Discourses 182
International Parliament of Writers 211
Interpretation of Dreams (Freud) 35
'Interpretations at War' (Derrida) 158
Introduction to the Work of Marcel Mauss (Lévi-Strauss) 66
Inverted Bell (Riddel) 121
'Is Ontology Fundamental?' 57

Jabès, Edmund 58
Jacques Derrida (Derrida/Bennington) 177–8, 185

Jakobson, Roman 66
Jameson, Fredric 100, 123, 233n.
Jan Hus Association 151, 159
Jan Hus Educational Foundation 151
Johns Hopkins conference, Baltimore 59, 69, 82, 98
Johnson, Christopher 215, 217
Jospin, Lionel 185
Joyce, James 39, 54, 90, 115, 150, 153–4, 157–8, 234n.5
Judaism 10, 13, 15–16, 21–2, 29, 164, 166–8, 171, 175, 179, 205
Jünger, Ernst 137, 228
justice 97, 153, 170, 171, 193, 212

Kafka, Franz 90, 151, 153
Kamuf, Peggy 138
Kant, Immanuel 9, 21, 26–8, 43–6, 52, 76, 139, 148–9, 182–3, 202, 205, 211
'Kant, the Jew, the German' (Derrida) 161
khora 90, 97, 158–9, 171, 173
Kierkegaard, Søren Aabye 20, 127, 176
Klossowski, Pierre 109
Kofman, Amy Ziering 222, 225
Kofman, Sarah 109, 116, 209
Kojève, Alexandre 34
Krell, David Farrell 111
Kristeva, Julia 87, 89

'La parole soufflée' (Derrida) 58–9
La Pensée 68 (Ferry/Renault) 161
La philosophie en effet 116
Lacan, Jacques 31, 34–6, 45, 59, 60, 63, 65, 67, 69, 70–3, 74, 88–9, 111, 117, 130–2, 134, 149, 150, 188, 232–3n.8, 235n.5
Lacoue-Labarthe, Philippe 109, 116, 145, 147, 154, 164
language 111, 112, 142, 175, 179, 208–9
l'avenir 96
law 97–8, 107, 109, 131, 153, 155, 204, 205, 208, 211, 214
Leavis, F. R. 100
'Letter on Humanism' (Heidegger) 56, 234n.1
Leverkühn, Adrian 154
Lévi-Strauss, Claude 33, 60–2, 65–8, 71, 74, 77, 235n.2
Levinas, Emanuel 21, 27–30, 37, 51, 56–9, 63, 65, 104, 145, 146–7, 207–9
liberalism 201, 213
life *see* death/life
Limited Inc. (Derrida) 125–6
literature 103, 152–4, 155
Living On: Borderlines (Derrida) 137, 138, 147
Logical Investigations (Husserl) 25, 76, 232n.2
logocentrism 37, 53–4, 68, 77, 93, 103–4, 137, 147, 168, 230
logos 51–2, 68, 146, 228
Luxembourg, Rosa 33

Lyotard, Jean-François 35, 42, 58, 81, 107, 109, 147, 148, 156, 173, 214, 218
Lyotard and Us (Derrida) 218

Machiavelli, Niccolò 221
McMullen, Ken 150
Madness and Civilization (Foucault) 30, 37, 109, 185
Major, René 70, 235n.5
Malabou, Catherine 94–5, 184, 210
Mallarmé, Stephane 87–8, 90, 150
Mandela, Nelson 117, 238n
Mann, Thomas 154
Marburg, University of 46
Margins of Philosophy (Derrida) 84, 85, 87, 105, 114
Marivaux, Pierre 57
Marquis de Sade, le 112
Marx en jeu (Derrida/Guillaume) 209, 210
Marx, Karl 34, 63, 69, 70, 169, 193–5, 204–5
Marxism 31–5, 45, 53, 55–6, 58, 70, 82, 89, 105–7, 163, 170, 184, 186, 189, 191, 200, 209
Mauss, Marcel 66, 67
May '68 80–3
meaning 54, 57, 64, 69, 114, 130, 202
media, the 215
Meditations (Descartes) 111
Memoires of the Blind (Derrida) 92, 94, 139, 174–6
Memoires for Paul de Man (Derrida) 99, 101, 102, 124, 152
memory 68
Mensah, Patrick 208
Merleau-Ponty, Maurice 25, 30, 45
messianism 162, 190, 195, 198, 204–5
metaphor 86
metaphysics 21, 62, 77, 96, 106, 135
Meyer, Michael 215, 217
Mill, John Stuart 205
Miller, J. Hillis 122, 123, 239n.4
Mitsein 58
Mitterand, François 117, 119–20, 151, 158, 160
Monk, Ray 127
Monolingualism (Derrida) 18, 208
Montaigne, Michel de 92, 93, 189, 196, 197
Moses and Monotheism (Freud) 178

Nancy, Jean-Luc 58, 109, 116, 121, 145, 147, 218
'Nation, Nationality Nationalism' (Derrida) 161
nationalism 134, 189, 190, 192
'natural light' 86
Nazism 6, 80, 97, 105, 140–1, 143, 146, 153, 154, 161, 166, 168–72
New Criticism 59, 122–41
New International 197

New York 59, 99, 144, 218, 220
New York University 99
Nietzche, Friedrich W. 2, 17, 20–2, 24, 30, 34, 36, 42, 56–7, 60–3, 65, 68, 78, 84, 86, 88, 92–3, 96–8, 106–8, 122, 127, 130–1, 135, 140–3, 154, 170, 172, 180, 184, 190, 196–203, 205, 228, 234n, 243n
'Nietzche and the Machine' (Derrida) 190, 201
nihilism 137, 187, 228, 229–30
Nombres (Sollers) 89
'Nomos, Logos, Topos' (Derrida) 161
Norris, Christopher 3, 107, 177, 215, 217

objectivity 28, 52, 124
objet petit a 69, 72
Of Grammatology (Derrida) 25, 30, 35, 40, 52, 60, 62, 64, 70, 74, 77, 79, 102, 103, 111, 122, 232n.4, 236n
Of Spirit (Derrida) 134, 138, 162–3
On An Apocalyptic Tone (Derrida) 146, 147
On Cosmopolitanism and Forgiveness (Derrida) 210–11, 214
On the Phenomenological Psychology of E. Husserl (Derrida) 47
One 197
ontology 5, 55, 59, 77, 86, 193, 226
origin 53, 135
'Origin of Geometry, The' (Husserl) 39, 40, 45, 47, 49–51, 52, 158, 218
'Origin of the Work of Art, The' (Heidegger) 139
Other Heading, The (Derrida) 182, 183, 215
Other, the 28–9, 34, 37, 52, 56–8, 71, 78, 93–8, 104, 107, 110, 121, 125–6, 129, 134, 139, 145–9, 162–3, 166–7, 170–1, 174–6, 179–81, 184, 190–2, 194, 196, 198, 203–4, 206, 208–10, 217, 224
Otobiographies (Derrida) 93, 107, 138, 139, 142, 202
'Ousia and Gramme' (Derrida) 85, 216
Overbeck, Franz 200

Paris 22–4, 25, 59, 97
Parti communiste français (PCF) 33, 55, 81, 89, 105
Pascal, Blaise 92
'Paul de Man's War' (Derrida) 104
Phallus 132, 207, 244n
pharmakon 87, 89, 90
phenomenology 24–6, 30, 45, 47, 50–1, 79, 181, 191
Phenomenology of the Consciousness of Internal Time (Husserl) 76
Phenomenology of Spirit (Hegel) 90
'Philosopher's Hell, The' (Derrida) 168
Philosophy of Arithmetic, The (Husserl) 27, 28
Philosophy in a Time of Terror (Derrida) 172, 218
Pilger, John 173
'Pit and the Pyramid, The' (Derrida) 85

Plato 5, 26, 50, 65, 84, 87–90, 92, 127–8, 159, 196, 198, 222, 226–7, 230, 245n
'Plato's Doctrine of Truth' (Heidegger) 90
'Plato's Pharmacy' (Derrida) 87, 89
Plotnitsky, Arkady 215, 217
Poe, Edgar Allen 69, 88, 132, 188
poetry 123–4
Poetry, Language, Thought (Heidegger) 234n
politics 151, 152, 196, 199, 221–2
Politics of Friendship, The (Derrida) 92, 161, 189–91, 216
Pompidou, Georges 80
Ponge, Francis 42, 90, 150
Positions (Derrida) 106
Post Card, The (Derrida) 7, 36, 70, 121–2, 125, 128–31, 135, 140, 152, 216
post-modernism 68, 173
Poulet, Georges 59
Pound, Ezra 123–4
power 29, 67, 69
pragmatism 2–3
Prague 151
Prayers and Tears of Jacques Derrida (Caputo) 204
presence 21, 64, 76, 77, 148, 193
present, the 68, 149, 191
Prix Cavailles 47, 233n.5
'Problem of Genesis in the Philosophy of Edmund Husserl, The' (Derrida) 25, 26
Proust, Marcel 56–7
Psyche (Derrida) 133, 134, 148, 149, 150, 210
psychoanalysis 111
Purloined Poe, The (Lacan) 71, 239n
'Purveyor of Truth, The' (Derrida) 132

Question of Being, The (Heidegger) 111, 137, 228
questioning/the question 51, 216
Quine, Willard van Orman 39

rationalism 148
Real, the 69, 72, 123, 172, 195
Reason 51, 68
Rée, Paul 200
religion 46, 51, 68, 124, 148–9, 153, 158, 176–7, 182–3, 195, 204–8, 214–15, 215, 241n.2
'Religion' (Derrida) 205
religion without religion 195
Remembrance of Things Past, The (Proust) 56, 57
representation 134, 173
Resistances of Psychoanalysis (Derrida) 185, 187, 188
responsibility 51
'Retrait of Metaphor, The' (Derrida) 130
Revue de métaphysique et de morale 30, 146
Richards, I. A. 123
Ricoeur, Paul 27, 55, 56, 65, 86, 144, 147
Riddel, Joe 121, 152, 185

Right to Philosophy from the Cosmopolitan Point of View, The (Derrida) 118–19, 222
Rorty, Richard 2, 113, 178, 223, 226
Rose, J.-Ch. 150
Rosenberg, Alfred 154
Roudinesco, Elizabeth 35, 65, 70, 152, 210
Rousseau, Jean-Jacques 17, 22, 62, 74, 77, 102, 103–4, 124, 126
Rousset, Jean 57
Russell, Bertrand 4, 207

Safar, Moses 10
Sallis, John 215, 217
Sartre, Jean-Paul 19–20, 26, 30, 61, 65, 81, 112, 236n.1
Saussure, Ferdinand de 53, 59, 66, 67, 71, 74, 77, 103, 111
Savary, M. 156
Schmitt, Carl 189, 196, 197, 199
Scholem, G. 158
Schopenhauer, Arthur 127
science 75, 77, 183, 206–7, 217
Science of Logic (Hegel) 85
Scruton, Roger 1, 6–7, 94, 151, 187, 204
Searle, John R. 105, 114–15, 126, 140
Sec 140
self 75, 94, 190
Serres, Michel 23
Servière, Michel 209
Sharon, Ariel 16
Shehan, Thomas 186
'Shelley Disfigured' (De Man) 137
Shelley, Percy Bysshe 137–8, 142
Sickness Unto Death, The (Kierkegaard) 176
sign, the 63, 67–9, 71–2, 75–6, 78, 85–7, 111, 130
'Signature, Event, Context' (Derrida) 105, 126
'Silk Worm Of One's Own, A' (Derrida) 205
Silverman, H. 138
simulcra 107, 172, 191
singularity 191
Socrates 89–90, 128, 222–3
Sollers, Phillippe 87, 88, 89, 105
Sorbonne, the 47, 55, 65, 117, 144
soul, the 21, 85
spectrality 54, 226
Spectres of Marx (Derrida) 55, 139, 163, 186, 189–91, 194, 197, 204
speech 50, 53
Speech and Phenomena (Derrida) 25, 40, 74
Spender, Stephen 244n.1
Spengler, Oswald 220
spirit 30, 164, 165–8, 194
Spivak, G. C. 155
'Spurs' (Derrida) 106, 107, 121–2, 141, 202
Stalinism 31, 32, 33, 68
Steiger, B. 208
Stirner, Max 194

structuralism 2, 8, 23, 29, 31, 42–3, 56–7,
    59–62, 65–8, 69–73, 77, 81–2, 105, 111,
    117, 121–2, 145–6, 150, 161, 181, 233n.2
'Structure, Sign and Play' (Derrida) 59, 60, 61,
    149
subject 72, 111
subjectivity 43, 68, 127
supplementarity 102
Szondi, Peter 83, 110

Tacitus 88, 155
teaching 119–20
technology 206, 228
Tel Quel 58–9, 63, 74, 87, 88, 89, 90, 93,
    105–6, 108, 150
Thing 72, 123
Third Critique (Kant) 139
thought, thinking 45, 51, 75, 77–8, 183, 195
Thucydides 88
'Time and Being' (Derrida) 135
Todorov, Tzvetan 59
Totality and Infinity (Levinas) 28–9
Toynbee, Arnold 243–4n
trace 57, 58, 61–4, 67, 70–3, 77–8, 84–6, 88,
    125, 130, 131, 137–8, 145–6, 214, 230
Trakl, Georg 164
transcendence 45, 52, 70, 77, 84, 111, 124,
    136, 145–7, 217
transcendental reduction 27, 28, 45, 46
Triumph of Life (Shelley) 137, 138, 142
truth 24, 89–90, 106–7, 115, 164, 172,
    199
Truth in Painting (Derrida) 122, 139

Ulmer, Gregory 114
Unconscious 34, 35, 36, 69, 70, 71, 72, 73,
    114, 130, 132
United Kingdom 118–19
United Nations 219–20

United States of America 39, 59, 69, 82,
    98–102, 118–19, 121–7, 150, 197, 219–21
unknown 35, 70, 136, 174, 176, 188

Van Gogh, Vincent 139
Vattimo, G. 205
Vernant, Jean-Pierre 59, 151, 158–9
violence 171
'Violence and Metaphysics' (Derrida) 28, 146,
    216
Virgil 155
void 72, 124
Voiles (Derrida) 222
Voltaire 205, 206

Wagner, Richard 155
Wahl, Jean 55
Weil, Simone 20, 23
West, the 6, 7–8, 18, 33, 37, 54, 61, 68, 111,
    136, 148, 168, 172–3, 189, 203, 219, 229,
    234n.3
What Are Poets For? (Heidegger) 137
What is Literature? (Sartre) 20
Who's Afraid of Philosophy? (Derrida) 222
Wiener, John 104
Wittgenstein, Ludwig 100, 101, 127, 217
Wolin, Richard 6–7, 104, 168–9, 186
Work of Mourning, The (Derrida) 59, 107, 222
writing 52–3, 56, 57, 64, 75–8, 86–8, 90–1,
    141, 147, 155
Writing and Difference (Derrida) 30, 40, 58, 74,
    77
Wyschogrod, Edith 145

Yale School, the 122–4
Yale University 99, 121–3, 137, 152

Zarathustra (Nietzsche) 56, 57
'Zur Kritic der Gewalt' (Benjamin) 170